Programming Techniques
Volume 3

Numbers in Theory and Practice

Blaise W. Liffick, Editor

"BOOKS OF INTEREST TO COMPUTER PEOPLE"

Library of Congress Cataloging in Publication Data (Revised)

Main entry under title:

Programming techniques.

   CONTENTS: [1] Program design. -v. 2. Simulation. -v. 3. Numbers in
theory and practice.
   1. Electronic digital computers - Programming 2. Computer simulation.
3. Mathematics - Data processing. I. Liffick, Blaise W.
QA76.6.P7518   001.6'4'4   78-8649
ISBN 0-07-037827-4 (v. 3)

Printed in the United States of America

TABLE OF CONTENTS

RANDOMIZING

GRAPHICS AND MATHEMATICS

FROM THE EDITOR

Programming Techniques is a series of books specifically designed to help make programming easier and more enjoyable for the personal computer enthusiast. This is done by providing articles which detail successful techniques for designing and implementing programs. Each book is a collection of the best articles on the selected subject from past issues of BYTE magazine, plus new material which has not appeared in print before. This provides the reader with vital information from previous BYTE issues which might have been missed, new material that has not appeared in the magazine, plus a book covering one specific theme for quick, easy reference.

The first volume in this series, **Program Design** (ISBN 0-931718-12-0), provides a look at several different methods for designing programs more efficiently and effectively. Included in the topics covered are structured program design, modular programming techniques, program logic design, designing tables, and binary tree processing.

Volume 2 of **Programming Techniques** is **Simulation** (ISBN 0-931718-13-9). Its purpose is to familiarize the reader with both a general overview of the vast area of computer simulation as well as details of specific types of simulations. The term simulation can cover a lot of territory, but for this book only three categories were chosen: artificial intelligence, motion, and experimentation.

Numbers in Theory and Practice, the book you now hold in your hands, is Volume 3 of the series. It covers many areas of numbers and computational methods for microcomputers. There are two main reasons for the development of this book. First, a person using a microcomputer must be more aware of number representations and formats than, say, the user of a large IBM computer. This is a result of the current memory constraints of most microcomputer systems and the frequent use of assembly and machine language programming in the field. Second, microcomputer users are more and more coming to need good numerical methods to solve the large range of programming problems for which the microcomputer is being used (the areas of simulation, statistical analysis, and graphics come readily to mind), but packages of numerical methods programs are not yet readily available to the microcomputer user.

This book, then, should serve the reader as an introduction to number systems, floating point numbers, numerical methods, random number generators, and the mathematics of computer graphics. There are many practical programs included in this book, as well as numerous references for further study of the subjects.

Blaise W. Liffick
Editor

TO BEGIN WITH

About This Section

Well, everything starts somewhere. This book begins with a section for the novice in need of background information about how computers use numbers.

Binary arithmetic is not all that difficult. And although a programmer seldom uses binary numbers in day-to-day activities, knowledge of the fundamentals of numbering systems is essential for certain types of work. In "An Introduction to Numbers", Webb Simmons introduces the concepts of fixed, scaled, and floating point numbers. Here you'll find some basic forms for each type, how the forms differ from each other, and how each can be used. "Making Binary Numbers Respectable" proposes that certain binary representations be given names. We can call 1000 a "thousand" in the decimal system, but what do we call that number if it's binary?

The second part of this section deals with the arithmetic used in microcomputers. Wayne Ledder describes the details of addition, subtraction, multiplication, and division in "A Novice's Eye on Computer Arithmetic." If you are uncertain as to how these basic operations are performed, this article should help. Many microprocessors do not have multiplication and division instructions, however, and so these operations must be implemented in software. "Two's Complement Multiplication" by Ray Bagley and "An Overview of Long Division" by Geoffrey Gass provide the background needed to write routines for these functions.

Working with large numbers can soon tax the limits of a calculator or even a microcomputer. Helpful "Procedures for Large Numbers" will get you through this difficulty. Michael Finerty even tells why you would want to represent a number as large as 10^{100}.

Finally, where there are numbers, there are also numerical errors. An important area of numerical calculations is the control of these errors: rounding errors, truncation errors, and so on. Daniel R Buskirk has some insights to this very necessary study in "Sources of Numerical Error."

An Introduction to Numbers

Webb Simmons

The concept of fixed point numbers, scaled numbers and floating point numbers originated in the scientific computer environment at a time when a computer was generally considered to be either a scientific computer or a business computer rather than the general purpose computer of today. Business computers used fixed point numbers but designers felt no need to describe them as such because that was the only kind of number used. Some business computers used decimal arithmetic rather than binary arithmetic and allowed a variable amount of decimal digits for various variables and values of programs. Some business computers referred to their decimal digits as characters and regarded every character whether or not it was a decimal digit as having a decimal digit value. But here we're concerned with the wider concepts of number representation in a general purpose computer.

In the general purpose machine we regard all numerical values to be binary numbers in some sense. The point in fixed point and floating point is not a decimal point but is a binary point. A binary point in a binary number plays the same role as the decimal point in a decimal number. The binary number 101 (meaning 101.) has the decimal value of 5. The binary number 10.1 has the decimal value of 2.5. The binary digit to the left of the binary point has the place value, positional value, of one; the binary digit next further left has the place value of two, then four, then eight, etc. The first binary digit to the right of the binary point has the

place value of one half, then one fourth, one eighth, etc. Binary 1010.1010 is decimal 10.625. Conversion is seen by adding the digit's place values 10.625 = 8 + 2 + 0.5 + 0.125.

The binary value in a register or memory location contains only binary digits as a succession of binary zeroes and ones. It has nothing in it that is explicitly a binary point. It is the responsibility of the programmer to decide the assumed position of the binary point. If the binary point is assumed to be to the right of the least significant binary digit, the value is an ordinary integer. Such a value is often called a "fixed point" number as in FORTRAN or PL/I. The binary point can be assumed to lie anywhere within the word or anywhere outside of the word. When the binary point is assumed to be fixed at any place other than at the right of the least significant bit (LSB) it is commonly called a scaled value, or scaled fixed point value. Any other fixed placement is a scaled binary number.

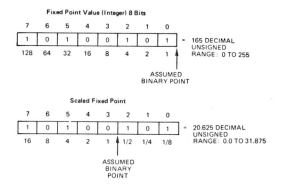

The values which can be represented as an integer in one 8 bit byte are from zero to 255 when all values are considered to be unsigned, and therefore positive. In signed two's complement notation the fixed point values in one byte are the integers from −128 to +127. In either case there are 256 different values possible, of which all are integers with no fractions permitted.

Scaled fixed point binary is not often used except as a part of a floating point word. When scaled numbers were widely used in earlier computers, the binary point was frequently placed, or assumed to be placed, in the center of a long computer word of 36 bits, 48 bits or 60 bits in length. Another common placement used was at the left of the most significant bit (MSB) but to the right of the sign bit of a two's complement number. In scaled values of this type the values are always less than one and greater than minus one. Many modern large computers have instructions to facilitate operations on these fractional scaled values.

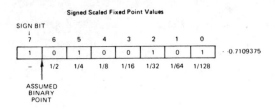

Signed Scaled Fixed Point Values

Scaled fixed point values will not figure strongly in our futures, except in those rare cases where speed or other application dependent criteria require optimization.

For signed and scaled fractional two's complement numbers, the largest binary value is 0 .1111111 and the smallest binary value would be 1 .0000000 where the digit to the left of the binary point is the sign bit; however, if we are to limit the range to fractional values, we must throw out the 1.0000000 state and treat 1.0000001 as the most negative value. This leaves us with 255 states ranging from +(127/128) to −(127/128) or performing the division, +.9921875 to −.9921875.

Extending Precision

The fact that a particular computer uses bytes for its memory storage and registers does not mean that a datum must be one byte. A unit of data can be any number of bits regardless of the computer word length. It can be 19 bits on a 13 bit word machine if you program such a construction. This would be unusual but it certainly is possible. It is customary to define the numerical data so that it will use 1,2,3 or some other whole number of bytes or words. Dividing data on

memory address boundaries eases and simplifies programming.

Scaled values were useful enough for many purposes but their use was troublesome to the programmer. If a value got too large, there was danger of overflow. If a value got too small, there was a loss of significance caused by too many leading zeroes and the danger of the value becoming zero. Special scaling factors had to be used from time to time to keep the problem in hand, and of course the effects of the scaling factors had to be removed when the computations were completed. The invention of floating point numbers cured most of the scaling difficulties.

Enter Floating Points

A floating point number has two parts for each value. One part is a fraction which is a scaled fixed point number as described above. The fractional part has many names. It may be called the fraction, mantissa or coefficient. The typical floating point number has a fraction whose absolute value is always less than one. The minimum fractional value is determined by the base of the other part of the floating point number. This other part of a floating point number has been called the exponent, power or characteristic depending on whose description you read. It is the exponent or power to be applied to some base (also called the radix) that forms a scaling factor. The value of the number is the fractional part multiplied by the base raised to the power of the exponent's value.

For many years the base for the exponent part of a floating point number was almost invariably two. For a base radix of two a nominal minimum absolute value for the fractional part is one half. We set up our hardware or software to force the most significant bit of the mantissa to be one, in order to "normalize" our numbers. Similarly, for each possible base we constrain the fractional value: For a base of four the minimum fraction value is one fourth. For a radix of eight the minimum fraction is one eighth and for 16 it is one sixteenth. IBM System 360/370 uses a radix of 16 for the exponent base in floating point numbers and so do various other computers and systems. Whatever the radix for the exponent, whenever the fraction is greater than or equal to the minimum value for that base, the floating point number is said to be normalized (in other words, it is the "normal" or "best" form).

There is very little standardization among floating point numbers. The radix for the exponent's base may be two or it may be ten or even 16. Within a floating point word the bits for the exponent can be either before or after the fraction. The number of bits for the exponents vary widely in different systems as do those for the fractions. There are various schemes for showing the signs for the exponents and the signs for the fractions.

The dynamic range of values allowed for a floating point number is determined primarily by the radix for the exponent and the number of bits in the exponent. The IBM System 360 and 370 hardware uses an 8 bit exponent of which one bit is used to take care of the sign for the exponent (it is not truly a sign bit but the overall effect is much the same) and one bit handles the sign for the fraction which leaves six bits to determine the value of the exponent. The largest value in six bits is 63 which, when applied to a base of 16, produces 16^{63} or approximately 7×10^{75}. The smallest positive exponent is equivalent to 16^{-64} or approximately 9×10^{-78}. These exponents must be multiplied by some fraction between 0.0625 and 1 to get the final value of a floating point word. The exponent for a Univac 1100 series computer is nine bits which loses two bits for the signs. The remaining seven bits would seem better than the remaining six for the System 370 except that the radix of the exponent is two. The largest exponent is 2^{127} or approximately 1.7×10^{38} and thus much smaller than that for the IBM version. The Univac double precision floating point word allows numbers to 2^{1024} or approximately 1.8×10^{308} which is pretty impressive.

The precision, or accuracy limit, of a floating point number is determined by the number of bits in the fraction part. Just in case you're mistakenly tempted to regard accuracy and precision as being the same, let us learn to distinguish between them. Precision relates to the ability to differentiate between value representations that are nearly the same. In terms of decimal values the precision can be to eight significant digits but if the accuracy is less than the precision then some or all of these eight digits are nonsense. Accuracy cannot exceed precision. Precision can be defined as the maximum possible relative accuracy. You cannot easily ascribe a precision to a 1 bit field because there is only one nonzero value possible.

In spite of slight conceptual error it is often convenient to regard the precision as the representional error caused by the variation of one in the least significant bit position for a field width in bits that does not include leading zero bits. Using this method for two bits we can stipulate four values, so we can say the precision is about 25%.

From this point let us decide to give

Bits	Number of Values	Maximum Error	Decimal Digits
2	4	.250	0
3	8	.125	0
4	16	.063	1
5	32	.031	1
6	64	.016	1
7	128	8E-3	2
8	256	4E-3	2
9	512	2E-3	2
10	1K	1E-3	3
11	2K	5E-4	3
12	4K	2E-4	3
13	8k	1E-4	3
14	16K	6E-5	4
15	33K	3E-5	4
16	66K	2E-5	4
17	131K	1E-5	5
18	262K	4E-6	5
19	524K	2E-6	5
20	1M	1E-6	6
21	2M	5E-7	6
22	4M	2E-7	6
23	8M	1E-7	6
24	17M	6E-8	7
25	34M	3E-8	7
26	67M	1E-8	7
27	134M	7E-9	8
28	268M	4E-9	8
29	537M	2E-9	8
30	1G	9E-10	9
31	2G	5E-10	9
32	4G	2E-10	9

Table 1: This is a summary of the nominal maximum relative error that occurs for different field widths. The field widths are measured in bits. The maximum error column is calculated as being the maximum error or change in value that occurs if the least significant bit is lost or changed. The decimal digits column indicates the number of decimal digits which are unaffected by relative error in the representation.

precision as the precision in bits in the bit field that does not include leading zero bits. Then, for each such precision, we can compute an error that will have nothing at all to do with accuracy beyond placing a limit on the accuracy. This is equivalent to saying that a method or procedure which produces a value can be totally wrong but this does not reduce the precision in the value as it is represented. We can claim the square root of 4 to be 1.389567. This square root is quite precise but not very accurate.

When one thinks of errors it is usually errors caused by all inaccuracies rather than just those errors caused by precision of expression. However, for the remainder of this article I will take a narrow view of errors and assume they are all caused by precision only. The nominal maximum relative errors for different field widths, measured in bits, are summarized in table 1.

Our approximate rule for the maximum error in a 2 bit value gave us 25% when the true value was about 20%. As the field width in the number of bits increases the approximate rule improves and is close enough in any case. It is important to remember that the effective field width does not include leading zeroes.

The floating point fraction on the Univac 1108 (Univac calls it the mantissa) is 27 bits wide and the most significant bit is always set for positive values. Thus the precision, expressed as the maximum representational error, is about one part in 10^8 and is equivalent to seven or eight significant decimal digits. The single precision floating

| hexadecimal | 4 | 1 | 1 | 0 | 0 | 0 | 0 | 0 |
| binary | 0100000100010000000000000000000 |

Table 2: The breakdown of a sample number of a 32 bit word into binary and hexadecimal digit groups.

point fraction on the IBM System 370 computers is allowed a width of 24 bits but because the exponent radix is base 16, the normalized fraction can have from none to three leading zeroes. The precision therefore varies from an error of about one part in 10^8 for 24 bits to one part in 10^7 for 21 bits. The equivalent decimal precision is about six or seven significant decimal digits. The IBM fraction is not quite as good as Univac's but the dynamic range allowed by the floating point exponent is greater. Both are greatly inferior to the CDC machines with their 12 bit exponent and 48 bit mantissa in a word of 60 bits.

It is not customary to use a signed value in the exponent part of floating point numbers. The more usual arrangement is to bias the exponent by adding a constant. The exponent range for the IBM floating word is from 16^{-64} to 16^{63}. The 16 is not shown but is assumed. IBM adds 64 to the exponents so that the floating exponent part for the value 16^{-64} is zero and for 16^{63} is 127. A floating value of one is equivalently $16 \times 1/16 = 1$ which yields binary 0100000100010000000000000000000 as a single, 32 bit value. In hexadecimal this is 41100000. The exponent part in hexadecimal is 41. Table 2 shows a summary of the binary and hexadecimal digit placement as used by IBM.

Negative floating values are typically formed one of two ways. The word as a whole is simply arithmetically inverted or else only the sign bit is inverted. Either of these methods is satisfactory and neither changes the dynamic range of the exponent nor the precision of the fraction.

Many IBM users go to double precision floating point because the precision equivalent to 6 decimal digits is not sufficient for their needs. In this case the exponent, and therefore the dynamic range, is not changed but the fraction width is increased to 56 bits which is equivalent to about 17 decimal digits. Double precision on the Univac allows 12 bits for the exponent, versus the single precision 9 bits, and 60 bits for the fraction, versus the single precision 27 bits. Double precision on the CDC machines is almost ridiculous — the exponent is essentially repeated in the second word which allows 96 bits for the fractional part which is equivalent to more than 30 decimal digits!

If I were writing a complete programming system for an 8 bit byte machine, I would not use a 4 byte copy of the IBM floating word but would use two bytes for the exponent with an exponent base radix of two rather than 16 and four bytes for the fraction part. A 32 bit fraction is equivalent to about nine significant decimal digits and the exponent range would be ridiculously large. Or maybe one should use the IBM method but add two bytes to the fraction part. My point here is that I personally do not like a word with only six decimal digits of precision.■

Making Binary Numbers Respectable

Webb Simmons

For some reason binary numbers have not quite made the grade with certain people. Professional computer programmers have, of necessity, fully accepted binary numbers for a very simple reason: their livelihood depends upon them. The ordinary man appears to be in a world of hurt when faced with the little binary beasties. The reason for this must be found and corrected.

One reason decimal numbers are so popular is that we have names for them. Not just the names "one" through "nine," but names for larger magnitudes such as "thousand" and "million." In the binary numbers, we have "one" and "zero," adopted from decimal numbers, but there it stops. One seldom hears "one thousand" or "binary one thousand" for 1000 base 2, and no one is guilty of "one million" for 1000000 base 2. We need names for larger entities, but we should not use decimal names; there is confusion enough as it is. Yet it would be better to avoid the invention of totally new words because there would be little acceptance for them (consider the lack of acceptance for Esperanto and other word inventions). We must adopt meaningful words which relate to the binary numbers and that are already accepted in the English language.

Believe it or not, such names do exist. It is amazing that we have not already associated them with ordinary binary numbers. How many of us have noticed the remnants of various number systems other than base ten that exist in English: "score" for twenty, "dozen" for twelve, "minute" for 1/60 part and "second" as the abbreviation for "second minute" or 1/60 part of 1/60 part? For two we have many words, "both," "pair," "duo"; and for four we have "quad." This line of approach is doomed quickly because, even though we find "octo" for eight, where are 16, 32, etc? If we but open our dictionaries, the words are with us, and they are in a coherent system.

There is a large collection of words whose future prospects are dim because of the trend towards adoption of the metric system of weights and measures with its decimal scales of value. Let us adopt these soon-to-be-obsolete words to retain them for

Chaldron	=	256	gallons
Butt	=	128	gallons
Seam	=	64	gallons
Coomb	=	32	gallons
Strike	=	16	gallons
Bushel	=	8	gallons
Bucket	=	4	gallons
Peck	=	2	gallons
Gallon	=	1	gallon
Pottle	=	1/2	gallon
Quart	=	1/4	gallon
Pint	=	1/8	gallon
Cup	=	1/16	gallon
Gill	=	1/32	gallon
(Noname)	=	1/64	gallon
Ounce	=	1/128	gallon

Table 1: This is a compilation of names, soon to be obsolete due to conversion to the metric number system, which are associated with binary values in American and British volume measurement. With the exception of COOMB, all these units have at some point in time been associated in common practice with the power of 2 multiples shown.

posterity while, at the same time, enriching the vocabulary of a noble field: the binary number system.

In table 1 I show the results of an iterative sort-merge procedure on the words used in both the American and British languages for both fluid (liquid) and dry volume measures. Modesty prevents me from describing the elation and exultation that I felt when the full impact of my discovery sank home. Here we have a full set of defined words just begging to be used. Naturally, we will remove any impression of volume measurements previously associated with their use and, for uniformity, we will truncate all of them to their first four letters. There will be no loss to our weights and measures since for these we will be using liters anyway, as well as the modifications kiloliters, deciliters, and so forth. The final results are shown in table 2.

An examination of table 2 discloses that we need no longer say "one" for binary one, but will instead say **gall**. This raises the question of "zero"; what shall we use for this? "Nogallon" is obviously zero, so let us adopt **noga** for this important concept.

Imagine if you will the sheer convenience

Chal	=	100,000,000.	= 256
Butt	=	10,000,000.	= 128
Seam	=	1,000,000.	= 64
Coom	=	100,000.	= 32
Stri	=	10,000.	= 16
Bush	=	1,000.	= 8
Buck	=	100.	= 4
Peck	=	10.	= 2
Gall	=	1.	Unity
Pott	=	.1	= 1/2
Quar	=	.01	= 1/4
Pint	=	.001	= 1/8
Cupa	=	.0001	= 1/16
Gill	=	.00001	= 1/32
Nona	=	.000001	= 1/64
Ounc	=	.0000001	= 1/128

Table 2: By shortening the names in table 1, a set of positional names for the binary number system is obtained.

and immediate impact of being able to say **coom-bush-buck-peck** for the awkward "binary 101110." Consider the fluidity in such as **pott-cupa-nona** for "binary 0.100101." **Stri** will join "taxi" as an English noun ending with the letter **i**. When a variable value drops to less than one, we can say it has gone to **pott**. If you need a small amount of something, you can ask for a **cupa**. An open question, however, is the proper pronunciation of **ounc**. ∎

A Novice's Eye on

Computer Arithmetic

Wayne Ledder

Now that you have your shiny new microcomputer you want to use it for something. No matter what the application, someplace in it you have to use numbers: to count, do arithmetic, input from a keyboard, or output to a terminal of some sort. If you are operating with a higher level language such as BASIC or FORTRAN there is no problem since all the number manipulation programs are already included. Most of us, however, must work in assembly language or even machine language, and if you have never been there before it can be a discouraging situation when you don't get the expected results.

The purpose of this article is to explain how simple numbers are often represented in a computer and how to do the four basic arithmetic operations. Since the real world of people is decimal, not binary oriented, we have to convert from one to the other. Since most computer peripherals talk in a language called ASCII, I will also show how to translate that into binary and vice versa.

Binary Number System

All the computers you are liable to run into operate on the binary number system, where each element has two possible states, usually designated as 1 and 0. Let's consider an arbitrary 8 bit computer, meaning that the internal arithmetic and logic of the computer handles data that consists of eight bits at a time.

When counting in either the binary or decimal number system the first number is designated by 0 and the second number by 1. We run into difficulties when we try to express the number 2. In the decimal number system it is easy, 2. In the binary number system we have already used up the two allowable states with the first two numbers. What we need is an additional bit of information. When this bit is added we can now designate the number 2 by 10. This extra digit on the left represents a weight of $2^1 = 2$. (The rightmost digit has a weight of $2^0 = 1$.)

Each digit position in a number is assigned a weight dependent on where in the number it occurs. To obtain these weights take the base number and raise it to a power equal to the position of the digit in the number. The rightmost digit is the least significant digit and has the position index of zero. Following these two rules the weights for the decimal number system are: $10^0 = 1$, $10^1 = 10$, $10^2 = 100$, etc. In the binary number system the base number is 2 instead of 10. Substituting, we have the following weights: $2^0 = 1$, $2^1 = 2$, $2^2 = 4$, etc.

To translate a binary number into a decimal number just add up the weights of the digits which are 1s. Table 1 shows how the decimal numbers from 0 through 16 are written in binary and two other forms of numbering common in computers: hexadecimal, which uses a base of 16, and octal, which uses a base of 8.

The octal and hexadecimal forms are used to save you from writing out long strings of 1s and 0s which are hard to read and give plenty of opportunity for mistakes. For hexadecimal notation six new digit value graphics are needed to allow a total of 16 different digits, representing four bits. To fill this need the letters of the alphabet A through F are used to represent the numbers 10 through 15. To convert a binary number to hexadecimal start at the

Decimal Number	Binary Number					Hexadecimal		Octal	
	Weights = 16	8	4	2	1	Weights = 16	1	Weights = 8	1
0	0	0	0	0	0	0	0	0	0
1	0	0	0	0	1	0	1	0	1
2	0	0	0	1	0	0	2	0	2
3	0	0	0	1	1	0	3	0	3
4	0	0	1	0	0	0	4	0	4
5	0	0	1	0	1	0	5	0	5
6	0	0	1	1	0	0	6	0	6
7	0	0	1	1	1	0	7	0	7
8	0	1	0	0	0	0	8	1	0
9	0	1	0	0	1	0	9	1	1
10	0	1	0	1	0	0	A	1	2
11	0	1	0	1	1	0	B	1	3
12	0	1	1	0	0	0	C	1	4
13	0	1	1	0	1	0	D	1	5
14	0	1	1	1	0	0	E	1	6
15	0	1	1	1	1	0	F	1	7
16	1	0	0	0	0	1	0	2	0

Table 1: Binary, octal, decimal and hexadecimal equivalents of the decimal numbers 0 through 16.

least significant (right) end and count off binary digits in groups of four. If the last group does not contain four digits visualize additional 0s to make four binary digits. Consider each 4 digit group as a separate number and write its hexadecimal equivalent (refer to table 1). For example:

binary	1101011100100011				
separated	0001	1010	1110	0100	0111
hexadecimal	1	A	E	4	7

To convert from hexadecimal to binary notation just reverse the procedure. Replace each hexadecimal digit with its binary equiv- alent, remembering to add leading 0s so that each of the hexadecimal digits forms a 4 digit binary number.

Octal conversion is the same except the binary number is broken into groups of three. For the previous example:

binary	1101011100100011					
separated	011	010	111	001	000	111
octal	3	2	7	1	0	7

Conversion from octal back to binary is done by replacing each octal digit with its 3 digit binary equivalent.

Let's return to our 8 bit computer. If table 1 is expanded to eight binary digits (bits) the largest number that can be formed would be decimal 255 (binary 11111111). Counting 0, this gives 256 different num- bers that can be expressed with eight bits. In some applications 256 numbers are enough, but if you were going to balance your checkbook a maximum balance of $2.55 would be rather useless. I will return to this limitation shortly and show you how to get around it; but first, in the context of balancing checkbooks, what happens when a number is negative? If we accept 0 as a positive number then we can assign one bit of the number to be the sign, a 1 for negative and a 0 for positive. Notice that we have lost a bit from the numerical value and now can only have 128 different values each with two signs for a total of 256 dif- ferent numbers. However, −0 is not con- sidered a valid number, so there are only 255 usable numbers. This type of notation is called a sign-magnitude representation of a number. Using this notation, −1 is written as:

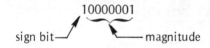

If you were going to add two signed numbers (say +3 and −1) your program would have to take into account several things first. First, if you simply added the two numbers, the result would be wrong:

+3	00000011	
−1	10000001	
sum	10000100	= −4

Wouldn't it be nice if there were a number notation that would allow identif- ication of positive and negative and give a correct answer when added together? Con- sider adding +1 to −1 to get 0. What 8 bit binary number added to 1 gives 0?

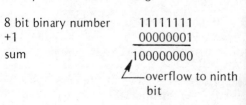

8 bit binary number   11111111
+1   00000001
sum   100000000
—overflow to ninth bit

The binary number which is all 1s can be called −1. What would −2 be?

−2	11111110
+2	00000010
sum	100000000

We can take any positive number up to 127 decimal (01111111 binary) and subtract it from 0 (assume there was a ninth bit equal to 1 so 0 is really 100000000). The resultant binary number is called the 2's complement. The most significant (leftmost) bit is a true sign bit in the 2's complement notation, but negative numbers have an altered magnitude value. When two such 2's complement notation numbers are added the answer is correct. Consider the previous example of adding +3 and −1:

+3	00000011
−1	11111111
sum	100000010 = +2 (in 2's complement notation)

Now consider adding +1 and −3:

+1	00000001
−3	11111101
sum	11111110 = −2 (in 2's complement notation)

One method of finding the 2's complement of a number has been mentioned which required subtraction from binary 0. A simple method that can easily be done on paper, especially if you are prone to making errors in binary subtraction like me, is to first rewrite the number substituting 1s for 0s and 0s for 1s, then add binary 1 to the result. For example, the 2's complement of +5 is:

+5	00000101
substitute	11111010
add 1	1
−5	11111011

To check, we should be able to take the 2's complement of −5 and end up with +5:

−5	11111011
substitute	00000100
add 1	1
+5	00000101

Substituting 1s for 0s and 0s for 1s is called complementing and is usually found as an instruction in the computer instruction set. Adding 1 is usually available as an instruction also. Sometimes both instructions can be combined into one step. In summary, to make a number negative (if you have no negate instruction):

- Clear the accumulator.
- Add the number to the accumulator.
- Complement the accumulator.
- Add 1 to the accumulator.

The accumulator now contains the negative of the original number in 2's complement notation. One interesting property which comes along with this 2's complement form is the fact that *all* states of the 8 (or n) bits are valid and there is only one zero state. The largest negative number, however, has no positive value equivalent.

Let's return to the problem of not having enough bits to make a big enough number. If we use two successive byte size memory locations to represent a number we have 2^{16} (65,536) possible numbers. Using 2's complement notation we can have any number from −32,768 to +32,767. If that is not enough you can expand in increments of eight bits until your needs are satisfied. There is a problem now, since the computer only operates on eight bits at a time. When a number is spread over more than one memory location it is called a multiple precision or extended precision number. If two locations are used for each number it is called double precision; if three are used it is called triple precision, etc. (However, it remains a binary number. In large machine floating point representations, this terminology has a different meaning.)

One more item needs to be mentioned before I describe multiple precision arithmetic. All computers have some sort of means to detect an accumulator overflow (or underflow). In our 8 bit example this is a ninth bit at the extreme left of the number. The status of this bit can be controlled and tested. It increases by 1 when the addition of the eight bits causes a carry and decreases by 1 when the subtraction of the eight bits causes a borrow. When a rotate instruction is executed this bit receives the most significant bit and loads the least significant bit on a rotate left. It receives the least significant bit and loads the most significant bit on a rotate right. This extra bit is known by different names, such as overflow, carry, and (in the PDP-8) the link.

The steps shown in the box on page 13 will vary from machine to machine, depending upon how the instruction set is organized. For example, the 6800 instruction set has ADC for add with carry input, and the 8080 instruction set has a similar variation. In these cases, there is no need to rotate the accumulator from the carry flag prior to the second addition, since the ADC instruction type takes into account the old value of the carry.

How do you do a 2's complement of a double precision number? Start with the accumulator and carry set to 0s. Add the least significant part of the number. Complement and add 1 as before. The accumulator now contains the 2's complement of the least significant part, so store it. Rotate left to load any carry into the least significant bit. Store the contents of the accumulator (the carry) in any convenient location. Add the most significant part of the number to the accumulator. Complement it only. Now add the previously stored carry. The contents of the accumulator are now the most significant part of the 2's complement. As in the simple addition case, machines with an ADC instruction can often use the previous setting of the carry flag as part of the addition.

Addition

All computers can add. They typically add some specified memory location to the contents of an accumulator (a built-in memory location in the processor). When adding two or more numbers together you must be careful not to allow the resulting sum to get so large that you get an incorrect answer. For instance, when using 2's complement notation you can add together two numbers which are positive and get a negative answer if a carry into the sign bit occurs. Also be sure the accumulator and carry are initialized to 0.

Subtraction

Some computers do subtraction directly, but be careful. They may only subtract magnitudes. You have to do checking of each number to see which is larger and in what order the subtraction takes place in order to determine ahead of time what the sign should be. Sign bits must be set to 0 so they don't give false indication of magnitude. The sign bits must be put back into the answer if you are using signed number notation. All of this takes a lot of extra software and time. If you are using 2's complement notation you can subtract directly and the sign will automatically come out correct. Most of the common microprocessors use 2's complement notation and have no problems subtracting directly.

If direct subtraction is not possible in your computer, all is not lost. Consider subtraction by addition of a negative number. If you want to perform A−B=C, for example, use 2's complement notation and first make B negative by taking its 2's complement and then add A to get the answer C. Notice that even if A or B is negative to begin with, the answer will still be correct in 2's complement notation without any extra software to keep track of the sign. This will also work for multiple precision numbers. You still have to be careful not to use numbers which are large enough to cause inadvertent sign bit changes.

Multiplication

Two problems immediately confront us when we consider multiplication. First, if you multiply two 8 bit numbers together, the result is 16 bits long; and second, you simply can't add up 2's complement numbers and always get the correct answer. For instance, if you add −3 three times the answer would be −9 (equivalent to 3 times −3) which is correct, but what would you do with a negative multiplicand as in −3 times −3? To solve this problem and use successive addition to do multiplication the first step is to convert all numbers to a positive absolute value without sign. If you have been using 2's complement notation it is an easy procedure to convert. Rotate left to load the sign bit into the carry bit. Test the carry bit. If it is 0, the number is positive; if it is 1, the number is negative. If the number is positive, just rotate right to restore it to its original value and set all 0s into a location assigned to be the sign of the number. If the number is negative, first rotate right to restore the original, then take the 2's complement of it to get the number positive and finally, with an all zero accumulator, set the carry bit to 1 and rotate right. Store this in the sign location. What we have done is separate the number into its sign and magnitude. Now if the signs are added we get the correct sign for the answer directly which should be stored in a location assigned to the sign of the answer. Two generalized techniques may be used to find the magnitude of the answer.

Successive addition may be used by adding A to itself B times. If the instruction set allows decrementing a number, use that instruction to decrease B by 1 each time you add A to the accumulator until B reaches 0. At that point you have the magnitude of the answer. If the instruction set allows incrementing but not decrementing, first take the 2's complement of B and use incrementing of the now negative number until it reaches 0. The disadvantage of using successive addition is that you have to do a potentially large number of additions which can take a lot of time.

A second technique that requires only a few operations is a direct copy of how you do binary multiplication by hand. For example, let's multiply two 4 bit binary numbers by hand:

$$\begin{array}{r} 1101 \\ X\ \underline{1010} \end{array} \begin{array}{l} = A \\ = B \end{array}$$

$$\begin{array}{r} 0000 \\ 1101 \\ 0000 \\ \underline{1101} \\ \hline 10000010 \end{array} \quad = C$$

Notice that all we have to do is add A, a shifted version of A, or 0, depending on which digit of B is used and whether it is a 1 or 0. Notice also that two 4 bit numbers produce an 8 bit answer, so if you don't restrict the number size, you have to use multiple precision shifting and addition.

A technique that is sometimes useful when you want to multiply by a constant is to recognize that shifting a number left one position is equivalent to multiplying by 2. Shifting left two positions is equivalent to multiplying by 4, three positions is multiplying by 8, etc. By shifting and adding the various shifted numbers in a fixed format you can do the equivalent of multiplying very quickly by a constant. For example, to multiply by 5, shift left twice and add it to the original:

$$5A = (4 + 1) A = 4A + A$$

Division

Division is the most difficult operation to do. First, handle the separation of magnitude and sign as under multiplication and use the same technique of adding signs to get the correct answer sign. The problem with division is that seldom does the answer come out exactly even. Usually there is a remainder. You have to decide how far you want to carry out the answer and what rules you are going to use for rounding off. You may also have the binary equivalent of a decimal point to consider.

One method of dividing is by successive subtractions. For example, to divide A by B, count how many times you can subtract B from A before the remainder is 0 or negative. If the remainder goes to 0, the value of the count is the exact answer. If the remainder becomes negative that means you went one step too far. Reduce the count by 1, add B back to A, and test the remainder to see how to round off. This will give you a whole number answer. It will also locate the binary equivalent of a decimal point if you want to carry the answer further.

Alternatively, you can add B successively, counting the number of times, until the sum equals or exceeds A. Equal to A means the answer is exact, and exceeds A means you went one step too far.

One very limited type of division is very easily done. If you are dividing by 2,4,8,16, etc, all you have to do is rotate the number to the right the appropriate number of times. However, you must be careful of rotating a 1 through the carry bit and having it appear in the most significant bit of the number. To avoid this be sure the carry bit is cleared to 0 before each rotate. A check of the carry bit after the last rotate can be used for

An Example of Double Precision Addition

Step Number	Procedure	Resulting Values	
		Carry Bit	Accumulator
1&2	Clear carry bit and accumulator.	0	0 0 0 0 0 0 0 0
3	Add A_2 to the accumulator.	0	1 1 1 0 1 0 0 0
4	Add B_2 to the accumulator (gives C_2 in accumulator).	1	1 1 0 0 0 1 0 0
5	Store contents of accumulator in the memory location assigned for C_2. Set accumulator to 0; preserve status of carry bit.	1	0 0 0 0 0 0 0 0
6	Rotate accumulator left one bit.	0	0 0 0 0 0 0 0 1
7	Add A_1 to the accumulator.	0	1 1 0 0 1 1 1 0
8	Add B_1 to the accumulator (gives C_1 in accumulator).	0	1 1 1 0 0 1 1 1
9	Store contents of accumulator in the memory location assigned for C_1. Set accumulator to 0.	0	0 0 0 0 0 0 0 0

To check, write out all 16 bits and add:

```
A = 1 1 0 0 1 1 0 1 1 1 1 0 1 0 0 0
B = +0 0 0 1 1 0 0 1 1 1 0 1 1 1 0 0
C = 1 1 1 0 0 1 1 1 1 1 0 0 0 1 0 0
```

$$A \begin{cases} A_1 = 1\ 1\ 0\ 0\ 1\ 1\ 0\ 1 \\ A_2 = 1\ 1\ 1\ 0\ 1\ 0\ 0\ 0 \end{cases} \qquad B \begin{cases} B_1 = 0\ 0\ 0\ 1\ 1\ 0\ 0\ 1 \\ B_2 = 1\ 1\ 0\ 1\ 1\ 1\ 0\ 0 \end{cases}$$

The simple addition of two double precision positive numbers, A and B, to obtain an answer C. In this example the subscript 1 denotes the most significant part of the number and the subscript 2 denotes the least significant part. To add two double precision numbers:

1. Clear the accumulator to all 0s.
2. Set the overflow, carry (or whatever the extreme leftmost bit is called) to 0. Often these two steps can be combined into one.
3. Add A_2, the least significant part of A, to the accumulator.
4. Add B_2 to the accumulator. At this point the accumulator contains the sum of the least significant parts of A and B. If any carry has occurred due to this addition the carry bit will be a 1. If no carry has occurred, it will be 0.
5. Store the contents of the accumulator in the memory location assigned for C_2. Set the accumulator to 0, but preserve the state of the carry bit.
6. Rotate the accumulator left one position. This will load the carry bit from the previous addition into the least significant bit of the accumulator.
7. Add A_1 to the accumulator.
8. Add B_1 to the accumulator. At this point the accumulator contains the sum of the most significant parts of A and B plus any carry from the least significant parts.
9. Store the contents of the accumulator in the memory location assigned for C_1.

round off determination. If it is a 1, round off the answer to the next higher number.

Interfacing to a Nonbinary World

As mentioned earlier, the world is decimal oriented and we should be able to talk to the computer with decimal digits, and indeed our terminals have decimal keys and decimal outputs. Our terminals, however, talk to our computers in yet another language, usually ASCII.

Notice the codes for the decimal ASCII digits 0 through 9 as seen in any table of ASCII codes. If you consider only the least significant four bits you have the binary value of the associated decimal digit. There are two ways of extracting the binary value from the ASCII code. You can first load the ASCII character into the accumulator and then subtract 0110000 or mask it by "anding" the accumulator with 1111. So now you have converted one decimal digit into its binary equivalent. Unfortunately, very often you need more than one decimal digit to make the number. The simplest way to handle this is to use a fixed format. This means you have to enter leading 0s so a number will always have the same number of digits and the order in which they are entered defines their decimal rank (units, tens, hundreds, etc). Since each digit is now known it may be placed in a location assigned to its rank after it has been converted to binary. You now have a fragmented number which is not usable for arithmetic. It must first be made into a single binary number.

As an example, let's assume we are using a 3 digit fixed format and the decimal number we are entering is 27. First we type a 0 for the hundreds digit which is stored in a location, HUNS, as a binary 0, using one of the ASCII to binary conversion techniques. Then we type a 2 and a 7 which are converted to binary and stored in locations TENS and UNITS, respectively. Now to make it all one big binary number.

First test the hundreds digit. It is 0 in this case, so jump to testing the tens digit. It is not 0, so multiply the binary equiv-

alent of 10 (1010) by the contents of the TENS location, in this case 2, and the contents of the UNITS location, and store it in the answer location. In the more general case what you do is multiply each decimal digit by the binary equivalent of its rank and add up all the partial products. Finally, you have to convert the binary number into whatever notation you are using for doing arithmetic.

After the arithmetic, or whatever, is completed, the next step is to output it in recognizable form (ie: ASCII to the output device). The procedure is essentially a reverse of the input steps.

First convert the binary number into its fragmented equivalent. Using the above example, first subtract the binary equivalent of decimal 100 (1100100). In this case, the first attempt produces a negative answer, which means there are zero hundreds in the number and the HUNS location should be set to 0. Next try subtracting binary 10s until the result goes negative, then add one back. The number of times you can subtract 10s before it goes negative is equal to the value of the 10's digit. The remainder is the value of the units digit. These digits may now be converted to ASCII by simply adding 0110000 to each digit location. The final step is to transfer each digit (now in ASCII) to the output device (TTY or CRT terminal, etc) in the proper order.

It is possible to write a program that will work under a variable format for input and output to eliminate the need for leading 0s. This is more complicated since you have to count how many individual entries of digits are made and then arrange them in reverse order knowing the last entry is the units digit regardless of how many digits there are.

One last point: always verify each arithmetic program you write, either in the computer (best way) or write it out step by step by hand. Use extreme values for numbers, like 0, 1, and the maximum number your program is supposed to work with. Finally, select a number at random and try it. If they all work correctly, chances are very good your program is totally correct.■

READING STRINGS

I read with great interest Wayne Ledder's description of how a string of ASCII digits can be read and converted to a binary number in "A Novice's Eye on Computer Arithmetic" (page 9). A faster, cleaner, and easier algorithm exists for this purpose.

To read a 3 digit number, Ledder recommends placing the first digit (after subtracting ASCII "0") into memory location HUNS, the second into TENS, and the third into UNITS. Then HUNS is multiplied by 100, TENS by 10, and these results are added; UNITS is added to this sum to give the final result. Clearly, this method works. However, it is inconvenient to use for two reasons. First, the program itself must be modified if one wishes to input, say, four digit numbers. Second, the number must be typed using a fixed number of digits. Now, how would you feel if your tiny BASIC made you type things like 00001, or interpreted 0001 either as something ridiculous or an error?

I think there is a better way. The following algorithm is cleaner and as easy to implement.

1. Set NUM to 0.
2. Get a digit from input. If it is not a digit (eg: a blank or a new line), terminate.
3. Otherwise, convert the digit from ASCII by subtracting the code for ASCII "0" from it.
4. Multiply NUM by 10. Then add the digit to it.
5. Go to step 2.

When the algorithm terminates, the value of NUM will be the binary number corresponding to the ASCII coded input.

Several comments are in order. First, the multiplication in step 4 can be performed quickly by adding the value of NUM shifted left three times to the value of NUM shifted left once. Second, the processing of the first digit should probably be moved outside of the loop. This facilitates checking for a negative sign, avoids an unnecessary multiplication in step 4 on the first iteration, and makes it possible to check for a completely blank line (which should be treated as an error, not as zero).

This algorithm requires no leading zeroes and works for numbers of any length. It is also quite fast; in reading numbers less than 65,536, it requires only $3 \times n$ 16 bit shifts and $2 \times n$ 16 bit adds, to read an n digit number. Unfortunately, I can claim no credit for it since it has been in existence for many years.

Eric Hamilton
Dunster D-11
Harvard University
Cambridge MA 02138

Printed in the letters column in the May 1978 issue of BYTE.

Two's Complement Multiplication

Raymond B Bagley

Does your personal computer have a multiplication instruction? No? Let's solve the problem and design a software multiplication routine. Pure positive numbers are easy, but problems arise when the values are signed two's complement numbers [see "A Novice's Eye on Computer Arithmetic" on page 9 for an explanation of two's complement notation . . . BWL].

A popular approach for taking care of signed values is to set both input values positive. These values are multiplied to obtain the product. Next the signs of the inputs are checked. If the signs differ, we take the two's complement of the product to make the result negative. However, it is possible to carry out a signed multiplication directly.

Consider the simpler problem of addition. Two's complement notation is convenient for this operation. The hardware simply adds the two input values as pure magnitudes. This means that the sign bits are just more bits of magnitude to be combined with the sum. If the signs of the two inputs are different, the carry bit is ignored; lo and behold, the result is the proper signed sum.

To illustrate this point, consider the two four-bit values 1011 and 0001. These binary values have decimal magnitudes of 11 and 1. The decimal sum is 12. The binary value of this sum is 1100. Now reinterpret these numbers as two's complement values. The binary value 1011 represents decimal −5, the binary value 0001 represents +1. The proper sum is −4. The two's complement representation of −4 is 1100. This is precisely the same bit pattern as the magnitude result. The designers of addition and subtraction processes know that the signs take care of themselves. We can carry this idea over to multiplication. Let's design a multiplication routine in which the signs take care of themselves.

Fundamentally, binary multiplication is quite simple. The multiplication table consists of just the digits 0 and 1. Zero times anything is 0, and 1 times a number is simply

the number. For example, the calculation of 6 times 5 in binary is:

```
   110
   101
  ----
   110
  000
 110
 -----
 11110
```

We call this way of multiplication the sum method. The product is formed from the sum of the partial products.

The absolute sum algorithm in table 1 multiplies two non-negative numbers. A combination of right and left shifts is used to achieve multiplication and division by

1. [Let the multiplier be $m \geq 0$. Let the multiplicand be $n \geq 0$. Let l be the fixed word length. Let the partial product be p, with the length of p as 2 l. Let i be the word length counter.] Initialize p to 0. Initialize i to l.
2. Test the low bit of m. If this bit is 1 then add n to p.
3. Shift m right one place, dropping the low bit. Shift n left one place. Set i to i−1.
4. If i is not 0 go to step 2. If i is 0 the product is in p and the algorithm terminates.

Table 1. The absolute sum method of binary multiplication. The product is formed from the sum of the partial products. The method as presented here assumes that the values to be multiplied together are positive.

1. [Let the multiplier be m. Let the multiplicand be n. Let l be the fixed word length. Let the partial product be p, with the length of p as 2 l. Let i be the word length counter. Let j be a sign indicator.] Initialize p to zero. Initialize i to l. Set j = 0 if the signs of m and n are the same. Otherwise set j = 1. Set m to |m| and set n to |n|.
2. Left shift p one place, ignore overflow. Left shift m one place. If the shifted out bit of m is 1 then add n to p. Set i to i − 1.
3. If i is not zero, go to step 2.
4. [i is zero] If j = 1 then set p to (−p). The product is in p and the algorithm terminates.

Table 2. The sum method of two's complement multiplication. This variation scans the multiplier from the high end, chiefly for greater efficiency when implemented on the 8080 microprocessor, which can shift data in its registers to the left more easily than to the right. The algorithm here allows negative values to be multiplied.

powers of 2. If **m** had a 1 in some bit position j, then 2 raised to the j power times **n** was added to the partial product.

The algorithm scans the bits of the multiplier starting from the low end. The multiplier could be scanned starting from the high end just as easily. Scanning from the high end would allow us to devise an algorithm which did not use right shifts. This is an advantage for a system like an 8080 where 16 bit right shifts are not efficient.

The sum method in table 2 adds the logic to take care of the signs. Notice an important difference between the algorithms in table 1 and 2. The absolute sum algorithm in table 1 shifts the multiplicand each time we travel around the loop. The sum algorithm in table 2 shifts the partial product each time through the loop. For some computers, the absolute sum algorithm can be devised so that the partial product is shifting into the positions vacated as the multiplier shifts right. This is the technique normally used when the resulting product is to be double precision. Some machines are built with this idea in mind. Such a computer may have two registers called A and M. The finished product will have the upper half of the answer in register A and the lower half of the result in register M (multiplier register).

A binary number is a sum of powers of 2. The binary number 101 represents the sum:

$$2^2 + 2^0 = 4 + 1 = 5$$

The key point is that this is not the only interpretation of the binary representation. Consider the binary value 0111. This is the sum of three powers of 2:

$$2^2 + 2^1 + 2^0 = 4 + 2 + 1 = 7$$

This number is a string of consecutive 1 bits. Such a number of **p** consecutive 1 bits

is called a *Mersenne number* and is of the form:

$$2^p - 1.$$

The number 7 is:

$$2^3 - 1 = 8 - 1 = 7$$

Seven can be represented as the sum of three powers of 2 or as the difference of two powers of 2. 1 is, of course, 2 raised to the 0 power.

Any consecutive sub-sequence of 1 bits in a binary number represents the difference of two powers of 2. The binary representation of decimal 14 is 1110. This is just 2 times 7 or:

$$14 = 2(8 - 1) = 16 - 2 = 2^4 - 2^1$$

which is the difference of two powers.

Look at the binary value 0111100111-0011. This number can be represented as the sum of nine distinct powers of 2. The sums yield:

$$(2^{12} + 2^{11} + 2^{10} + 2^9) + (2^6 + 2^5 + 2^4) +$$
$$(2^1 + 2^0) = 7795.$$

Grouping the clusters as differences we have:

$$(2^{13} - 2^9) + (2^7 - 2^4) + (2^2 - 2^0) = 7795.$$

We use the power of two from the position just to the left of a cluster for the first value in a difference. The power of 2 represented by the rightmost 1 bit of a cluster is the number to be subtracted in the difference.

The difference method does not always result in fewer arithmetic operations than the pure sum method. If a cluster is three or more bits long, the difference method yields fewer calculations. If the cluster is two bits long both methods yield two arithmetic operations. When a cluster is just a single 1 bit the sum method yields fewer calculations.

Let us evaluate the difference calculations for a fixed word length of four bits. The binary number 1101 is calculated from a difference calculation as:

$$(16 - 4) + (2 - 1) = 13.$$

Think about the signed two's complement representation. This number is negative since it has a leading one bit. Evaluate the number by the difference method and then subtract 16 if the leading bit is 1. Another way is to write -16 first and then write the difference calculation:

$$-16 + (16 - 4) + (2 - 1) = -16 + 13 = -3.$$

MERSENNE NUMBERS

Marin Mersenne (1588-1648) was a French theologian, philosopher, and number theorist. A Mersenne number is defined as a number of the type:

$$M_p = 2^p - 1$$

where p is a prime number. Mersenne asserted that the only primes for which M_p is a prime are 2, 3, 5, 7, 13, 17, 19, 31, 67, 127, and 257. It has been found that M_{67} and M_{257} are not primes; however, mathematicians have since discovered Mersenne primes for p = 61, 89, 107, 521, 607, 1279, 2203, 2281, 3217, 4253, 4423, 9689, 9941, and 11213. The largest of these, M_{11213}, is 3376 decimal digits long.

If we regroup the negative 16 into the first set of parentheses, the 16s will cancel. This is the key to the technique we are going to devise. The calculation can now be written as:

$$(0 - 4) + (2 - 1) = -3.$$

We can state a rule for evaluating signed two's complement numbers by the difference method:

When the number is negative, substitute 0 for the first term of the leftmost difference cluster.

With this rule we see that the difference method calculates the value of a signed two's complement number.

To multiply some value n by a negative value such as -3 we have:

$$(-3)n = [(0 - 4) + (2 - 1)]n = -4n + 2n - n.$$

The product is formed by adding *and* subtracting various partial products.

The difference algorithm in table 3 is more complex than the absolute sum method in table 1. The added complications involve the testing and setting of the flag j in order to detect transitions of 1 bit and 0 bit clusters.

If the method is to be implemented in hardware, some elegant variations have been developed that look at the multiplier two bits at a time to produce a very fast multiplication. With hardware implementations the introduction of flags like j usually cost nothing in time and not much in additional hardware.

Flag testing in software is usually an additional time overhead. We can improve the software time element of the difference algorithm to the point where it is just as good as the sum algorithm in table 2. This will cost us a moderate amount of repeated code.

The difference algorithm tests the low order bit of the multiplier. Logically, we could have started at the other end of the multiplier and tested the high bit. Then we would arrange the shifts as in the reversed difference algorithm in table 4.

Starting from the high end of the multiplier m causes some inconvenience. Notice that m is shifted left $l+1$ times. This is because we have to detect the transition of the least order bit of m. The reason for reversing the difference algorithm is that some microprocessors (such as the 8080) can shift left more efficiently than they can shift right.

The fast difference algorithm in table 5 revises the reversed difference algorithm by

completely removing the flag j. Steps 5 and 6 could have been combined into one step and the "go to step 6" command in step 1 changed to "go to step 5". The reason for separate steps 5 and 6 is that it does not change the amount of code written and we save some time by avoiding the extra operation of step 5.

Steps 2, 3, and 4 in the fast difference algorithm are the same sort of process as steps 5, 6, 7, and 8. The fast difference algorithm has four more steps than the reversed difference algorithm but the number of operations to be performed is less for

1. [Let the input values be **m** and **n** of fixed length l. Let the partial product be **p**, with the length of **p** as 2l. Let the length counter be i. Let j be a flag to detect cluster patterns.] Initialize **p** to zero. Initialize i to l. Shift **m** left one place, put the carry in j.
2. Shift **p** left one place, ignore overflow. [The first time through the loop **p** is not actually changed.] Shift **m** left one place, call the carry **q**. Set i to i − 1.
3. If **q** ≠ j and j = 0 then add **n** to **p**. If **q** ≠ j and j = 1 then subtract **n** from **p**.
4. Set j = **q**. If i is not zero go to step 2. If i is zero then the product (with sign) is in **p** and the algorithm terminates.

Table 3. The difference method of multiplication. This algorithm is slightly more complex, due to the use of the flag j to detect the transitions of one bit and zero bit clusters. This method automatically handles two's complement (positive or negative) values.

1. [Let the input values be **m** and **n** of fixed length l. Let the partial product be **p**, with the length of **p** as 2l. Let the length counter be i. Let j be a flag to detect cluster patterns.] Initialize **p** to zero. Initialize i to l. Initialize j to zero.
2. Test the low bit of **m**. Call this bit **q**. If **q** ≠ j and j = 0 then subtract **n** from **p**. If **q** ≠ j and j = 1 then add **n** to **p**.
3. Set j = **q**. Shift **m** right one place dropping the low bit. Shift **n** left one place. Set i to i − 1.
4. If i is not zero go to step 2. If i is zero then the product (with sign) is in **p** and the algorithm terminates.

Table 4. The reversed difference multiplication method. The shifts are reversed for efficiency. The algorithm starts from the high end of the multiplier m, and therefore is shifted left $l+1$ times. This is to detect the transition of the least order bit of m.

1. [Let the input values be **m** and **n** of fixed length l. Let the partial product be **p**. Let the length counter be i.] Initialize **p** to zero. Initialize i to l. Shift **m** left one place. Call the carry **q**. If **q** = 1 then go to step 6.
2. Shift **p** left one place, ignore overflow. Shift **m** left one place. Call the carry **q**.
3. If **q** = 1 then add **n** to **p** and go to step 8.
4. Set i to i − 1. If i is not zero go to step 2. If i is zero then the product (with sign) is in **p** and the algorithm terminates.
5. Shift **p** left one place, ignore overflow.
6. Shift **m** left one place. Call the carry **q**.
7. If **q** = 0 then subtract **n** from **p** and go to step 4.
8. Set i to i − 1. If i is not zero go to step 5. If i is zero then the product (with sign) is in **p** and the algorithm terminates.

Table 5. The fast difference multiplication method. This version has completely eliminated the flag j. Steps 5 and 6 are kept separate to save time in execution. The total number of steps is greater than the reversed difference algorithm, but the elimination of the flag j has reduced the total number of operations.

19

the fast difference algorithm since we no longer have a flag, j.

The advantage of the difference method over the sum method is the automatic handling of signed two's complement values. In some cases the difference method will save on the number of arithmetic operations. In other cases the sum method will save on the number of arithmetic operations.

Unlike the difference method, the sum method does not change very much when we start the multiplier scan from the opposite end. This is because the operation with each bit is independent of the context of the other bits.

8080 Implementation

To illustrate the algorithms, the sum and fast difference methods are coded using 8080 microprocessor instructions. The sum method is coded as a subroutine called SMPY (listing 1). The fast difference method is coded as a subroutine called FMPY (listing 2). Notice that some program steps could have been saved if the multiplicand was originally in the BC register pair.

The main purpose of program FMPY is to gain speed over the method of SMPY. Even though FMPY has some repeated code, it still saves eight bytes of space over SMPY. The time formulas for SMPY and FMPY are:

$$T(SMPY) = 150A + 103N + 47M + 983$$
$$T(FMPY) = 442.5A - 18N + 951$$

where:

A := Probability of performing an addition or subtraction of the multiplicand during a given time around the loop.

N := Probability that the multiplier or multiplicand is negative.

M := N^2

The timing is in terms of 8080 cycles. For many 8080 computers the times may be converted to microseconds with a division by 2 (1 cycle = 0.5μ seconds). The time saved by using FMPY rather than SMPY is:

$$V = T(SMPY) - T(FMPY) =$$
$$-292.5A + 121N - 47M + 32.$$

Consider some reasonable values for A and N; say A = N = 0.5, then:

$$V = -65.5 \text{ cycles.}$$

What happened? Program FMPY did not save us time. In fact we lost 65.5 cycles. The difficulty rests with the fact that double precision subtraction is very time consuming on the 8080. To perform the double precision addition was simple and cost only 1 byte and 10 cycles. The double precision subtraction cost 6 bytes and 28 cycles. In addition it cost two more bytes and 21 cycles of overhead to save and restore the loop counter during the subtraction. This overhead killed the advantages of using the fast sum algorithm. Had SMPY and FMPY been programmed for the more versatile Z-80 microprocessor, FMPY *would* be faster than SMPY. So a blind implementation of an *improved* technique does not always yield the expected results.

```
;   CALLING SEQUENCE:
;
;       HL = MULTIPLICAND
;       DE = MULTIPLIER
;       CALL    SMPY
;
;   ON RETURN THE 16 BIT PRODUCT IS IN HL.
;   DE AND BC ARE SAVED.
;
0100          SMPY     EQU    $
0100 C5                PUSH   B
0101 E5                PUSH   H     ; SAVE FOR SIGN CALCULATION!
0102 D5                PUSH   D     ; SAVE REGISTERS.
0103 97                SUB    A
0104 B2                ORA    D
0105 F20E01            JP     SMPY1 ; MULTIPLIER IS NON-NEGATIVE.
0108 2F                CMA          ; VALUE IS TWO'S COMPLEMENTED.
0109 57                MOV    D,A
010A 7B                MOV    A,E
010B 2F                CMA
010C 5F                MOV    E,A
010D 13                INX    D
010E 44       SMPY1:   MOV    B,H
010F 4D                MOV    C,L   ; MULTIPLICAND.
0110 97                SUB    A
0111 67                MOV    H,A
0112 6F                MOV    L,A   ; INITIALIZE P. PROD. = 0.
0113 B0                ORA    B
0114 F21D01            JP     SMPY2 ; MULTIPLICAND NON-NEGATIVE.
0117 2F                CMA          ; VALUE IS TWO'S COMPLEMENTED.
0118 47                MOV    B,A
0119 79                MOV    A,C
011A 2F                CMA
011B 4F                MOV    C,A
011C 03                INX    B
011D 3E10     SMPY2:   MVI    A,16  ; THE LOOP LENGTH COUNTER.
011F 29       SMPY3:   DAD    H     ; LEFT SHIFT P. PROD.
0120 EB                XCHG
0121 29                DAD    H     ; LEFT SHIFT MULTIPLIER.
0122 EB                XCHG
0123 D22701            JNC    SMPY4 ; NEXT BIT = 0.
0126 09                DAD    B     ; NEXT BIT = 1, ADD TO P. PROD.
0127 3D       SMPY4:   DCR    A
0128 C21F01            JNZ    SMPY3 ; LOOP AROUND.
012B D1                POP    D
012C F1                POP    PSW   ; A = ORIGINAL H VALUE.
012D C1                POP    B     ; RESTORE REGISTERS.
012E AA                XRA    D     ; TEST SIGNS OF INPUT VALUES.
012F F0                RP           ; RETURN ON LIKE SIGNS.
0130 97                SUB    A     ; PRODUCT IS TO BE NEGATIVE.
0131 95                SUB    L
0132 6F                MOV    L,A
0133 3E00              MVI    A,0
0135 9C                SBB    H
0136 67                MOV    H,A
0137 C9                RET
;
;   FINISHES SMPY.
;
```

Listing 1: SMPY, a multiplication subroutine based on the sum method of table 2, as written for the 8080 processor. It is called with the 16 bit multiplier contained in the D and E registers, and with the 16 bit multiplicand in the H and L registers. It returns with the 16 bit product contained in the H and L registers. Note that multiplication of two 16 bit numbers may result in a product up to 32 bits long, causing left truncation of the product value.

Observe that the multiplicand which is pushed into the stack from the H and L registers at hexadecimal location 0101 is popped into the A register and status flags at hexadecimal location 0126. This is so that the sign of the multiplicand can be tested.

Improved Implementation

It is possible to improve the fast difference program so that it is faster than the sum program. The techniques used demonstrate the creative aspects of assembly language programming. These techniques are oriented to the particular instruction set of the 8080 processor, and other methods would have to be used on other types of computers.

To be perfectly fair, we can also improve the sum program. The execution time of the sum program can be reduced at the cost of using two more bytes of memory space. Observe that when the basic multiply loop is reached the numbers to be multiplied should always have leading 0 bits. Hence we skip over these bits and only have to go around the loop 15 times rather than the original 16 times. The improved version is called ISMPY and appears as listing 3. The time formula for ISMPY is:

$$T(ISMPY) = 150 A + 103 N - 47M + 944.$$

The improved sum multiplication program saves 39 cycles over the original.

The improvements which we can make to the fast difference program are more subtle. The idea is to reduce the overhead caused by the saving of the loop counter. Notice that the program FMPY essentially starts with the second bit of the multiplier and continues the scan one iteration after the last bit has been processed. An extra bit was used to create a transition in pattern at the end as needed by the algorithm. After the last shift the remaining multiplier is always 0. We may therefore check the multiplier for a value of 0 rather than using a loop counter. When the multiplier is 0, the loop is completed.

A problem does arise, however, if the multiplier reduces to 0 *before* the last bit is shifted out. We deal with this problem in the following manner. At the beginning of the program FMPY, the multiplier is shifted to remove the first bit. We then set the low bit of the shifted multiplier to 1. Now the multiplier cannot reduce to 0 until this bit is shifted out. We can dispense with the loop counter.

Now a new problem appears. The last shift will have the wrong test value for determining the operation to be done. This is taken care of by reversing the test when we know that we are at the end of the loop.

These extra operations cost us space. We do get a reduction in the time necessary to execute the subroutine since an end of loop test is not needed when the next multiplier bit is 0. These improvements in the fast dif-

```
;   CALLING SEQUENCE:
;
;       HL = MULTIPLIER
;       DE = MULTIPLICAND
;       CALL   FMPY
;
;   ON RETURN THE 16 BIT PRODUCT IS IN HL.
;   DE AND BC ARE SAVED.
0138              FMPY    EQU     $
0138 C5                   PUSH    B
0139 D5                   PUSH    D       ; SAVE REGISTERS.
013A 42                   MOV     B,D
013B 4B                   MOV     C,E     ; MULTIPLICAND.
013C 3E10                 MVI     A,16    ; THE LOOP LENGTH COUNTER.
013E 110000               LXI     D,0     ; INITIALIZE P. PROD. = 0.
0141 29                   DAD     H       ; LEFT SHIFT MULTIPLIER.
0142 DA5401               JC      FMPY3
0145 EB                   XCHG
0146 29            FMPY1:  DAD     H       ; LEFT SHIFT P. PROD.
0147 EB                   XCHG
0148 29                   DAD     H       ; LEFT SHIFT MULTIPLIER.
0149 EB                   XCHG
014A D26101               JNC     FMPY4
014D 09                   DAD     B       ; ADD MULTIPLICAND.
014E 3D            FMPY2:  DCR     A
014F CA6501               JZ      FMPY5   ; LOOP TEST.
0152 29                   DAD     H       ; LEFT SHIFT P. PROD.
0153 EB                   XCHG
0154 29            FMPY3:  DAD     H       ; LEFT SHIFT MULTIPLIER.
0155 EB                   XCHG
0156 DA4E01               JC      FMPY2
0159 F5                   PUSH    PSW     ; SAVE COUNTER.
015A 7D                   MOV     A,L     ; SUBTRACT MULTIPLICAND.
015B 91                   SUB     C
015C 6F                   MOV     L,A
015D 7C                   MOV     A,H
015E 98                   SBB     B
015F 67                   MOV     H,A
0160 F1                   POP     PSW     ; RESTORE COUNTER.
0161 3D            FMPY4:  DCR     A
0162 C24601               JNZ     FMPY1   ; LOOP TEST.
0165 D1            FMPY5:  POP     D
0166 C1                   POP     B       ; RESTORE REGISTERS.
0167 C9                   RET
;
;   FINISHES FMPY.
;
```

Listing 2: FMPY, a multiplication subroutine based on the fast difference method of table 5, coded here in assembly language for the 8080 processor. It uses less memory space than the program SMPY in listing 1; however, the time consuming process of 16 bit subtraction causes FMPY to execute more slowly than SMPY. The subroutine calling sequence is the same here as in SMPY. Note the possible product value truncation.

ference program appear in listing 4 as the subroutine IFMPY. The time formula for IFMPY is:

$$T(IFMPY) = 607.5 A + 10 N + 691.$$

IFMPY uses seven more bytes than FMPY.

Using the improved programs, the time saving of the fast difference method (IFMPY) over the sum method (ISMPY) is:

$$W = T(ISMPY) - T(IFMPY) =$$
$$-457.5 A + 93 N - 47 M + 253.$$

Using A = N = 0.5 (M = 0.25) we obtain:

$$W = 59 \text{ cycles.}$$

So the improved fast difference method does save both time and space over both the original and the improved sum algorithm. ∎

```
;   CALLING SEQUENCE:
;
;        HL = MULTIPLIER
;        DE = MULTIPLICAND
;        CALL  ISMPY
;
;   ON RETURN THE 16 BIT PRODUCT IS IN HL.
;   DE AND BC ARE SAVED.

0168          ISMPY   EQU    $
0168 C5               PUSH   B
0169 E5               PUSH   H        ; SAVE FOR SIGN CALCULATION!
016A D5               PUSH   D        ; SAVE REGISTERS.
016B 97               SUB    A
016C B4               ORA    H
016D F27601           JP     ISMP1    ; MULTIPLIER IS NON-NEGATIVE.
0170 2F               CMA             ; VALUE IS TWO'S COMPLEMENTED.
0171 67               MOV    H,A
0172 7D               MOV    A,L
0173 2F               CMA
0174 6F               MOV    L,A
0175 23               INX    H
0176 42      ISMP1:   MOV    B,D
0177 4B               MOV    C,E      ; MULTIPLICAND.
0178 97               SUB    A
0179 57               MOV    D,A
017A 5F               MOV    E,A      ; INITIALIZE P. PROD. = 0.
017B B0               ORA    B
017C F28501           JP     ISMP2    ; MULTIPLICAND NON-NEGATIVE.
017F 2F               CMA             ; VALUE IS TWO'S COMPLEMENTED.
0180 47               MOV    B,A
0181 79               MOV    A,C
0182 2F               CMA
0183 4F               MOV    C,A
0184 03               INX    B
0185 29      ISMP2:   DAD    H        ; DON'T NEED LEADING ZERO BIT!
0186 EB               XCHG            ; P. PROD. TO HL.
0187 3E0F             MVI    A,15     ; THE LOOP LENGTH COUNTER.
0189 29      ISMP3:   DAD    H        ; LEFT SHIFT P. PROD.
018A EB               XCHG
018B 29               DAD    H        ; LEFT SHIFT MULTIPLIER.
018C EB               XCHG
018D D29101           JNC    ISMP4    ; NEXT BIT = 0.
0190 09               DAD    B        ; NEXT BIT = 1, ADD TO P. PROD.
0191 3D      ISMP4:   DCR    A
0192 C28901           JNZ    ISMP3    ; LOOP AROUND.
0195 D1               POP    D
0196 F1               POP    PSW      ; A = ORIGINAL H VALUE.
0197 C1               POP    B        ; RESTORE REGISTERS.
0198 AA               XRA    D        ; TEST SIGNS OF INPUT VALUES.
0199 F0               RP              ; RETURN ON LIKE SIGNS.
019A 97               SUB    A        ; PRODUCT IS TO BE NEGATIVE.
019B 95               SUB    L
019C 6F               MOV    L,A
019D 3E00             MVI    A,0
019F 9C               SBB    H
01A0 67               MOV    H,A
01A1 C9               RET

;
;   FINISHES ISMPY.
;
```

Listing 3: ISMPY, a subroutine based on the sum method of multiplication, which has been optimized to reduce the time necessary for its execution. This program skips over the leading zero bits of the numbers which are being multiplied. This results in 15 loop iterations, rather than 16. Note the possible product value truncation.

```
                    ;   CALLING SEQUENCE:
                    ;
                    ;       HL = MULTIPLIER
                    ;       DE = MULTIPLICAND
                    ;       CALL    IFMPY
                    ;
                    ;   ON RETURN THE 16 BIT PRODUCT IS IN HL.
                    ;   DE AND BC ARE SAVED.
                    ;
01A2                IFMPY   EQU     $
01A2 C5                     PUSH    B
01A3 D5                     PUSH    D       ; SAVE REGISTERS.
01A4 42                     MOV     B,D
01A5 4B                     MOV     C,E     ; MULTIPLICAND.
01A6 110000                 LXI     D,0     ; INITIALIZE P. PROD. = 0.
01A9 29                     DAD     H       ; LEFT SHIFT MULTIPLIER.
01AA 23                     INX     H       ; SET END OF WORD MARK.
01AB D2B901                 JNC     IFMP3
01AE C3C601                 JMP     IFMP5   ; MULTIPLIER IS NEGATIVE.
01B1 7D             IFMP1:  MOV     A,L     ; SUBTRACT MULTIPLICAND.
01B2 91                     SUB     C
01B3 6F                     MOV     L,A
01B4 7C                     MOV     A,H
01B5 98                     SBB     B
01B6 67                     MOV     H,A
01B7 29             IFMP2:  DAD     H       ; LEFT SHIFT P. PROD.
01B8 EB                     XCHG
01B9 29             IFMP3:  DAD     H       ; LEFT SHIFT MULTIPLIER.
01BA EB                     XCHG
01BB D2B701                 JNC     IFMP2
01BE 7A                     MOV     A,D
01BF B3                     ORA     E
01C0 CAD601                 JZ      IFMP6   ; MARK GONE, FINISHED!
01C3 09                     DAD     B       ; ADD MULTIPLICAND.
01C4 29             IFMP4:  DAD     H       ; LEFT SHIFT P. PROD.
01C5 EB                     XCHG
01C6 29             IFMP5:  DAD     H       ; LEFT SHIFT MULTIPLIER.
01C7 EB                     XCHG
01C8 D2B101                 JNC     IFMP1
01CB 7A                     MOV     A,D
01CC B3                     ORA     E
01CD C2C401                 JNZ     IFMP4
01D0 85                     ADD     L       ; A FAST "MOV A,L" SINCE A=0.
01D1 91                     SUB     C       ; SUBTRACT MULTIPLICAND.
01D2 6F                     MOV     L,A
01D3 7C                     MOV     A,H
01D4 98                     SBB     B
01D5 67                     MOV     H,A
01D6 D1             IFMP6:  POP     D       ; RESTORE REGISTERS.
01D7 C1                     POP     B
01D8 C9                     RET
                    ;
                    ;   FINISHES IFMPY.
0000                        END
```

Listing 4: IFMPY, a subroutine which employs the fast difference algorithm, which has been improved to reduce its execution time. The loop counter has been removed, and with it the steps in which it is used are saved. This saves program steps and time. The end of the loop is found by monitoring the multiplier. When it reduces to 0, the loop is ended. At the beginning of the program, the multiplier is manipulated to prevent it from reducing to zero prematurely. Once again note the possible product value truncation.

An Overview of Long Division

Geoffrey Gass

On the very simplest level, a division problem starts with two numbers, a *dividend*, which we want to divide by a *divisor*, to obtain a third number, a *quotient*. In terms of grade school long division:

```
              Quotient
            ┌──────────
Divisor     │  Dividend
                        + Remainder
```

The quotient (integer portion) is simply the number of times the divisor can be subtracted from the dividend and still leave a positive remainder.

The simplest computer program for this calculation goes as follows:

- Put the dividend into register N.
- Put the divisor into register D.
- Clear a quotient register Q.
- Assign a remainder register R.
- Subtract D from N and put the result in R.
- Test R.
- If R is positive, increment Q, transfer R into N, and go back to the *subtract* step.
- If R is negative, exit. Q is now the (integer) quotient and N contains the remainder.

There is nothing basically wrong with this procedure, but it's not very useful. If N is 1,000,000 and D is 2, it will take 500,000 operations of the program to get Q. If D is 797,236, the program will quickly tell us the answer is 1, with a remainder.

Let us check off the chief deficiencies.

First, if the two numbers are very different, the program will give us an accurate answer, but will take a long time doing it. Second, if the two numbers are very close in value, the program will be very quick, but not very precise. Third, if D is larger than N, zero is the only answer. Fourth, if D happens to be zero, the program will loop forever trying to get Q up to infinity.

What we'd prefer is a quicker program that gives us an answer correct to at least as many places as the significant digits of the numbers we put in, regardless of the magnitude of the numbers. But won't that take a more complicated program and won't a more complicated program take longer to execute? A program 2,000,000 instructions long could be quicker to execute than one which loops through six instructions 500,000 times. And it certainly won't take two million instructions to make a quite thorough, precise, accurate, and quick division program.

To get speed and precision, start out just as a previous generation was taught in grade school, by juggling the decimal points around (or binary points if we are working in binary). To put it another way, multiply the divisor and dividend some number of times by the base of the number system (10 or 2, for example) until the dividend is only slightly larger than the divisor. Note how many places it is necessary to shift the numbers so they are nearly equal. (In old-fashioned long division, the divisor is shifted until it is an integer, and the dividend is shifted the same number of times. The rest of the necessary shifting is done by relocation of the quotient with respect to a fixed location for the decimal point.)

To start, set up an array of registers large enough to hold the largest numbers we want to deal with. The quotient register is twice as large as the others, since dividing a very small fraction by a very large number produces a yet smaller fraction, and dividing a very large number by a small fraction gives an even larger quotient. Then arbitrarily define some point in each register as the decimal or binary point. A convenient place is between two memory words, as shown in figure 1. Although a more common technique is to use only three registers (no R register), using four is a little easier, and you'll never notice the slightly increased time required for putting R into N after every successful subtraction. However, extra time is only needed for BCD (binary coded decimal) division. In binary arithmetic, the extra time for an addition after every *unsuccessful* subtraction approximately balances the time wasted in transfers.

The first operation is to load in the numbers, being careful to locate them in the proper position with respect to the decimal point. If the dividend N is nn00, it will go into the word just to the left of the point in N. If the divisor is 000d, it will go in the corresponding word of register D. All other locations must be cleared to 0000, if not already done. Table 1 shows our starting arrangement. Because the program is general purpose, and must be able to operate with any kind of numbers that can be fitted into its registers, it can't "know" how big N and D are. Its first job is to find out their magnitudes so it can set them to be nearly equal.

The easiest way to do this is to start by shifting register D to the left and insert zeros at the least significant digit position of the fraction part of the register until something pops up at the most significant digit position at the left of the integer part of the register. In this operation we must set a limit to the number of shifts allowed, so when we have done 16 shifts and still get nothing at the top of the register, we can stop. Division by zero is not allowed, of course, and the computer has better things to do than spend hours shifting empty registers. Then do the same thing with register N, shifting it left until its most significant digit shows at the top of the register. We can use the same counter used for D to keep track of how many shifts it takes, starting with the count left over from counting D's shifts and counting in the opposite direction. Our final count will reflect the difference in magnitude between the two numbers. That number is saved for later. Again, with N, it is necessary to set a limit to the count or we'll be shifting forever if N happens to be zero. The limit needn't be exact (it can't be, because we don't know what number we started with in the counter), but that's not critical. All that's needed is something that will get us out if the count starts looking like infinity. A limit of −20 or +20, depending on which way the counting starts, is adequate. In the example of table 1, the saved number is 3 (the difference between the seven shifts it took to get D to the top of the register and the four shifts required for N).

Before starting subtraction, counting, and shifting, a certain number of operations must be set. Since we started with possible 16-position numbers, 16 operations should give 16 position answers, which is what we were looking for. We will be moving quotient digits into the Q register at a point 15 places to the right of the binary/decimal point. If the answer is 1, 16 shifts will put that first and only digit of the answer just to the left of the binary/decimal point in Q.

Now, with a starting count of 16, and the D and N numbers in position, subtract D from N and put the result in R. Is R negative? (If binary coded decimal notation is used D could be larger than N, and R could therefore be negative. If binary notation is used, N must equal D, so R could not in the specific example be negative; but we test for it anyway.) If R is negative, go immediately to the next operation. If R is positive, transfer R to N and increment Q. If working in binary arithmetic, go to the next operation at this point, since another subtraction can not be done. If working in binary coded decimal, however, N could be 9 and D could be

N			0000	nn00	.	0000	0000		
D			0000	000d	.	0000	0000		
R			0000	0000	.	0000	0000		
Q	0000	0000	0000	0000	.	0000	0000	0000	0000

Table 1: Starting arrangement of the registers for division. The dividend and divisor have been loaded; all other registers are cleared.

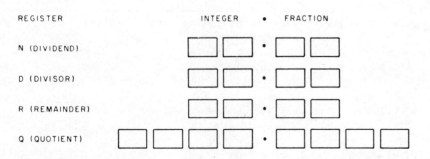

Figure 1: Four registers for division, each with two words for integers and two for fractions, except register Q which is double size. The registers are usually strung out serially in adjacent memory locations, but it is convenient to think of them in block form as shown.

1, and there are eight operations yet to go. So for binary coded decimal, loop back and keep on subtracting and swapping R back into N until R is finally negative, then stop. Don't transfer R or increment Q, just get on to the next operation.

At this point, the most significant digit of the quotient is in the least significant digit position of register Q. Now shift D one position to the right and shift Q one position left, marking the end of one operation in our operations counter. Keep repeating the above process until all 16 shifts have been done. At this point, the first Q digit is one position to the left of the binary or decimal point in Q. Now, go back and look at the magnitude difference count obtained at the start of the program. If it is positive, shift Q to the left that many times; if it is negative, shift Q to the right that many times. (We could have checked the magnitude difference count when the operations counter was set: if the magnitude difference was negative, set that many fewer operations for the program. We would not have added any positive number, however; that would set up a divide by zero for the 17th operation.) Register Q now has the correct quotient.

We neglected the small problem of loading the digits into the registers in their proper positions, and didn't get into fine detail on how a subtract or shift operation might be performed in a multiword register; however, the general outline of the algorithm can now be imagined, and that's half the battle. And there are some details of it that can help us along to the next step.

When the numbers were shifted up to the tops of their registers in the earlier example, we were actually going through the process of converting fixed point to floating point numbers, by normalizing the digits, with a saved exponent indicating how far they'd been shifted. In that specific example, we saved only the difference in exponents, but this gave us the information needed to create a conventional notation number from our floating point answer in Q.

Our next step is to establish a full floating point format in order to avoid the magnitude limitations forced on us by fixed point data. Because most processors are equipped with binary coded decimal arithmetic aids, there is no need to bother with binary coded decimal to binary conversions (and vice versa) when handling numbers input via the keyboard. Also, battling with the attendant conversion problems can be avoided (ie: decimal fractions that can only be approximated by binary fractions and rounding operations which don't come out the same in binary coded decimal and binary).

In floating point format, every number is stored as a string of digits, with the most significant nonzero digit at the top of the register and the decimal point *location* saved in a separate register. The programmer can arbitrarily say that the imaginary decimal point is anywhere in the normalized string of digits as long as the program is internally consistent. For ease of output in standard scientific notation, however, it's best to say that the 0 position of the decimal point is immediately following the most significant digit in the register. That is, the number stored is 1 or greater and less than 10, and is to be multiplied by 10 to the power indicated to obtain conventional notation.

The number 6045.35 is stored as:

EXP   NUMBER
03   604535

with the number in EXP indicating how many places further to the right of the first digit the decimal place must be moved for conventional notation. If EXP is 00, the number is 6.04535; if EXP is FD (−3 in hexadecimal form), the number is .00604535. In addition to the number and the base exponent, we also need something to indicate the sign of the number.

In binary operations, the most significant bit of a number can be considered the *sign* bit, providing a single byte with the range of values +127 to −128 decimal. Arithmetic performed under this convention gives consistent answers (except under overflow conditions for which most processors have detection circuits and warning flags). For binary coded decimal, the topmost *digit* position is the sign *digit*: 0 for a positive number, and 9 for a negative number. Negative numbers are generally handled in *tens complement* form, obtained by subtracting the absolute value from 999999999 . . . . 9 and then adding 1 to the least significant digit (this is the way many early adding machines handled subtraction).

Without going into the detail of how it got that way, simply assume that all data in our division problem will be available to us in tens complement form, in the format shown in figure 2. The exponent could be in binary coded decimal form (maximum values + and − 79, with the most significant

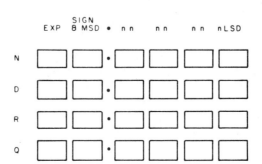

Figure 2: Register arrangement for floating point binary coded decimal division. Note that it is no longer necessary to provide a double size register for Q. The imaginary decimal point is located immediately following the most significant digit.

bit used as a sign bit), but it's easier to keep it in binary form, allowing a value range of +127 to −128, limited by the program to plus and minus 99. The format gives nine significant digits, of which we may elect to hold out two or three as guard digits, and display only six or seven, rounded off according to the value of the guard digits.

There is one more complication in our division routine: *signs*. The operation we want to perform here is repeated subtraction of absolute values, not just the simple signed subtraction for which the tens complement form can give correct answers. When dividing +956 by −3, we do not want the remainder to become larger and larger! So first of all, look at the sign digits of the two numbers (if a number is negative, the 9 at the most significant digit position will set the N bit of a condition code register, just as for binary operations) and determine the proper sign for the quotient. Store this flag away for the moment.

Next, if the dividend is negative, use a tens complement routine to get its absolute value, and put it back in register N. We might also test it for 0 at this point, and do an early exit if the answer is going to be 0. This would be appropriate only if we had already checked D, since D might also be 0, and 0/0 would be an indeterminate value, not 0. So don't bother with the zero check at this point if register N is being processed first.

What we do with register D depends on the processor being used. Some processors have decimal subtract operations, or a binary coded decimal adjust instruction which is effective after a subtraction. In the Motorola 6800, the DAA instruction works properly only after an ADD operation with register A (ADD A, ADC A, or ABA). For the 6800, then, the subtraction function requires register D to be in tens complement negative form, so our subtraction can be performed with an addition instruction. For other processors, D must be in absolute (positive) form if a subtract instruction is to be used, or in complemented form for an add instruction, depending on what is available in the machine.

So we do or don't run the data in register D through a tens complement operation depending on its present form and the form required by our division routine. While checking the sign, we can also note if D is 0; if it is, we set an error flag and exit. If D is not 0, check here to see if N is 0, and exit early if it is (assuming register Q is already cleared), thus saving a little processing time.

Next, look at the exponent data to discover what the final exponent will be. Subtract the D exponent from the N exponent, but before storing it away check for over-

flow (a carry into the sign bit, effectively reversing the sign from what it should be), or, if we have set limits of + and − 99, check for a number exceeding these limits. If the magnitude of the answer is going to be out of limits, we may choose to reject the problem, set a warning flag, or simply set Q to 0 or 999999E99 to indicate that the result is beyond the capacity of the machine if the program is simply a calculator program without programmability or other exotic features. For a scientific program, this sort of thing could lead to serious and probably undetectable errors, and would never do. For an interpreter program, the exponent overflow should spring out to an error message and halt the program. If the exponent is within limits, store it as the tentative exponent for Q, subject to later adjustment.

Now, we're finally ready to divide. We can skip the procedure done earlier in running data up to the tops of the registers. First, set up a count of nine (the number of digits desired). Subtract D from N, with binary coded decimal adjustment as required, and store the difference in R. If R is positive (checking byte 1 in R), increment the least significant bit in register Q (no need for binary coded decimal adjustment here — the digit will never exceed nine), transfer R to N and repeat until R is finally negative. Leave R alone this time and do not increment Q. Shift Q one digit (four bits) left, starting at the least significant byte of the register and shifting it one bit left, repeating the process four times. Then shift D one digit (four bits) right, starting at the most significant byte of the register and going through it four times. One more operation must be remembered when working with D in tens complement form and doing additions: the sign digit of D must be extended back to the top of the register. Do this by adding 90 to the most significant byte after we have completed the shifting above. When we get down to the last operation, register D should be all 9s except for the least significant digit.

Before going back to the subtract operation, step the operations counter by one, and exit if the counter indicates completion. When the subtracting is done, check the most significant digit of register Q. If it is 0, the result of the first subtraction was no good and the initially assigned exponent for Q was too large. Under these circumstances we shift Q one more digit to the left and reduce the exponent that was calculated earlier by 1.

Now, everything is taken care of except the sign. If we have a simple calculator program, we can just look at the sign flag stored away and either do or don't output a minus sign, followed by the register Q data in absolute form. However, for most applications, Q will have to be stored away for future use in machine usable form (as previously discussed in figure 2), just as we got the N and D data to start with.

So look at the sign flag. If it says Q is negative, send Q through the tens complement routine, then store the result wherever it belongs. If Q is to be positive, store it as is, with 0 for a sign digit. In either case, "park" the exponent data next door, so it can be retrieved along with Q's digits whenever needed.

Well, we did it. A whole long division program in binary coded decimal, with a constant precision answer. Of course, we haven't actually formatted the digits for output, or converted our binary exponent to signed ASCII, or decided whether to output the number in conventional or scientific notation (there really isn't room on the average printer for 99 zeros). We also haven't figured out how to use the exponent to locate the decimal point in the printout of conventional notation data. But these things are incidental. Once past the conceptual problem of the "engine" in this dividing machine, the design of the transmission, differential, seat cushions, and bumpers should be no barrier to rapid progress in any direction that suits the user.■

Procedures for Large Numbers

Michael Finerty

Now that you have bought your new programmable calculator or microcomputer and have done some work with its available software, your manual tells you that you have calculating power between $10-100$ and 10^{100}. This is staggering, considering that many of us never use number values over a trillion in normal calculations. For some calculations, even the range of a microcomputer or programmable calculator is inadequate. Take this example: Experimenting with the factorial program [n x (n—1) x (n—2) x . . . x (n—(n—2)) x (n—(n—1))] you find that you top out at 69 factorial (69!). 70! causes your computer to flash its display or inform you by other methods that you have erred. Thus, many simple problems seem to lie outside of the scope of some computers.

For instance, in 1609 William Shakespeare published his *Sonnets*. There are 154 of them and they are not in the order in which they were written. Since then, various scholars have tried to establish the original order of composition. It would be interesting to know how many ways the *Sonnets* can be arranged to assess the specific degree of futility. The answer is 154! or 154 x 153 x 152 x . . . x 3 x 2 x 1. "Alas", you say, "This lies beyond the power of my machine." Not true. If your machine possesses the logarithmic function $\log_{10}(x)$, and the corresponding antilogarithmic function, 10^x, you can solve this and many other similar problems.

For example: 20,000! equals 1.8 x $10^{77,337}$ and 256 to the 65,536 power equals 2.596 x $10^{157,826}$. The latter is the number of different messages that can be stored in a 64 K by 8 bit machine, correct to four digits. I used logarithms to arrive at these numbers.

From algebra we know that the exponents of two numbers are added when the numbers are multiplied:

$$10^5 \times 10^8 = 10^{5+8} = 10^{13}.$$

In this equation the values 5 and 8 are the logarithms of 100,000 and 100,000,000. If you multiply these numbers together, you get 10,000,000,000,000 or 10^{13}. But 13 is the logarithm of 10^{13}. When we are working with logarithms we can write:

$$\log(10^{13}) = \log(10^5) + \log(10^8).$$

This says that 5+8=13. Every positive number has a logarithm. (Logarithms of base 10 are called *common* logarithms, compared with the *natural* logarithms, based on the irrational number e. All logarithms in this article are common logarithms.) To multiply any two numbers together we have to find the logarithms of the two numbers, add the two numbers together and raise ten to the power of the result of our addition.

The logarithm of most numbers is an irrational number. That is, it never repeats its order of numbers and it never terminates. This causes problems if you are a stickler for precision. For most purposes, however, an approximation to a certain number of digits is sufficient.

Taking a specific example, we know that 20 equals 2 x 10, so we expect the logarithm of 20 to be equal to the logarithm of 2 plus the logarithm of 10. Using a calculator, we find that the common logarithm of 2 is 0.3010 and the logarithm of 10 is 1. Adding these two numbers together gives 1.3010, which is the logarithm of 20. This is important. It means that any number can be written as a product of a number between 1 and 10 and a power of 10. It also means that 20 may be written as:

$$10^{\log(2)} \times 10^{\log(10)}$$

or

$$10^{(0.3010 + 1)}$$

Changing the order of addition does not change the result of addition since addition is communtative. If we write the sum the first way, we are writing logarithmically. If we write it the other way, we are setting it up to be written in scientific notation, where 1 is called the *characteristic* and 0.3010 is called the *mantissa*. Notice that the characteristic is the exponent of 10 in scientific notation. There is no need to take the antilogarithm of the characteristic if we intend to write our result in scientific notation. We can subtract it or record it, making sure to subtract it before taking the antilogarithm of the number we are looking for. This is the most important step in dealing with big numbers. If the characteristic is greater than 99 or less than −99, the machine will overload.

Now let us proceed step by step to find the number of all possible messages that can be stored in a 64 K by 8 bit machine:

$$2^8 = 256$$
$$2^{16} = 65,536$$

That is, 256 messages can be stored in an 8 bit byte, and 65,536 bytes can be addressed by a 16 bit address code. The total number of messages is $256^{65,536}$. The problem is converting this number to base 10. We know that 256 equals 10 raised to the logarithm of 256. Therefore; the number of messages is equal to:

$$N = \left(10^{\log(256)}\right)^{65536}$$

Reviewing algebra we find:

$$N = 10^{65536 \times \log(256)}$$
$$= 10^{157,826.4144}.$$

If we subtract out the characteristic and raise 10 to that power:

$$N = 10^{0.4144} \times 10^{157,826}.$$

Now all we have to do is find $10^{0.4144}$, which is 2.596. The final answer is:

$$N = 2.596 \times 10^{157,826}.$$

To how many places is our result good? As a general rule, the result is good to one fewer digits than there are digits in the mantissa. How do we know this?

There are three general properties to the logarithmic curve that need to be studied to arrive at the answer. First, the logarithm of x is defined only for positive real numbers. Second, as x increases, the logarithm of x also increases. Third, the tangent line to the logarithm curve always has positive slope and that slope is always decreasing. So, a small error in the calculation of the logarithm of a large value x leads to a large error in the associated values of x. The further we go in the positive direction, the larger the errors are. What doesn't change is the error ratio. If x is 10 times as great as y, the same error in the mantissa of x will give exactly ten times the error found in the mantissa of y. Therefore, to evaluate error, we need only look at the mantissa and the range of values which the mantissa may assume. The greatest error will be on the high side of the mantissa; in 4 place logarithms this will be at 0.9999; in 5 place logarithms, 0.99999. In both cases the next mantissa is 0.0 and the characteristic is 1, the logarithm of 10. All we need do is find the antilogarithms of 0.9999 and 0.99999 and subtract them from 10 to determine how much error is introduced by the truncation of the logarithm.

$$\text{antilog } (0.9999) = 9.99769768$$
$$10 - \text{antilog } (0.9999) = 0.00230232$$

That is, an error of 1 in the least significant digit leads to an error of 2.30323 in the third digit of the antilogarithm. Because we do not know the actual method of roundoff, there is an inherent error of 1 to .5 in the last place of our logarithm. An answer to three digits is the best we can do. Different calculators have different numbers of significant digits. Mine has 13 calculating digits; others have 10 or 8. I can get powers of large numbers with little effort and with good accuracy. In fact the range of my calculator, a Texas Instruments SR−51A, is from $10^{999,999,999}$ to $10^{-999,999,999}$ to three digit accuracy.

Even on a small calculator, a number of interesting problems can be tackled. One of the most famous problems in probability is the *monkey* problem: Given a certain number of monkeys typing at random on the same number of typewriters, how long will it be before one of them types the complete works of Shakespeare? The answer depends on a number of parameters, including the number of separate functions on a typewriter keyboard. On my typewriter there are 92 characters (counting upper and lower case as different keys), including carriage return. Suppose that Shakespeare's works (first folio) contains N characters including a blank character for a space. The number 92^N represents the total variability of messages up to and including a message the same length as the works. I don't propose to count all the letters and blanks and carriage returns in the complete works of Shakespeare, but anyone really interested in the problem will have to. There are probably

Table 1: Algorithm for determining the factorial of a large number.

fewer than a billion characters, if that is any consolation.

Other problems in genetics may be more to the point. It is quite possible to calculate the probability of coding DNA to produce long chains such as collagen alpha (I), which is approximately 1000 units (amino acids) long, simply by assessing the probability of a broken chain: $P = 1 - (61/64)^N$. The probability of a broken chain is very large, but that probability doesn't tell the entire story. Another important parameter is the variability of protein molecules up to 1000 units long. Given 20 amino acids and one unit (amino acid) to signify the end of a chain, we find that the variability is $21^{1,000}$. Because the genetic code is degenerate, we may also wish to know the average redundance for 1000 unit proteins: $R = (61/20)^{1,000}$. These numbers are now in the range of simple hand-held calculators. More sophisticated analyses can be done on programmable calculators and microcomputers.

One of the functions which often appears in probability and statistics is the factorial function:

$$N! = N \times (N-1) \times (N-2) \times \ldots \times (N-(N-2)) \times (N-(N-1)).$$

This can be rewritten in logarithmic form:

$$\log(N!) = \log(N) + \log(N-1) + \log(N-2) + \ldots + \log(N-(N-2)) + \log(N-(N-1)).$$

This form is ideally suited to solution by the method developed for exponentiation as shown in table 1. Modifications can be made for permutations and combinations. You can write the program for combinations:

$$nCr = \frac{n!}{(n-r)!r!}$$

and then in the permutations program substitute 1 for r before running the program, giving:

$$nPr = \frac{n!}{(n-1)!1!}$$

Finally, in the factorial program, substitute 1 for both r and (n−r) leaving:

$$n! = \frac{n!}{1! \times 1!}$$

One more word of caution. When programming for large n and r, save memory space by using the following formulas:

$$\log(nCr) = \log(n!) - \log((n-r)!) - \log(r!)$$
$$\log(nPr) = \log(n!) - \log((n-r)!) - \log(1)$$
$$\log(n!) = \log(n!) - \log 1 - \log 1.$$

For error calculations, it is best to assess the maximum error in the worst case, which in this case is the largest value of N. Multiply the maximum error by N and use that to set the limits of error.

Using such a program I was able to ascertain that there are approximately 3.09×10^{271} ways of arranging Shakespeare's sonnets.

I hope some of the techniques discussed in this article will help you in using large numbers on computers.■

Sources of Numerical Error

Daniel R Buskirk

A growing number of microcomputer enthusiasts are finding the need to perform control operations, evaluate complicated mathematical expressions and analyze statistical data. In short, many hackers want to tackle problems conventionally left to larger computers. To do this, they must become acquainted with error analysis.

Programmers need to be concerned about errors in any program involving the evaluation of a function or algebraic expression, or one which involves a large number of simple but repetitive operations. Even in control applications, it is often critical to be aware of the potential for error.

What do we mean by error? The numerical analyst, a professional mathematician involved with the design and analysis of numerical algorithms, recognizes three distinct types of error. The first is the *blunder*, which is not an error at all in the mathematical sense. A blunder is a gross error: a mistake in program logic, a typographical error, or perhaps only a misplaced decimal point. The mathematician, like the rest of us, must shrug his shoulders at a blunder, and hope to do better next time. Blunders need not concern us here.

Certainly blunders account for the vast majority of errors; but what other types of errors are there if we ignore blunders? One type is the truncation error. For example, take the infinite series representation of the function $sin(x)$:

$$sin(x) = \frac{x}{1!} - \frac{x^3}{3!} + \frac{x^5}{5!} - \ldots$$

If we were to use this relation to evaluate $sin(x)$ in a computer, we could not carry this series on forever. Whenever we stop, we have failed to evaluate the remaining terms in the expression, or *truncated* the series. Those who understand a little calculus will recognize that this series *converges;* that is, it gets arbitrarily close to the correct value when sufficiently many terms are calculated. But there must always be a small but finite truncation error (if this computation is carried out on a digital computer).

Another calculation involving truncation error is the evaluation of integrals using the trapezoidal rule. Though an infinite series of trapezoids, each approaching zero width, will give us the area under the curve (its definite integral) exactly, any computer evaluation must settle for a finite number of trapezoids. Thus there will be truncation error. To be sure, it is generally possible to avoid the consideration of truncation error by simply requiring that the truncation error be less than the precision of the whole calculation. However, the clever programmer recognizes that there are usually several different infinite series representations of any function. Often, one of these series will require significantly fewer terms to come within the required precision.

The error of most concern to numerical programmers is not truncation error but rather *roundoff error*. Since the word length in most computers is fixed, any number that exceeds this length must be rounded off before it can be stored in the computer's memory. This error is the most significant, so we shall consider it in more detail.

Although almost all "big" computers store numbers in binary digits, the following examples are given in base ten because it is more familar (and it is similar to the binary coded decimal format often used in microcomputer floating point packages).

Most computers store a real number by breaking it down into a mantissa and an exponent, much like scientific notation. A word which looks like this:

mantissa   exponent

would represent the real number 0.7352 x 10^5 or 73520. Now, if we wish to store a number larger than four decimal places, we must round it off. (It is true that our exponent here is limited to two decimal places. Any exponent with three or more places in this case represents an *overflow* condition. Since overflow is generally easily avoided, we will not discuss it here.) Consider the numbers 8,931,724 and 0.761253. In the first case, rounding off to 0.8931 x 10^7 represents an error of 724. The error in rounding the second is 53 x 10^{-6}. Thus, it is most common for the numerical analyst to speak of relative error rather than absolute error. In this case, both errors will be on the order of 10^{-4} of the value being stored in memory.

If this error seems trivial, let us look at an example, albeit a contrived one (more realistic examples will be examined later). For instance, if we wish to evaluate the expression:

$$\frac{1}{a-b}$$

where a = .89136 and b = .89134. Rounding a and b and subtracting, we get 10,000 rather than 50,000, the correct answer. Thus our answer was off by a factor of five even though our round off error was very small. It might be argued that double precision calculation would have eliminated the problem completely. Clearly, accuracy increases with increased word length, but roundoff never disappears. Since some hand calculators use up to 13 decimal digits in storing numbers while displaying ten digits, we might expect them to have "more than enough" accuracy. But in many engineering and statistical problems, calculators can make significant errors. The reader concerned with calculator accuracy might wish to read the short article by Bernard Cole in the November 25 1976 issue of *Electronics*.

The reason for the problem with roundoff, even with 13 digit accuracy, is the situation most frustrating for numerical programmers. Roundoff occurs at every step of any program. In a very long program, roundoff error may have been introduced many millions of times. This error may propagate itself and accumulate into a very large error in the result. Programs in which this propagation of error is likely to occur (finding the inverse of a large matrix, for instance) are generally so complicated that it is impossible to predict precisely what the effect of constant rounding off will be. Often the numerical analyst resorts to probability theory to get an idea of how much error is likely to be in the results.

Errors often become critical when functions are calculated. Let us assume we have a value for the variable x stored in memory. There is some error associated with x (perhaps roundoff error, or maybe x is the result of a physical measurement). We'll call this error δ. Thus $x = x_0 + \delta$, where x_0 is the unknown true value of x. It may be very easy to calculate some function of x, $f(x)$, but what is the error of the result? Let us define the error of the result as ϵ. Then:

$$f(x_0) + \epsilon = f(x_0 + \delta)$$

If we know our initial error δ is small, we would like to assume the error ϵ is small as well. If the function is simple, or involves only one variable, we can be confident the resulting error is not large if neither δ nor the derivative of the function at x_0 is large. But what about functions of more than one variable? What about complex algorithms such as the solution to simultaneous equations, often done using a process mathematicians know as Gaussian elimination? Very often, small errors in the input values will yield results which are off by a significantly large amount. So large, in fact, that the results are worthless and the programming is futile. This situation is distressingly common in everyday problems in science, engineering and the social sciences. Numerical analysts call a problem *well posed* if small errors in input still result in a reliable answer. However, even a well posed problem can be solved inaccurately if the programmer has not chosen his algorithm cautiously.

With all this talk about errors, what can be done? Is there any hope at all of obtaining consistently reliable results? Unfortunately, there are no general methods. However, the programmer who is aware of how errors can occur is in a better position to compensate for them. For instance, let's look at the general quadratic equation:

$$x^2 + 2bx + c = 0$$

[Note: *The expression on the left side of this equation is equivalent to the familiar form used to generate the quadratic formula, $ax^2 + bx + c$. However, it leads directly to the computationally simpler form of the two roots X_1 and $X_2 \ldots$ CM*]

If we have a computer of word length **t**, we might reasonably hope to solve for **x** by using the formulas

$$x_1 = -b + \sqrt{b^2 - c}$$
$$x_2 = -b - \sqrt{b^2 - c}$$

These formulae work well in most cases, but the astute programmer should notice that there is a problem if $b < 0$ and

$$\frac{|c|}{b^2} < 10^{-T}.$$

In that case:

$$x_2 = -b - \sqrt{b^2 - c}$$

will give an erroneous result. A programmer who tests for this condition can then calculate the corre t result simply, using the relation

$$x_2 = c/x_1$$

For another example, consider the experimenter who wishes to record the temperature of his home hourly, 24 hours a day, and print out the average of the last 24 readings (perhaps he also wants to execute some control operation based on this average). Being inclined toward efficiency, this fellow decides that after having added 24 readings for the first average, for each of the succeeding averages he need only add the newest reading and subtract the oldest from his running total, rather than read all the readings every hour. What might happen here is that small errors which occur during the arithmetic are never disposed of and can accumulate without any upper limit. Perhaps the error might eventually become as large as the measurement itself! If this programmer were not quite so "efficient" and calculated using the last 24 readings each hour, the error would be, at most, 24 times the error for each data point.

Folk wisdom claims, "There's more than one way to skin a cat." Likewise, there's more than one way to do most calculations. A+B—A does not always equal B to a computer. Algebra tells us that A(B+C) = AB+AC, but again, the computer sometimes disagrees. It is the programmer's responsibility and challenge to understand his algorithms and to choose them wisely. The reward for the trouble is results he can trust!■

REFERENCE

Ralston, Anthony, *A First Course in Numerical Methods*, McGraw-Hill, New York, 1965.

FLOATING POINT NUMBERS

About This Section

A very real limitation of many high level languages implemented on microcomputers is their inability to deal with real numbers. Many BASIC interpreters, for instance, can operate only on integer values. However, if you intend to use your computer for sophisticated arithmetic operations, it is necessary to have a floating point arithmetic package. Adding floating point calculation abilities to your microprocessor can represent a quantum leap forward in performance.

"Math in the Real World" by Joel Boney, "What's in a Floating Point Package" by Sheldon Linker, and "Floating Point Arithmetic" by Burt Hashizume provide three looks at how to add an economical floating point package to your system and improve your number crunching facilities.

Next, Henry A Davis discusses "Evaluating a Floating Point Package." This article will help you learn how to test a floating point package and avoid the sources of numerical error discussed in the previous section.

However, if your computer is currently running a programming language that allows only integer manipulation, don't despair. You can still have a lot of fun exploring real numbers. Jef Raskin describes how to perform "Unlimited Precision Division" using only an integer BASIC package.

Math in the Real World

Joel Boney

Your system is completed. You bought a kit with lots of memory and spent many hours assembling it. The manufacturer's manuals are dog eared. You've read various works on computer programming which inspired you to write integer multiply and divide routines and create your own mathematical statement processor. The routines are thoroughly debugged and now you are ready to enter your first mathematical statement: $5 \div 2 =$. The computer promptly responds with '2'. Well, that's not really wrong in integer arithmetic where remainders are often dropped, but most of us learned in the third grade that $5 \div 2$ really equals 2.5. How do you get your computer to answer 2.5 instead of 2? Read on. The answer lies in floating point or **real** representation and manipulation of numbers.

Floating Point

A floating point number is a number that can be representated by an integer portion and a fractional portion. The number 2.5 is a floating point or real number; so are 3.3, 0.9 and 2.0. All can be represented by an **integer part and a fractional part.** The numbers 1, 8, and 17 are **not real** since they have no fractional portion. Numbers in scientific notation such as 2.37×10^8 are real.

Before jumping head first into how to represent floating point numbers in the computer, an understanding of how floating point numbers are represented in base ten is instructive. For example, in the number 125.76, the digit positions correspond to:

$$
\begin{array}{rcr}
1 \times 10^2 & = & 100.00 \\
2 \times 10^1 & = & 20.00 \\
5 \times 10^0 & = & 5.00 \\
7 \times 10^{-1} & = & 0.70 \\
6 \times 10^{-2} & = & 0.06
\end{array}
$$

The decimal point merely tells where the boundary exists between the positive powers of ten and the negative powers of ten. Numbers to the left of the decimal point are positive powers of ten and those to the right are negative powers of ten. In binary (base 2) numbers the same rule applies. The base 10 equivalent of the binary number 101.11 is:

$$
\begin{array}{rcll}
1 \times 2^2 & = 1 \times 4 & = 4.00 \\
0 \times 2^1 & = 0 \times 2 & = 0.00 \\
1 \times 2^0 & = 1 \times 1 & = 1.00 \\
1 \times 2^{-1} & = 1 \times .5 & = 0.50 \\
1 \times 2^{-2} & = 1 \times .25 & = \underline{0.25} \\
& & 5.75
\end{array}
$$

The '.', which is now called a binary point, denotes the division between positive and negative powers of two. This concept can be expanded to any base, but here we will only consider base 10 and base 2. In general the '.' might be called the "base point."

Quite often it is more convenient to represent real decimal numbers in scientific notation. This allows both very small and very large numbers to be written with the fewest number of digits (eg: 3.75×10^{-10}, rather than 0.000000000375). Numbers in

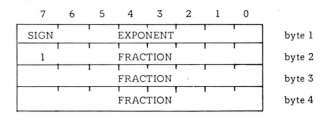

Figure 1: Format for the arrangement of data in the computer's memory for the binary floating point representation described here. The high order bit of byte 2 will usually be '1' because of normalization. The only time that this will not happen is when the number being represented is zero.

Binary									Decimal
00000000	.10000000	00000000	00000000	=	0.5	x	2^0	=	0.5
00000001	.10000000	00000000	00000000	=	0.5	x	2^1	=	1.0
00000001	.11000000	00000000	00000000	=	0.75	x	2^1	=	1.5
10000001	.11000000	00000000	00000000	=	−0.75	x	2^1	=	−1.5
01111111	.10000000	00000000	00000000	=	0.5	x	2^{-1}	=	0.25
11111111	.10000000	00000000	00000000	=	−0.5	x	2^{-1}	=	−0.25
00000000	.10000000	00000000	00000001	=	0.50000006	x	2^0	=	0.50000006

scientific notation are represented by three parts: integer portion, fractional portion and exponent. In order to conserve memory within the computer and to make calculations have fewer steps, it is more convenient to represent all real numbers with only a fraction and an exponent. This is accomplished by moving all digits to the right of the base point while adjusting the exponent appropriately. Thus all numbers are of the form: $.FFF \times 10^{EE}$ in base 10 (where "FFF" are the fractional digits and "EE" is an expression for the power of ten exponent). This change of form does not in any way alter the value of the number or change the accuracy of the subsequent calculations. For example: 3.75×10^2 becomes 0.375×10^3 thus eliminating the integer portion of the number.

If the fractional portion of a number has a fixed number of digits as is the case within a computer, then the greatest accuracy is achieved if the digit following the base point is nonzero. Using a 5 digit fraction, the number 0.37868×10^5 is more accurate than 0.03787×10^6. We now have formulated two rules that will make calculations easier and maintain maximum accuracy:

- Floating point numbers will consist of only a fraction and an exponent.
- Floating point numbers will be adjusted so that no zeros immediately follow the base point.

```
Begin
    Clear exponent and integer of answer
    Clear fraction of answer (4 bytes)
    Do while input character ≠ '.'
        If input character = '−' then set fraction sign = 1
        If input character is a number then
            Convert input character from ASCII to binary
            Integer: = integer * 10 + input number
        Endif
    Enddo
    N: = 1
    Do while input character = number and N < 8
        Convert input character from ASCII to binary
        Fraction: = fraction + (Table(N) * input number)
        N: = N + 1
    Enddo
    Do while integer > 0
        Shift integer and fraction one bit right
        Increment exponent
    Enddo
    Normalize answer
    Roundup answer
    Delete integer portion and fraction byte 4
End
```

The only exception to these rules is the number zero which is allowed to violate rule two. Manipulating numbers so that they conform with the above rules is called normalization.

All of the above examples were in base ten, but as might be expected the concepts are just as valid in base two except the exponent is now a power of two instead of ten. Therefore, numbers are of the form: $.FFF \times 2^{EE}$ (where FFF and EE are now hexadecimal representations of binary numbers). At this point we must decide upon a specific format to use within the computer that will give sufficient accuracy without wasting memory. A fraction containing 24 bits gives an accuracy of $1/2^{24}$ or about seven decimal places. A two's complement exponent of base 2 containing seven bits gives an exponent range of approximately $\pm10^{\pm19}$. This format has sufficient magnitude range for many applications and can represent numbers over 38 decimal orders of magnitude.

There are several common formats for floating point numbers. In some, the exponent is a power of 16 and a fraction is considered normalized if any of the four most significant bits are set. Exponents are often represented in "excess" form instead of two's complement form. In this form some appropriate number is added to all exponents so they are all positive. The specific format I chose consists of four 8 bit bytes for each number and is shown in figure 1. The high order bit (bit 7 typically) of byte one is the algebraic sign of the number (1 = −). The low order seven bits of the first byte (bit 6 to bit 0) are the signed two's complement value of the exponent. Bytes two, three and four contain the normalized unsigned fraction with the understood binary point preceding byte two. Note that bit seven of byte two is 1 for all normalized numbers except zero because of normalizing rule two.

Some sample numbers and their decimal equivalents are given in table 1.

Ins and Outs

Now that we've defined a format for real numbers, how can we put it to use? Several subroutines will be required. We need to be able to read real numbers from a terminal and convert them to our defined format and vice versa. Also, we need to outline how we can operate on real numbers once they are converted. First, the ins and outs.

The conversion to and from the terminal is the most difficult part of handling floating point numbers. An attempt is made here to outline a procedure that is well adapted to microprocessors. Several other algorithms are outlined in *The Art of Computer Programming, volume 2* by Donald Knuth (see references following this article) including information on converting to and from scientific notation.

Suppose the input string 13.05 is typed at a terminal. Since the computer will see the characters as they are typed left to right, the program in listing 1 can easily convert any number preceding the decimal point into a binary integer. In this example the 13 becomes 00001101, assuming an 8 bit integer. Once the decimal point is read the fraction can be calculated if a table of unnormalized fractions corresponding to the binary equivalent of 10^{-n} is stored in memory. Since there is no need for n to be larger than the accuracy of the final format, table 2 was calculated with n equal to seven. Table 2 was calculated using a BASIC program to determine which bits in the fraction should be set. Note that the fractions in this table are 32 bits wide instead of the 24 bits required in the final answer. This is done to insure the accuracy of the conversion. Using this table and starting with a zero exponent byte and zero in a 4 byte fractional portion in the answer, when the first number following the decimal point is typed on the terminal it is multiplied by the table value of the fraction for 0.1 and added to the fraction of the answer. Subsequent inputs are multiplied by 0.01, 0.001, etc, and added to the answer until the bottom of the table is reached after seven inputs or the input string is exhausted. Since the input numbers are 0 thru 9, it is easier and takes less time in a microprocessor to do the multiplication by successive additions. For the example input, 13.15, the fraction is calculated by example 1. Including the integer portion and the exponent the input becomes the representation in example 2. Normalizing this by shifting the integer and fraction four bits to the right and adding 4 to the exponent it becomes example 3.

Now the integer portion and the low order byte of the fraction can be deleted after incrementing the next to low order byte if bit seven of the low order byte was set (rounding up). See example 4 for the final value in the correct 4 byte format. Had the input number been −13.05 instead of

+13.05, the only difference in the number generated would be bit seven of the exponent (fraction sign bit) would be set. Note that if the input had been something like 0.005 the normalizing process described above would require left shifts of the frac-

Table 2: Decimal fraction to binary equivalent conversions. The table covers only the first seven digits since the accuracy of the routines we are considering is only seven places. This conversion assumes that the exponent is set to zero.

Decimal		Binary					
0.1	=	00011001	10011001	10011001	10011001	=	10^{-1}
0.01	=	00000010	10001111	01011100	00101000	=	10^{-2}
0.001	=	00000000	01000001	10001001	00110111	=	10^{-3}
0.0001	=	00000000	00000110	10001101	10111000	=	10^{-4}
0.00001	=	00000000	00000000	10100111	11000101	=	10^{-5}
0.000001	=	00000000	00000000	00010000	11000110	=	10^{-6}
0.0000001	=	00000000	00000000	00000001	10101101	=	10^{-7}

Example 1.

1	x	0.10	=	1	x	00011001	10011001	10011001	10011001
+ 5	x	0.01	=	5	x	00000010	10001111	01011100	00101000
						00100110	01100110	01100110	01100001

Example 2.

Integer	Fraction				Exponent
00001101	00100110	01100110	01100110	01100001	00000000

Example 3.

Integer	Fraction				Exponent
00000000	11010010	01100110	01100110	01100110	00000100

Example 4.

Exponent	Fraction		
00000100	11010010	01100110	01100110

Table 3: Portion of table used to convert the exponent of 2^e into decimal notation of the form $F \times 10^{Exp}$.

e (index)	Exp (1 byte)	F (3 bytes)		
.	.	.		
.	.	.		
.	.	.		
4	00000010 (2)	00101000	11110101	11000001 (0.16)
3	00000001 (1)	11001100	11001100	11001100 (0.80)
2	00000001 (1)	01100110	01100110	01100110 (0.4)
1	00000001 (1)	00110011	00110011	00110011 (0.2)
0	00000000 (0)	00000000	00000000	00000000 (0)
1	00000000 (0)	10000000	00000000	00000000 (0.5)
2	00000000 (0)	01000000	00000000	00000000 (0.25)
3	00000000 (0)	00100000	00000000	00000000 (0.125)
.	.	.		
.	.	.		
.	.	.		

```
Type entry = record of
        Exp: 8 bit binary
        F: 24 bit fraction
Var conv-table: array |-64..63| of entry
    table: array |1..7| of 24 bit fraction
(* e is the base 2 exponent of the number to be output*)
Begin
    Fraction: = conv-table|e|.F * fraction of number to be output
    If Fraction sign = 1 then print '-'; endif
    Print decimal point
    N: = 1
    Do while N <8
        CTR: = -1
        Do while fraction is positive
            Fraction: = fraction-table(N)
            CTR: = CTR + 1
        Enddo
        Fraction: = fraction + table (N)
        Convert CTR to ASCII and print it
    Enddo
    Print 'E'
    If conv-table|e|.Exp is negative then print '-'; Endif
    Convert conv-table|e|.Exp to decimal ASCII and print it
End
```

becomes the number to print. After the number is printed, the fractional value of 0.1 is added back into the fraction. This whole process is effectively a binary divide by 0.1. After 0.1 is added back, the procedure is repeated for 0.01, 0.001, etc, until all seven output digits are printed. This process is summarized in listing 2.

It should be noted that the above algorithms pose particular problems on various implementations and the programmer should be cautious of such things as overflow and carry flags as well as round off errors while doing the multiprecision operations.

The Arithmetic

Now we have a format for floating point or real numbers and we know how to input and output them. All that remains is the internal manipulation subroutines. All these subroutines require two normalized real arguments, which in the following text and listings will be referred to as argument 1 (ARG1) and argument 2 (ARG2). They all create a normalized real answer (ANS). We will use the predefined format except that during the internal manipulation some extra bits are occasionally needed at the right of the fraction to retain accuracy. Only a couple of bits are necessary, but since most microprocessors have 8 bit words, it is easier to add a whole byte to each fraction thus creating a 4 byte fraction instead of the prescribed three bytes. This fraction will be rounded to a 3 byte fraction in the defined format before returning to the caller of the manipulation subroutines.

Addition is defined as ARG1 + ARG2 = ANS. Once again the base 10 analogy will be useful in understanding how to implement an algorithm. If we desire the sum of the two normalized real numbers 0.375×10^5 and 0.22×10^4, we must first make the exponents equal before we can add the fractions. Once the exponents are equal, the fractions can be added and the answer given the common exponent. Thus, the example becomes:

$$
\begin{array}{r}
0.375 \times 10^5 \\
+\ 0.022 \times 10^5 \\
\hline
0.397 \times 10^5
\end{array}
$$

To make the exponents equal in this example, the number with the smaller exponent was shifted right n decimal digits and its exponent incremented by n. It is desirable to adjust the smaller number since shifting the larger number would require left shifts that might result in numbers being shifted into the integer portion which would violate the defined format. Any shifting, however, can create accuracy

tion while decrementing thus creating a negative exponent.

Outputting real numbers is slightly more difficult. The fraction and exponent part must be dealt with simultaneously since conversion of the exponent from base 2 to 10 will affect the fraction. Due to this complexity, it is preferable to output real numbers in scientific notation. The output form that is used is 1305 E + 2 instead of $0.1305 \times 10^{+2}$.

To accomplish the conversion we will need a rather large (4 by 128 byte) table to convert 2^e (where e is the exponent of the real number to be output) to $F \times 10^{Exp}$ (where F is an unnormalized fraction in our 3 byte notation and Exp is the power of 10 of the number we wish to print). A portion of the middle of the table is given in table 3.

The base 2 exponent e is not a member of the table, but is used as the index into the table to retrieve values of Exp and F. Using e we access the table and multiply the fraction F times the fraction of the number we wish to output using a multiply fraction subroutine described later. The resultant fraction of this multiplication will be the fraction that must be converted and printed followed by the letter E and the decimal value of Exp, including its sign, from the table to obtain the desired scientific notation.

Printing of the fraction uses the same table as used for converting to real format. In the first iteration the binary fraction for 0.1 is subtracted from the fraction until the fraction goes negative. For each subtraction except the last a counter is incremented and problems in a fixed digit (or bit) computer, since if the magnitude of two numbers differs by a large amount, their sum will be equal to the larger number. For example, if we had a calculator with six digits for a fraction and we added 0.300×10^8 and 0.20×10^0, the answer would be 0.300000×10^8 since shifting 0.20 seven digits to the right would cause it to become zero.

Binary real addition is identical to the above decimal example except the shifts are by n binary bits and the exponent is a power of 2. The algorithm in listing 3 first checks to see if the exponents are equal. If not equal, the fraction of the smaller argument is shifted one place right and its exponent incremented. This continues until the exponents are equal. Since our format stores the fractions as absolute unsigned values, all the fractional portions of negative fractions must be two's complemented before addition can proceed. Once the negation of any negative fractions is completed, the fractions can be added by a multiprecision addition. The fractional portion of the answer is then composed of the sum of the adjusted fractions and the exponent becomes the common exponent. This answer may need to be normalized. In fact, all the manipulation subroutines will require a check for normalization before exit, and therefore a subroutine to normalize arguments is desirable.

Subtraction is defined as ARG1 − ARG2 = ANS. The subtraction routine is identical to the addition routine except a multiple precision subtract is substituted for the addition. In most implementations the addition and subtraction routines are the same routine with a flag to indicate whether a subtraction or addition of the fraction should occur.

Multiplication of real numbers is easier than addition since the fractions can be multiplied regardless of the exponents. The multiplication algorithm in listing 4 is defined as: ARG1 * ARG2 = ANS. The multiplication of the fractions involves a 32 bit by 32 bit multiplication, but only the most significant 32 bits of the result are necessary which reduces the complexity of the multiplication somewhat.

For details on writing a multiplication subroutine check the references, or better yet check the user group library for your microprocessor to see if one already exists. The biggest problem with real multiplication is that overflow or underflow of the exponent can occur during the addition of the exponents. Therefore, the subroutine must take precautions to check for overflow or underflow and flag the result as erroneous if either occurred. The answer obtained by the above algorithm may need to be normalized before returning it to the caller.

Listing 3: Algorithm for real addition and subtraction. Before additions or subtractions can take place the numbers must be manipulated so that their exponents are equal.

```
Begin
    Do while exponent ARG1 ≠ exponent ARG2
        If exponent ARG1 > exponent ARG2 then
            Shift fraction ARG2 right one bit
            Increment exponent ARG2
        Else
            Shift fraction ARG1 right one bit
            Increment exponent ARG1
        Endif
    Enddo
    If fraction ARG1 is negative then 2's complement fraction ARG1;Endif
    If fraction ARG2 is negative then 2's complement fraction ARG2;Endif
    If operation is addition then
        Fraction ANS: = fraction ARG1 + fraction ARG2
    Else
        Fraction ANS: = fraction ARG1 − fraction ARG2
    Endif
    Exponent ANS: = exponent ARG1 or ARG2
    Normalize ANS
    Roundup ANS
End
```

Listing 4: Real multiplication algorithm. When multiplying real numbers it is not necessary to worry about the exponents being equal. Multiplication can take place under any conditions.

```
Begin
    Fraction ANS: = fraction ARG1 * fraction ARG2
    Exponent ANS: = exponent ARG1 + exponent ARG2
    Set overflow flag if exponent overflowed or underflowed
    Normalize ANS
    Roundup ANS
End
```

Listing 5: The real division routine must check to see if the dividing number is zero. If it is, the overflow flag is set and the routine is ended. The fractional part of the number to be divided should always be smaller than the dividing number. This is assured by shifting the number to be divided one place left and incrementing the exponent.

```
Begin
    If fraction ARG2 = 0 then
        Set overflow flag
    Else
        Shift fraction ARG1 one bit right
        Increment exponent ARG1
        Fraction ANS: = fraction ARG1/fraction ARG2
        Exponent ANS: = exponent ARG1 − exponent ARG2
        Set overflow if exponent overflowed or underflowed
        Normalize ANS
        Roundup ANS
    Endif
End
```

Division is similar to multiplication and is defined as ARG1/ARG2 = ANS. Since most division algorithms will not terminate if ARG2 is equal to zero, the division algorithm in listing 5 first checks the fraction of ARG2 to see if it is zero. If it is zero, the algorithm should return with an overflow indication. Also, many division algorithms require that the fraction of ARG1 be smaller than the fraction for ARG2. The division routine could check to see if this condition exists, or better yet, since we know both numbers are normalized (ie: the most significant bit is set) and since we have added an extra byte for accuracy, we can always shift ARG1 one bit to the right and insure that it is less than ARG2. Of course, we must add one to ARG1's exponent to compensate for the right shift. Now we can proceed with a normal 32 by 32 bit divide of the fractions. Once the fractional portion of the answer is complete, the exponent of the answer is equal to the exponent of ARG1 minus the exponent of ARG2. Again precautions must be taken to insure (or at least flag) that no underflow or overflow of exponents has occurred. The answer may need to be normalized.

Conclusion

This article has attempted to give an overview of what is necessary to create a package of floating point subroutines that can be used for many applications. Floating point manipulation is not trivial and some microprocessors will be better adapted to the task than others. Instructions that can handle multiple precision arguments such as "add with carry," "subtract with carry" in conjunction with shifts and rotates on memory make the implementation simpler. Be cautioned that the procedures outlined are general and any particular microprocessor will require special procedures to adjust for processor peculiarities. In any case, it seems the majority of the code is dedicated to shifting fractions right or left to insure accuracy or in checking for various error conditions.

On the positive side, a good debugged binary floating point package takes less memory and runs faster than the decimal floating point implemented in many BASIC packages. The add, subtract, multiply and divide routines lay the framework for the programmer to create more exotic subroutines such as sine, cosine, etc. Best of all, when we ask our computer to divide 5 by 2, it responds with 2.5.■

REFERENCES

1. Boney, Joel, *Floating Point Package*, Motorola User Group Library, 1976.

2. *Digital Computer Design Fundamentals*, McGraw-Hill, 1962, pages 70 thru 73.

3. Knuth, Donald E, *The Art of Computer Programming, volume 2,* Addison-Wesley, 1969.

What's in a Floating Point Package?

Sheldon Linker

If you have been using computers for any length of time, or have used a calculator, you know the value of floating point numbers. In this article, I will endeavor to show how floating point works and how to use it.

Initially, you must understand the representation of real numbers. In the decimal system, a real number may have a sign, a decimal point, digits to the left or right of the decimal point, and an exponent. The general form is commonly referred to as scientific notation. This form is:

$$\pm N.NNNNNN \times 10^{\pm MM}$$

where N.NNNNNN is the "mantissa" and MM is the "exponent." Unfortunately, decimal numbers are hard to deal with, even with the decimal add or adjust instructions of some microprocessors. There are some simplifications that can be made without serious loss of precision:

1. It is easier to handle the numbers if all of the digits are on the same side of the decimal point. This simplifies the shifting used to "normalize" results after a multiply or divide instruction. The decimal form of this is:

$$\pm .NNNNNNN \times 10^{\pm MM}$$

2. The exponent base should, for simplicity of programming, be a power of 2. Assuming that a 6 bit (excluding sign) exponent is to be used, table 1 helps in selecting the base by giving the magnitude range (in decimal) for a 6 bit positive exponent.

For the sake of conformity to many existing floating point packages, you should either use a base of 2 or 16. A base of 2 gives somewhat limited dynamic range; so for the rest of the article, I will use base 16. The dynamic range is defined as the difference between the high decimal value of the exponent and the low value. This reduces the generalized form to a more specific case.

$$\pm .NNNNNNN \times 16^{\pm MM}$$

Another consideration is storage. So far, I have 6 bits allocated to the exponent, 1 bit for the sign of the exponent, 1 bit for the sign of the mantissa, and some amount for the mantissa itself. As one byte has already been used, another three would work out nicely. 24 bits gives a precision of 24Xlog2 or 7.22 digits of accuracy (which is treated as 7 for formatting purposes).

Taking all of the above into account, we now have the real number stored as in figure 1. *[This 4 byte format is similar to the format used in an IBM 360 or 370 for single precision floating point.]*

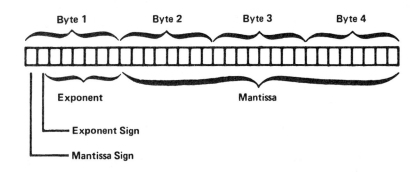

Example: The value of hexadecimal 013243F7
is hexadecimal $0.3243F7 \times 16^{1}$
or hexadecimal 3.243F7
or decimal 3.141593

Figure 1: Details how the floating point number may be stored in memory. In this format the first byte contains the exponent, the sign for the exponent, and the sign for the mantissa. Bytes two, three and four contain the mantissa of the number in absolute value form, with 24 bits of precision.

Table 1: *A summary of the dynamic ranges, difference between the lowest and highest expressable numbers, of several different bases. The bases are all powers of two since these are the easiest to handle on a computer. The range of the number is determined by assuming an exponent of 6 bits, excluding the sign.*

Base	Maximum Value (Base raised to 64th power)
2	1.84×10^{19}
4	3.40×10^{38}
8	6.28×10^{57}
16	1.16×10^{77}
32	2.14×10^{96}

Table 2: *Substitutions that may be made when adding or subtracting. This table reduces to a series of additions, subtractions and inversions which are performed by the routine of figure 2.*

Original Equation			Use
A+B	A≥0	B≥0	A+B
A+B	A≥0	B<0	A − |B|
A+B	A<0	B≥0	B − |A|
A+B	A<0	B<0	−(|A| + |B|)
A−B	A≥0	B≥0	A−B
A−B	A≥0	B<0	A + |B|
A−B	A<0	B≥0	−(|A| + B)
A−B	A<0	B<0	−(|B| − |A|)

We now come to what you've been waiting for: arithmetic. Addition and subtraction are the easiest, so I'll start with them. In the algorithms I'll present, addition and subtraction are simplest when using only positive terms; so the substitutions shown in table 2 can be made. Vertical bars denote absolute value as in |X| signifying the absolute value of X.

Table 2 actually boils down to a series of additions, subtractions and sign inversions. A flowchart of this process is given in figure 2.

When adding or subtracting, the first step is to determine whether a number is negative. When the first byte of a floating point number is negative, then the entire number is negative.

The second step is to change the sign of a number. This is done by adding or exclusive orring a hexadecimal 80 to the first byte of the number in this format.

You may notice that in the flowcharts I took no action to take the absolute value of either the A or B terms. This is because the mantissa bytes are actually in absolute value form.

You are now ready for the next step in

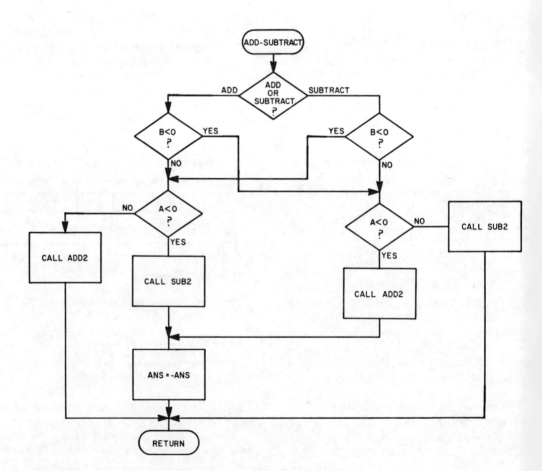

Figure 2: *Flowchart for a routine which will manipulate the two values to be added or subtracted according to the rules summarized in table 2.*

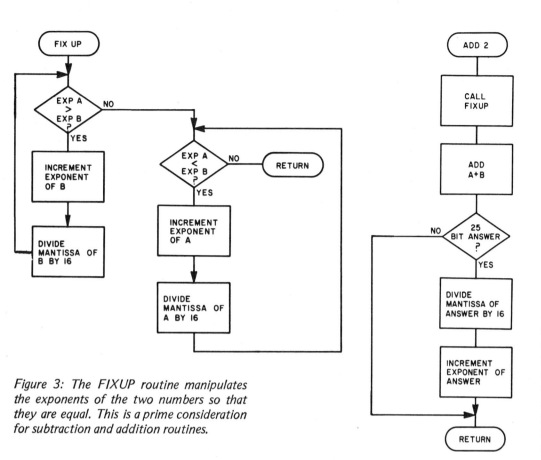

Figure 3: The FIXUP routine manipulates the exponents of the two numbers so that they are equal. This is a prime consideration for subtraction and addition routines.

Figure 4: This addition routine adds the two numbers and then checks if there has been an overflow into bit 25. If this condition exists, the mantissa is divided by decimal 16 and the exponent is incremented by one, thus giving a 24 bit answer.

addition or subtraction. Before the numbers can be used together, the exponents must match. This is done by incrementing the smaller exponent until it equals the larger exponent, while at the same time dividing the corresponding mantissa by 16. The larger exponent becomes the exponent of the answer up to this point. When comparing one exponent to another, you must keep in mind that the exponent occupies only the right 7 bits of the byte. To convert it to a standard signed number, you have to extend the sign by doing a shift left followed by an arithmetic shift right. Finally, you are about ready to do the actual addition or subtraction, but so that nothing is lost, you must treat the mantissas as 32 bit fields. A flowchart for the whole alignment step is shown in figure 3.

After the addition or subtraction you may have a 25 bit number, taking into consideration the carry of the 24 bit mantissas. If you do, divide it by 16 and add 1 to the exponent of the answer, as shown in figure 4. If the exponent of the answer is now 64, then you have the condition known as overflow. This is usually considered a severe error and warrants stopping the program, or substituting a "default" value.

After the subtract, you may be left with a negative number or zero. If you are left with a negative value, set the sign indicator bit of the answer to 1 and change the sign of the difference, as shown in figure 5. There is a

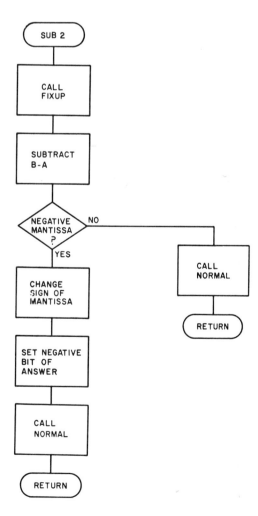

Figure 5: This subtraction routine subtracts two numbers and then determines the sign of the answer. If the sign is positive the answer is normalized and the number is then returned to the calling program. If the answer is negative a positive number is sent to the normalization routine and then the sign of the number is set negative before being returned to the calling routine.

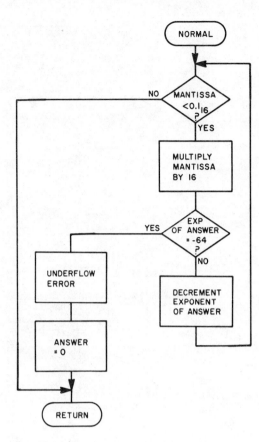

Figure 6: This is a normalization routine for the floating point format used in this article. The answer is set up so that the mantissa is hexadecimal 0.100000 to hexadecimal. FFFFFF. This is accomplished by multiplying the mantissa by decimal 16 and then incrementing the exponent until the high nybble of the mantissa is from hexadecimal 1 to 16.

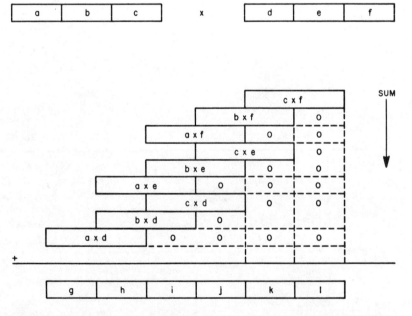

Figure 7: A summary of the method of multiplying two 24 bit mantissas to attain a 48 bit mantissa result. After the summation, the low order K and L bytes may be discarded as they will not show up in the final answer.

final step shown in figure 6, after the subtraction called normalization. If the mantissa of the answer is less than hexadecimal 0.100000, multiply it by 16 and subtract 1 from the exponent of the answer.

If the exponent is less than or equal to −64, you have a condition known as underflow. The underflow condition is considered a minor error, and the accepted response is to set the answer to zero, print a warning message, and continue execution of the program.

Continue normalizing until the mantissa is at least hexadecimal 0.100000.

To avoid the error of coming up with an answer of −0, apply this simple test: If the first 16 bits of the answer equals hexadecimal 8000, then the real answer is zero. Also, be sure to assemble the exponent into the final answer along with the sign and the mantissa.

After mastering addition and subtraction, we now forge onward to multiplication. As theory tells us:

$$(A \times 16^B)\,(C \times 16^D) = AC \times 16^{B+D}.$$

This makes things extremely simple. Step one is to multiply the two 24 bit mantissas together, giving a 48 bit result. Don't scream! You probably already have a method of multiplying two 8 bit numbers, giving a 16 bit result. The method of multiplying and summing for a 48 bit answer is shown in figure 7. After carrying out the nine 8 by 8 multiplies shown, sum vertically. Throw away bytes K and L of the result since they won't show up in the answer. Step two is to normalize bytes G, H, I and J. Bytes G, H and I now become the mantissa of the answer. Step three is to find the sign of the answer. Since table 3 applies to both multiplication and division, the exclusive or function can be used on bytes A and B to find the sign of the answer. Step four is to find the exponent. Separate the exponents, as in the FIXUP routine flowcharted in figure 3, and add them together along with the exponent given by the normalization process. Check for overflow and underflow.

The rule for division is stated as:

$$(A \times 16^B) \div (C \times 16^D) = A \div D \times 16^{B-D}.$$

This is similar to multiplication, except that the exponents are subtracted, along with the difference that you divide the mantissas instead of multiplying. To multiply, you took two 24 bit numbers and got a 48 bit product. To divide, you take a 48 bit dividend and a 24 bit divisor, giving a 48 bit quotient. Unfortunately, there is no way to chain partial quotients together as can be done with partial products. As you read the

Signs	Sign of Answer
A≥0 B≥0	+
A≥0 B<0	−
A<0 B≥0	−
A<0 B<0	+

Table 3: A summary of the sign of the answer given the sign of the numbers used in a multiplication or division.

description of 48 bit division, please refer to figure 8.

First, you must set up four 48 bit fields: the dividend, the divisor, the quotient and the hold register. Second, set the 24 high order bits of the 48 bit dividend to the 24 bit dividend and the 24 low order bits to zero. Third, set the high order 24 bits of the 48 bit divisor to the 24 bit divisor and the low order 24 bits to zero. Then, set the quotient to zero and the hold register to 1.

Now that the numbers are set up, normalize the divisor by multiplying it by 2 until the high order bit is on. Every time the divisor is doubled, the hold register is also doubled. Notice that if the divisor is zero, it will never get normalized; so it's a good idea to indicate an error condition and abort the program if this is the case.

The next step is the repeated subtraction: If the dividend is greater than or equal to the divisor then subtract the divisor from the dividend and add the hold register to the quotient. Then divide the divisor and the hold register by 2. If the hold register is still nonzero, then keep performing the repeated subtraction. This leaves only the normalization and sign operations, as in multiplication.

This completes the summary of basic floating point operations needed to do calculations in scientific notation. There are other formats which can be used, with more or less precision, using BCD coding for the mantissa and exponent, etc. The general steps required are all very similar. Other items which are useful to have, but which I have not covered here, include conversion routines for input and output, and transcendental function evaluations. But even if you can't calculate a sine or a cosine, and don't have a flexible FORTRAN style formatting output, the basic calculations of addition, subtraction, multiplication and division can prove a useful adjunct to your software.■

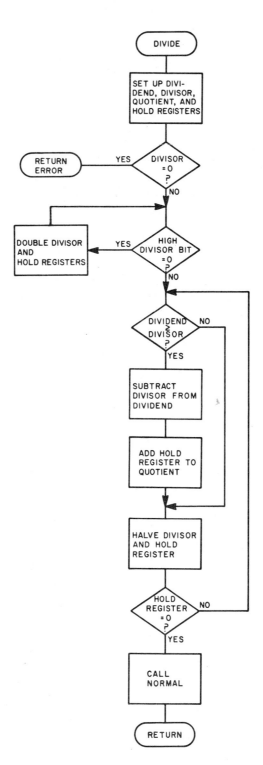

Figure 8: A division routine for floating point numbers. This routine starts with a 48 bit dividend and a 24 bit divisor to arrive at a 48 bit quotient. The routine then normalizes the answer before returning it to the calling program.

Comments on Floating Point Representation

Sheldon Linker's article "What's in a Floating Point Package?" on page 47 needs a refinement that might make a difference.

He states that the base of the exponent controls the dynamic range of the arithmetic. What he did not state is that the base also effectively controls the precision. The bigger the base, the greater the dynamic range and the poorer the precision. And this has nothing to do with stealing bits from the mantissa. Choosing the base is not an arbitrary matter of picking a hefty dynamic range.

The problem is illustrated when you attempt to add a single lowest order bit to a mantissa that has all the bits turned on. You can either up the exponent by 1 and renormalize (which is the procedure I read into Linker's article) or you can just not perform the addition. If the exponent is based on 2, then increasing the exponent causes a change in magnitude equal to the change that would be found if a bit were added to any other number. If the base is 16, the change is much greater. The net result is that the precision is much closer to six digits rather than seven.

Another way to look at it is to acknowledge first that all integer arithmetic takes place in finite steps; there are gaps between the numbers. Next, observe that the machine doesn't, through processes unknown, convert over to a continuous number machine when floating point is implemented. With floating point we just get the option of choosing the gap size as well as scaling the numbers.

The difference between base 2 and base 16 may seem trivial to the novice, and indeed must have seemed trivial to enough of the right people at IBM when they went hexadecimal. With base 2 you get seven digits throughout the dynamic range. With base 16 you *seem* to get seven digits most of the time, but are bound to get six now and then. In fact, with 2 and 16 as bases you get four and three digits of precision if your computations have any sophistication (like multiplication and summing) at all. The exact results, of course, depend on the numbers involved, but if you're interested in floating point and want precision, then base 2 cannot be beat. But remember that if you go double precision, then the range will probably be extended and you will have to extend the exponent field.

As an historical note, I heard somewhere that IBM put the exponent up front just to be different from Burroughs or Univac who had the exponent on the right.

R A Baker
2227 N Belmont
Richmond TX 77469

Originally appeared in September 1977 BYTE magazine.

Notes on Floating Point Representation

I would like to add a few comments on Sheldon Linker's article "What's in a Floating Point Package?," page 47. There are a few items that should be mentioned.

1. Usually one tries to keep all floating point information normalized. Let's consider an example: let the exponent be base 10 and assume we have four decimal digits of storage. Then

$$0.0025 \times 10^5 = 0.2500 \times 10^3 = 250$$

Clearly I have a choice of storage. But what about 2576? Then I can only use 0.2576×10^4. Chances are if my operands aren't normalized then the result may not be also.

2. In conjunction with normalized data, a hexadecimal base will yield a larger range than a binary base, but it will not carry the significance of a binary base. Hexadecimal base means that a leading hexadecimal digit of 1 will waste three binary bits!

3. In all my years of computing (14) I have never had a need for numbers greater than 10^{38} except for the legendary $24 Manhattan Purchase at 6% for 300+ years. I would suggest the following compromise.

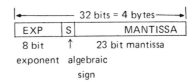

The exponent is a two's complement (excess 200) binary exponent. The dynamic range is 10^{76}. The sign bit is stored in place of the normalized most significant bit of the mantissa. Simple shifts or tests will determine the sign (and hence insertion of the MSB is easy).

Stephen R Alpert
Assoc Prof of CS, WPI
Vice Chairman, SIGMINI (ACM)
11 Ridgewood Dr
Auburn MA 01501

Originally appeared in November 1977 BYTE magazine.

Floating Point Arithmetic

Burt Hashizume

Many computer hobbyists are finding 8 bit integer arithmetic inadequate for a variety of mathematical applications. 16 and even 32 bit fixed point calculations are being used with increasing frequency because of their greater accuracy. However, these techniques are still inherently inadequate for calculations performed over a wide range of numbers.

Using a 16 bit integer format, only numbers from 0 to 65,535 can be represented. Larger or smaller numbers can be represented by moving the implicit radix point, but the range of discrete values still remains constant. The fractional part of the quotient in a division of one large number by another could be lost.

If one could dynamically slide the radix point, the number range would be dramatically increased. Using the same format, very small fractions and very large integers can be represented as floating point numbers. This is made possible by keeping track of the radix point's position separately with an exponent.

Floating Point Formats

There are many ways to represent floating point numbers, but there are only three basic formats; the others are variations. Two of these (the dominant ones in the traditional computer industry) use different binary representations. The third format, the one with the most variations, uses a binary coded decimal (BCD) representation, and is widely used in the electronic calculator and home computer industry.

The first format, shown in figure 1, is used by IBM in their implementation of FORTRAN on the System 360/370. It consists of a 24 bit mantissa, a 7 bit exponent, and a sign bit.

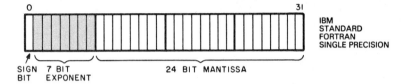

Figure 1: The floating point format used by IBM in their implementation on the System 360/370. It consists of a 24 bit mantissa, a 7 bit exponent, and a sign bit.

The mantissa represents a fraction with the radix point assumed to be to the left of the most significant digit. The exponent is in excess-64 notation, which is a 7 bit two's complement notation with the sign bit inverted, eg: a zero exponent (16^0) is 100 0000, the minimum exponent (16^{-64}) is 000 0000, and the maximum exponent (16^{+63}) is 111 1111. The algebraic sign bit of the value is associated with the mantissa, and the exponent's sign is inherent in its format: a one sign bit indicates the number is negative, and a zero sign bit indicates a positive number.

This is the data storage format of floating point numbers. All such data is assumed to be normalized (ie: the most significant digit in the mantissa is nonzero unless the number itself is zero, in which case all 32 bits are zero). Before a calculation, the numbers are assumed normalized; after a calculation they are normalized in the floating point accumulator before being stored.

The actual calculations take place in the floating point accumulator and other floating point registers. These registers can be in the hardware or in memory (software). Hardware floating point registers (expensive, but much faster than software) are used by large computers and many minicomputers, whereas most small computers implement floating point in software to keep costs down.

With the IBM format a "guard byte" is used in the floating point registers to maintain accuracy in performing the calculations.

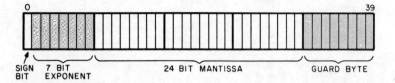

Figure 2: The IBM FORTRAN floating point format showing the location of the "guard byte." The guard byte is an extra field which holds portions of intermediate calculations so that the final calculated value can be rounded off rather than truncated prior to further use.

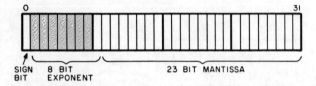

Figure 3: A binary floating point format used by Digital Equipment Corporation in BASIC interpreters on its PDP-11 series of computers. It consists of a 23 bit mantissa with a "hidden" bit, an 8 bit exponent, and a sign bit. The format assumes that the number to be represented is always normalized; that is, the most significant bit of the number is always understood to be 1 unless the entire number is equal to zero. This assumed "1" bit is the so-called "hidden" bit.

Table 1: Several decimal numbers along with their IBM FORTRAN floating point hexadecimal format equivalents (see figures 1 and 2).

Decimal Number	Hexadecimal Floating Point Number (Hexadecimal Digits)	
1.00	41	100000
6.00	41	600000
−1.00	C1	100000
0.50	40	800000
−0.50	C0	800000
100	42	640000
2^{16} (= 65,536)	45	100000
2^{-16}	3D	100000
$−2^{-32}$	B9	100000
0	00	000000
16^{-65}	00	100000
16^{+62}	7F	100000

Table 2: Examples of decimal numbers and their equivalents as encoded in the binary floating point format used in several BASIC interpreters (see figure 3).

Decimal Number	Binary Floating Point Number (Hexadecimal Digits)	
1.00	40	800000
6.00	41	C00000
−1.00	C0	800000
0.50	40	000000
−0.50	C0	000000
100	43	C80000
2^{16}=65,536	48	800000
2^{-16}	38	800000
$−2^{-32}$	B0	800000
0	00	000000
2^{-128}	00	800000
2^{+126}	7F	800000

The guard byte (see figure 2) is an 8 bit extension to the least significant end of the 24 bit mantissa, temporarily creating a 32 bit mantissa during calculations. By keeping track of 32 bits of accuracy throughout the operation, significance will not be lost when storing numbers because the 32 bits can be rounded off to 24 bits. If a guard byte is not used, no rounding off is possible, and the effect would be the same as truncation (which can result in loss of accuracy very quickly, as will be shown later).

Numbers from 1.00×16^{-65} to $F.FFFFF \times 16^{+62}$ can be represented by this format, resulting in an approximate range of from 10^{-79} to 10^{+76} with an accuracy of six or seven decimal digits. Table 1 lists several decimal numbers along with their hexadecimal IBM FORTRAN format equivalents.

The second format, shown in figure 3, is also a binary format that is used by Digital Equipment Corporation (DEC) in many of its BASIC interpreters. It has a 23 bit mantissa using a "hidden" bit, an 8 bit exponent, and a sign bit.

This format assumes that the number is always normalized. Therefore, the most significant bit (MSB) of the mantissa is always one unless the entire number is zero. If the number is zero, (indicated by the special case of a 0 exponent) then the hidden bit is also zero. The sign bit is zero for a positive number and one for negative. Because all nonzero numbers have an MSB of one, it need not be explicitly represented in the format; hence only 23 bits in the mantissa.

The exponent represents a power of two in excess-128 notation, which is similar to excess-64 notation. The largest exponent, 2^{+127} is represented by the largest number, 1111 1111, and the smallest exponent, 2^{-127}, by the smallest nonzero number, 0000 0001. An exponent of zero (2^0) is represented by 1000 000, while the number zero is reserved to indicate a zero mantissa.

As in the case of the first binary format, a guard byte must be used during calculations so that round off is possible before returning from the floating point accumulator for storage in memory. In this format it is also necessary to explicitly represent the hidden bit during calculations. This is accomplished by expanding the 4 byte format into six bytes: one byte for the sign, one byte for the exponent, and four bytes for the mantissa (including the guard byte). As a result there is a fair amount of processing necessary to load and store the floating point registers.

This format has a range of from 2^{+126} to 2^{-128} or from approximately 10^{+38} to 10^{-38} with a 7 decimal digit accuracy

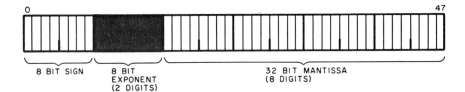

Figure 4: A BCD floating point format consisting of an 8 bit sign, an 8 bit exponent and a 32 bit (8 digit) mantissa.

(several examples are represented in table 2).

There are numerous BCD floating point formats currently in use. Mantissas range from as few as four digits to as many as 16 digits of accuracy, and exponents can typically range from 10^{+99} to 10^{-99}, or even 10^{+127} to 10^{-127}. The most popular format (see figure 4) has an 8 digit mantissa (four bytes of two digits per byte) with the decimal point assumed to be to the left of the most significant digit.

The mantissa sign is typically represented by a whole byte: 00 for positive and 0FF for negative. A variety of formats use one byte to represent the exponent.

One of the more frequently used formats is binary in the form of excess-128 notation. The exponent format itself is identical to the Digital Equipment Corporation format discussed earlier, but represents a power of ten instead of a power of two. Thus, an exponent of 84 base 16, using DEC's format, signifies two to the fourth power, and using the BCD format, ten to the fourth. The exponent represents the same power in both cases, but of different bases.

Eight digits are packed into four bytes in what is known as packed BCD (four bits represent one BCD digit).

The same format is usually used for both storage of data and actual calculations. This means neither a guard byte nor round off is used. The need for a guard byte is circumvented by using more significant digits than are actually necessary, eg: calculating to eight digits for 6 digit results, or calculating to nine digits for 8 digit results. This of course makes it necessary to use more memory per number for storage.

Some examples of numbers in this format are found in table 3.

Format Pros and Cons

Each of these basic floating point formats has its own particular advantages and disadvantages. Which format is best is dependent upon the requirements of the particular application: speed, small memory size, variable mantissa length, ease of coding in a given computer architecture, ease of interfacing to other software routines, etc.

The BCD format with its variations is by far the most popular in the personal computing field, probably because it is the easiest to program. The relative ease in converting from an ASCII representation

Decimal Number	BCD Representation (Hexadecimal Digits)		
1.00	00	81	10000000
6.00	00	81	60000000
−1.00	FF	81	10000000
0.50	00	80	50000000
−0.50	FF	80	50000000
100	00	83	10000000
$2^{16}=65,536$	00	85	65536000
2^{-16}	00	7C	15258789
$−2^{-32}$	FF	77	23283064
0	00	00	00000000
10^{+126}	00	FF	10000000
10^{-128}	00	01	10000000

Table 3: Several decimal numbers along with their equivalent floating point representations as encoded in BCD hexadecimal digits.

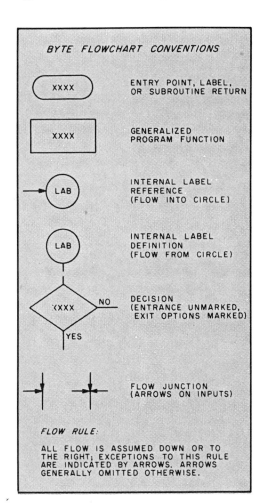

BYTE FLOWCHART CONVENTIONS

XXXX — ENTRY POINT, LABEL, OR SUBROUTINE RETURN

XXXX — GENERALIZED PROGRAM FUNCTION

LAB — INTERNAL LABEL REFERENCE (FLOW INTO CIRCLE)

LAB — INTERNAL LABEL DEFINITION (FLOW FROM CIRCLE)

XXXX — DECISION (ENTRANCE UNMARKED, EXIT OPTIONS MARKED)

FLOW JUNCTION (ARROWS ON INPUTS)

FLOW RULE:

ALL FLOW IS ASSUMED DOWN OR TO THE RIGHT; EXCEPTIONS TO THIS RULE ARE INDICATED BY ARROWS. ARROWS GENERALLY OMITTED OTHERWISE.

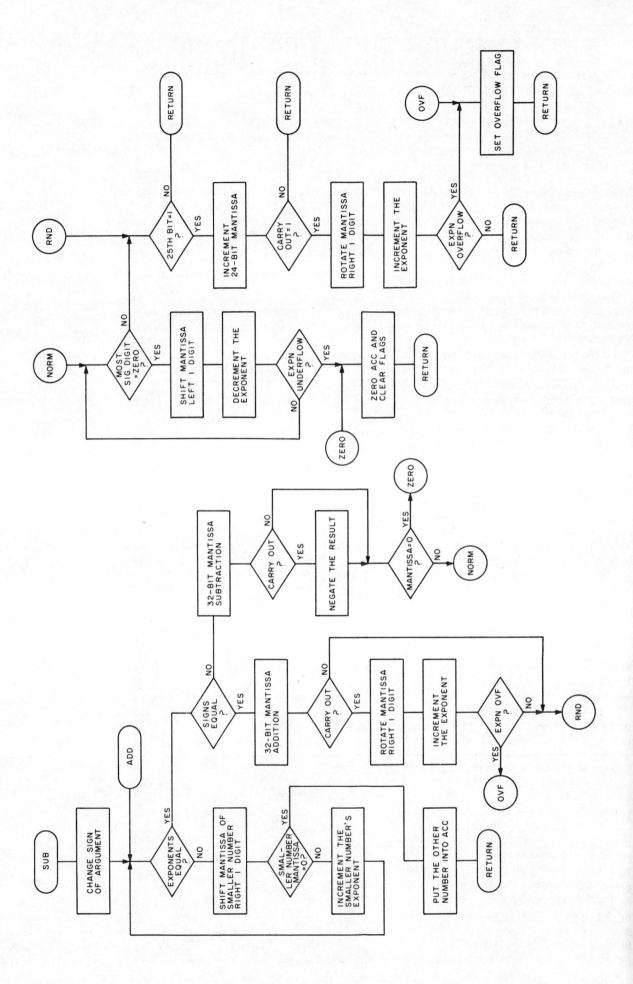

Figure 5: A flowchart of the floating point addition or subtraction routine.

of a number to the BCD format and back is a key factor, as is the ease with which the number of digits can be expanded.

This format has its list of disadvantages, though; but for these the commercial computer industry might have adopted it long ago. The program size required for performing just the basic operations and the conversion routines is about the same as for the other formats, but execution times are significantly slower. Many hobbyists are not as concerned with the number of milliseconds as with the number of bytes, but another disadvantage is the larger memory required to store the floating point numbers. For most assembly language applications the impact is negligible. It does become noticeable, however, when the floating point package is part of higher level language programs such as interpreters or compilers. One major disadvantage is more subtle. Many of the transcendental functions are best implemented using algorithms which are binary based. Using these algorithms, the BCD format is awkward at best and at worst consumes large quantities of time and memory.

The binary floating point format provides the fastest execution times, despite the fact that its format allows representation of 7 digit numbers at all times. Because the entire format is in binary, implementing the basic operations and all of the transcendental functions is easier than when using either of the other two formats.

The major drawback is the small range of numbers representable, relative to the other formats (10^{+38} to 10^{-38}). This is because its exponent is only a power of two compared with bases of 10 and 16 respectively. Two other minor drawbacks are the need for routines to convert floating point numbers from a decimal base to a binary base (and vice versa), and the need to expand the binary format to perform actual calculations.

The hexadecimal floating point format permits a much larger number range (10^{+76} to 10^{-76}) than the binary format, and the conversion routines are similar for both. Although slightly slower than the binary format, the hexadecimal format is still much faster than any BCD format of comparable capability.

It is somewhat more difficult to implement scientific functions such as square root, exponential and logarithm with this format than with the binary format, and its precision is not as great as the binary format's precision because it is digit rather than bit oriented. Even though the most significant digit is nonzero, the most significant three bits of the digit itself may be zeroes, resulting in only 21 bits of accuracy. This translates to only six digits of accuracy.

In describing the four basic floating point operations and the format conversions, the hexadecimal format will be used to illustrate examples.

Floating Point Operations

The software uses three floating point registers, an accumulator, argument register and scratch register. The floating point accumulator contains one of the operands prior to a calculation, and the result after the calculation is performed. The argument register contains the other operand, which is loaded by the routine, and the scratch register is used to hold temporary results.

In each of the basic operations there are two parts: exponent calculation and mantissa calculation. Fixed point operations require only the mantissa calculation, which turns out to be the easier of the two.

Add and Subtract Routine

Figure 5 is a flowchart of the add and subtract routine. The two operations are described together because the algorithms are identical except for a sign change before executing a subtract.

$$A = .100000 \times 16^1$$
$$B = .FFFFFF \times 16^0$$

Figure 6a: Two numbers A and B, which differ from one another by less than one part in 2^{24}, but which were represented as two different numbers.

	Mantissa	Guard Byte		
A =	.100000	00	X	16^1
B =	.0FFFFF	F0	X	16^1

Figure 6b: The same numbers as figure 6a, but with B shifted to the right one digit, and the extra digit stored in the guard byte in preparation for the subtraction shown in figure 6c. This shifting aligns mantissa radix points (makes exponents equal).

	Mantissa	Guard Byte						
A =	.100000	00	X	16^1				
−B =	−.0FFFFF	F0	X	16^1				
C =	.000000	10	X	16^1	=	.100000	X	16^{-5}

Figure 6c: The subtraction of B from A to give C. There is only one significant digit in the result, which is entirely located within the guard byte.

A =	.100000	X	16^1				
−B =	−.0FFFFF	X	16^1				
C =	.000001	X	16^1	=	.100000	X	16^{-4}

Figure 6d: If the guard byte is omitted, as in this example, the apparent result is off by a factor of 16 due to truncation prior to the mantissa addition (or subtraction).

The add and subtract routine consists of three functionally separate sections. The first prepares the numbers for the operation by aligning the radix points. This is analogous to aligning the decimal points for an addition or subtraction of decimal numbers. The addition or subtraction is then performed and the result normalized.

The radix points are aligned by shifting the mantissa of the smaller number right one digit and incrementing its exponent until the exponents are equal. When shifting right, the last eight bits shifted out are saved in the guard byte in order to maintain accuracy. During the shifting and incrementing loop, the 32 bit mantissa, including the guard byte, should be checked for all zeroes (a situation which implies that one operand is too small to affect the other). This is to avoid shifting insignificant zeroes. For example, 0.0001 added to 100000 will give 100000 because only six significant digits are retained.

In the second section the signs of the two operands are compared. If they are the same, addition is performed, and if they are different, subtraction is performed. Addition is a straightforward 32 bit fixed point add; the only normalization is a right rotate one digit and exponent increment when there is a carry out. An overflow can only occur if, on the right rotate, the exponent exceeds the maximum value when incremented. When this occurs, the current routine is exited, the overflow flag is set, and program control is returned to the caller.

If the mantissa signs are opposite, the argument mantissa is subtracted from the accumulator mantissa in a 32 bit fixed point operation. If the absolute value of the argument mantissa is greater than that of the accumulator mantissa, a carry out occurs and the result must be negated and the result sign complemented. The effect is the same as subtracting the smaller mantissa from the larger and using the sign of the larger.

The last section normalizes and rounds off the result and checks for exponent overflow and underflow. Normalization consists of shifting the mantissa digits left until the most significant digit is nonzero. For each shift, the exponent must be incremented and checked for overflow. Only 24 bits of mantissa are saved. Therefore, the 25th bit of the temporary result determines whether the mantissa is to be rounded up or not. For example, if the hexadecimal result were 10000094, it would be rounded up to 100001, whereas a result of 10000048 would not.

If the guard byte and a round off operation are not used in an addition, one bit of significance could be lost. By comparison, subtraction without a guard byte could mean a difference of an order of magnitude. Two numbers can be different by less than one part in 2^{24} and yet be represented as two different numbers (A and B in figure 6a). When one is subtracted from the other, the smaller must be shifted right in order to align the radix points. The guard byte stores the shifted out digit (figure 6b) and retains the only significant digit of the result (figure 6c). Without a guard byte the significant digit may be off by a factor of 16 (figure 6d).

Multiplication

Figure 7 is a flowchart of the multiplication routine. Calculation of the exponent for the multiplication and division routines is achieved by adding or subtracting the operand exponents respectively. Since the exponents are in excess-64 notation, the offset (64) will have to be subtracted from or added to the result. If the resultant ex-

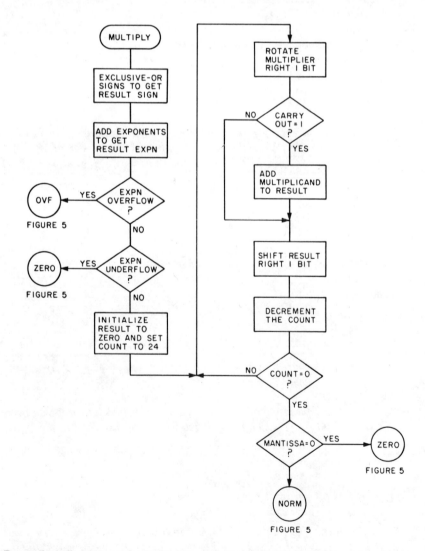

Figure 7: A flowchart for the floating point multiplication routine.

ponent is less than the smallest exponent or greater than the largest, an underflow or overflow condition exists and the appropriate action is taken (for example, displaying an error message or setting the result to a fixed value). Sign calculation for both multiply and divide is a simple exclusive or of the two operand signs.

The partial product method is the most widely used in fixed point multiplications, decimal or binary based. Using binary numbers, this algorithm rotates the multiplier right one bit and tests the bit rotated out. The multiplicand is conditionally added to the accumulated result if the bit is a one. The result is then rotated right one bit, retaining 32 bits, and the whole procedure repeated for all 24 bits of the multiplier. [An example of this algorithm implemented in hardware was found in the article "This Circuit Multiplies" by Tom Hall, page 36 in July 1977 BYTE . . . CH]

Though the fixed point calculation is straightforward and uncomplicated, it is extremely time consuming because the loop is repeated 24 times. One method of reducing the execution time is to cut out all subroutines within the loop and use only in line code. A complete multiplication routine can then have a worst case multiply time of about 2.5 ms using an 8080 processor with 2 MHz clock.

Division

Figure 8 is a flowchart of the division routine. The fixed point divide algorithm is analogous to the partial product method and is also commonly used. It compares the absolute value of the divisor to that of the dividend. If it is equal to or less than the dividend's absolute value, it is subtracted from the dividend, and a one is rotated into the least significant bit of the quotient. Otherwise there is no subtraction and a zero is rotated in. The dividend is then shifted left one bit and the loop repeated for a total of 32 times, generating a 32 bit quotient. Long division by hand goes through the identical procedure, but it operates on digits instead of bits.

Since more processing is done in each loop cycle than in the multiply routine, division execution times are longer than multiplication times. The worst case times are still around 5 ms for an 8080 with 2 MHz clock.

In both the multiply and divide routines, the normalization procedure is identical to the one in the subtract routine. Therefore it usually turns out to be shared code.

These routines are the core for other floating point functions such as format conversions and scientific mathematical func-

tions. Because of this it is important that these routines execute as fast as possible so that the other functions' execution times are not increased to several seconds instead of fractions of seconds.

BCD to Binary and Binary to BCD conversions are probably the most difficult to implement in a binary floating point package. There are several simple methods of converting integers from one format to the other, but I haven't seen any published literature to date on either floating point arithmetic or number base conversions.

The methods described here were chosen because of their simplicity rather than their speed. The slow base conversions are still relatively fast compared to the character oriented input and output operations in which they are used, so for most purposes the conversion speed is not noticeable.

Decimal to Binary Conversion

The Decimal to Binary (DB) routine

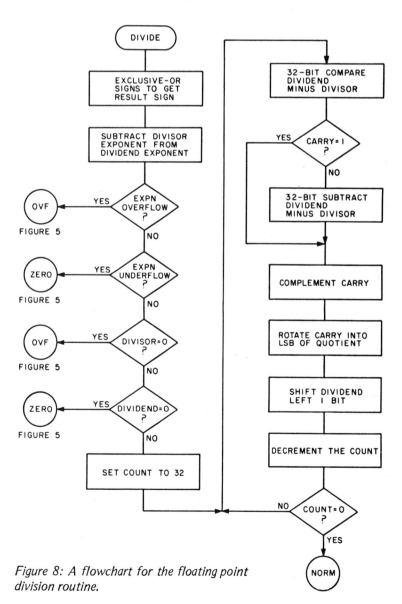

Figure 8: A flowchart for the floating point division routine.

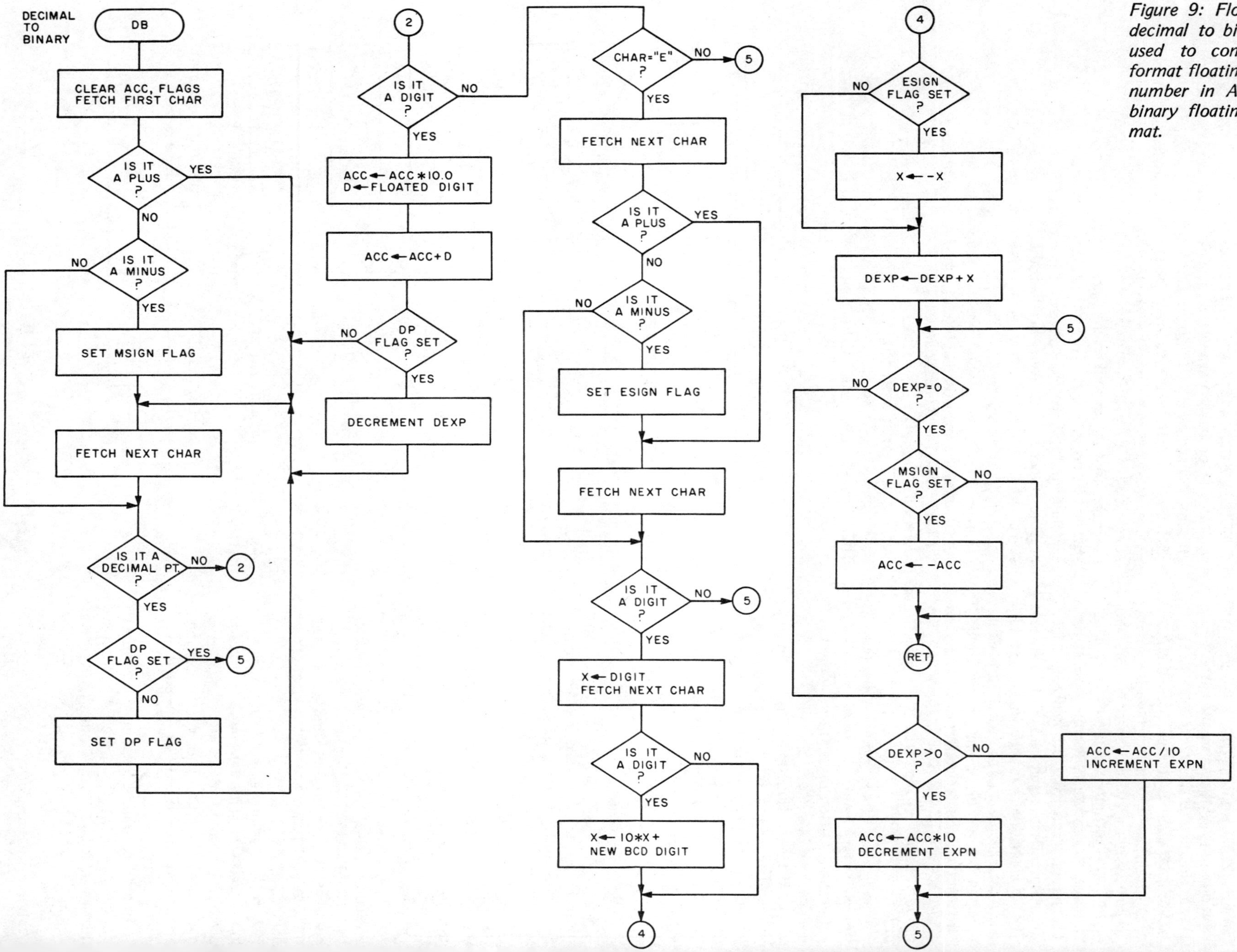

Figure 9: Flowchart of a decimal to binary routine used to convert a free format floating point BCD number in ASCII format binary floating point format.

(figure 9) converts a free format floating point BCD number in ASCII to binary floating point format, converting from ASCII BCD floating point to formatted BCD floating point, and then to binary floating point in one operation.

After initialization the DB routine first checks for a plus or minus sign, which is optional. It ignores a plus sign and sets a flag if there is a minus sign. It then reads in one or more digits (and possibly a decimal point). When it encounters a decimal point, it tests a flag to see if another decimal point has already occurred and sets the flag if not. If a decimal point has already occurred, the routine jumps to the last section. For each decimal digit input, the routine multi-

plies the accumulated result by ten in floating point format, creates a floating point number from the digit, and adds the number to the accumulated result. If a decimal point has previously occurred, a decimal exponent count is decremented, keeping track of the number of digits in the fractional part. This process is repeated until a character which is neither a digit nor decimal point has occurred, at which point control passes on to the exponent evaluation routine.

Here the decimal exponent of the number, if any, is processed. The routine first searches for the presence of an E character. If none is present, control jumps to the last section. If the character is present, one or two BCD digits are inputted with an optional

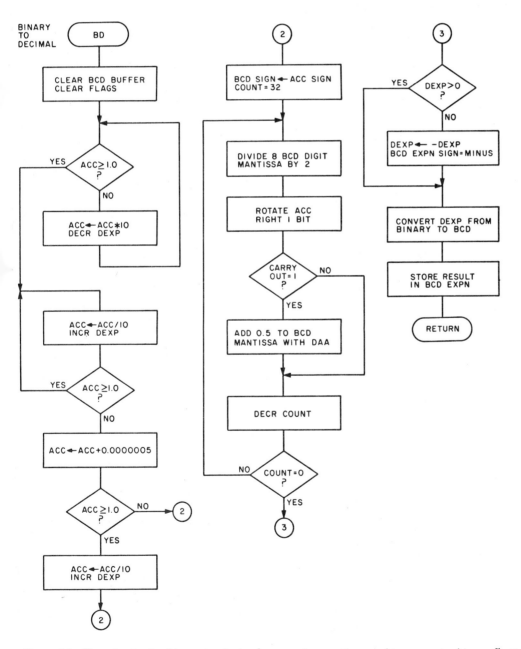

Figure 10: Flowchart of a binary to decimal conversion routine used to convert a binary floating point number to packed BCD floating point format.

plus or minus sign. The BCD digits are converted to an 8 bit binary, two's complement number and added to the decimal exponent count.

Finally, the mantissa is normalized by either repeatedly multiplying or dividing by ten, depending upon the decimal exponent count. Multiplication is performed if the count is greater than zero, and division is performed if it is less than zero. The count is either decremented or incremented respectively toward zero for every multiplication or division. When the count reaches zero, the sign is corrected if the number is negative, and the routine returns.

The Binary to Decimal (BD) routine shown in figure 10 converts a binary floating point number to packed BCD floating point. The number is left in packed BCD notation so the user can define his or her own format for the decimal point and exponent.

Initially, the binary number is normalized so that it is in the range of 0.1 to 1.0, with a decimal exponent kept separate. This is done by repeatedly multiplying or dividing by 10 until the number is equal to or greater than 1.0 and less than 10.0, and then dividing it by 10.0. During this operation, each multiplication or division by 10 is tabulated in a count. Next, a round off of 0.0000005 is added and a correction, if necessary, is made to make sure the number remains between 0.1 and 1.0.

The number is then converted to a binary fixed point fraction, and finally to a BCD fixed point fraction of eight digits, but accurate to only six digits because of the added round off.

After completing mantissa conversion, the binary count of the decimal exponent is converted to a signed BCD pair and stored with the BCD fraction.

These two algorithms for conversion of bases between BCD (base 10) and binary (base 2) are valid for any binary floating point format, not just the one used here.

Concluding Remarks

It is hoped that this discussion along with the flowchart specifications of the algorithms can be used by readers as a basis for coding a floating point arithmetic package for any general purpose microprocessor system. I have used this information in particular to code an 8080 version of the routines for the basic arithmetic functions, as well as extensions for functions such as square root, exponential, natural logarithm, sine and cosine, and arc tangent. The extensions all use the basic multiplication, division, addition and subtraction operations to evaluate the more complex functions involved. Readers interested in a complete 8080 floating point package including mathematical functions (square root and transcendentals) should write me for further information at POB 447, Maynard MA 01754.■

Evaluating a Floating

Point Package

Henry A Davis

Floating point arithmetic is often provided for microprocessor systems by software subroutines. While this works admirably for many applications, one drawback is the specific implementation of the floating point arithmetic package. Several "standards" exist for floating point format, but the IBM system 360/370 format is probably the most popular. Unfortunately the usability of each software package depends to a large extent upon the algorithms used by the programmer to realize the specific floating point functions. One common error in implementation is the truncation (chopping) after a fixed number of decimal places rather than rounding off. This practice results in substantial problems for digital filtering (especially large-ordered filters), least-squares numerical techniques, and even in conditional tests for skips or branches to subroutines. The problem is due to two factors. First, the mean of a sum of truncated random numbers is nonzero; and second, the relative error introduced by truncating a very large or small number becomes significant.

Knowledge of how your floating point package behaves can help in pinpointing possible problems before they occur. Unfortunately, few manufacturers or software houses provide listings of their packages. The burden of analysis falls on the user.

A program in FORTRAN (which easily converts to BASIC) for testing a floating point package and determining the relevant features simplifies matters considerably (see listing 1).

A floating point number system (let's call it F) assigns a radix (or base) and a mantissa (or decimal part) of a logarithm to each number. In general we can refer to the radix as R and the T-digit mantissa as M. Usually

R is 2, 8, 10, or 16, but is only restricted to being a positive integer greater than one. The exponent of the number is assumed to be greater than or equal to 0 and has no upper limit. Now we can represent a number N by:

$$N = (sign) .ddd...d(T)*R**E$$
$$(**signifies\ exponentiation)$$

where d's are integers in the range 0 through R−1. If the number N is not zero and the first digit of the fraction .ddd...d(T) is not zero, then N is said to be normalized. Thus, .01 would not be formalized; .1 would be. Because each number is represented by a finite number of binary digits in the machine, there is guaranteed to be a smallest positive floating point number Q such that when Q is added to one, the result is greater than one. This fact is the basis upon which we can compute the radix, the number of digits (T), and the machine error (Q).

Suppose the machine in question conforms to the definition above. Then the consecutive integers from zero to R**T can be represented exactly in the floating point system F. In addition, certain integers larger than R**T may be represented exactly. These are:

$$R**T, R**T+2R, R**T+3R,...., R**(T+1),$$
$$R**(T+1)+R**2...$$

So the difference between neighboring values is R on the interval:

$$R**T, R**T(T+1)$$

The first part of the algorithm must find this interval. This may be performed by testing successive powers of two until such a number A is found, and then adding successive powers of two to A until the next true representation (A+R) is found. Now R may be computed by subtracting A from the latter number. The most important part of the algorithm determines whether the numbers are truncated or rounded off. To determine this, add R−1 to A. This means that A will be in the interval:

$$R**T, R**(T+1)$$

Now T may be computed by:

$$T = floor(\log_R (A))$$

To avoid any inaccuracies introduced by the log base R function, T is the smallest power of R which will shift the least significant digit of an integer out of the mantissa.

Upper and lower bounds of the floating point exponent cannot be computed because overflow and underflow are not handled in a uniform manner.

The following FORTRAN program given in listing 1 will calculate R, T, and whether the system truncates or rounds off.

By using a subroutine similar to this it is possible to establish the environment in which floating point operations take place. In addition, the portability of software may be enhanced by writing mathematical subroutines in a very general sense and then calling a subroutine to fill in the details of the host computer.

Examples of such mathematical algorithms include zero-finder programs which must use a "machine epsilon" to determine when a 0 has been found, and iterative improvement algorithms which must stop interating when the corrections no longer affect the answer.■

```
      SUBROUTINE FLTCHK(R,T,RNDOFF)
      INTEGER R,T
      LOGICAL RNDOFF
      RNDOFF=.TRUE
      A=2.
      B=2.
C
C     FIND INTERVAL LOWER LIMIT, GOTO 20
      WHEN FOUND.
C
10    IF ((A+1.)−A.NE.1) GOTO 20
      A=A*2.
      GOTO 10
C
C     FIND UPPER LIMIT, GOTO 30
      WHEN FOUND
C
20    IF (A+B.NE.A) GOTO 30
      B=B*2.
      GOTO 20
C
C     CALCULATE RADIX
C
30    R=(A+B)−A
C
C     DETERMINE IF ROUNDING
C
      IF (A+(R−1) .EQ.A) RNDOFF=.FALSE.
      T=0
      A=1
C
C     DETERMINE NUMBER OF DIGITS
C
40    T=T+1
      A=A*R
      IF ((A+1)−A.EQ.1) GOTO 40
      RETURN
      END
```

Listing 1.

REFERENCES

1. Malcolm, M.A. "Algorithms to Reveal Properties of Floating-Point Arithmetic", C.S. Dept. Stanford Univ., STAN-CS-71-211, March 1972.

2. Redish, K.A. and Ward, W. "Environment Enquiries for Numerical Analysis" SIGNUM Newsletter 6(1), January 1971, 10-15.

Unlimited Precision Division

Jef Raskin

The Apple II, which I own, is a fine computer, especially since most programs that interest me get along quite well with integer arithmetic. Text editing, graphics, and the music programs I experiment with have little need of decimal notation or quantities. Besides, if I really need numbers like 3.14159 I can always load Apple's Applesoft BASIC which has *floating point* arithmetic.

The problems involved in using integer arithmetic show up occasionally when I need to perform a division, though. If you add, subtract or multiply two integers, you get an integer. But if you divide one integer by another, you may or may not get an integer result. From a mathematical standpoint, integers are *closed* under addition, subtraction, and multiplication, but not under division.

I started to write a program to do real division on the Apple II. I thought it would be difficult, but it turned out to be very easy. Let us say you want to divide X by Y and print the answer to N decimal places. Listing 1 does the job, assuming X, Y and N are defined elsewhere.

Line 1020 determines the integer portion of the quotient. If X is 10 and Y is 3, Q is calculated to be exactly 3. This is, after all, integer division. Since we have the whole number part of the answer, line 1030 prints it. The semicolon means leave no space between the item just printed and the next item to be printed. The next item is a period (used as a decimal point). The final semicolon makes sure that the rest of the answer will be printed immediately after the decimal point.

Line 1040 is the heart of the routine. It does what you do in long division. The original value of Q might not be exactly the right answer. Q is most likely too small (at best it is exactly right). By how much is it too small? You can find out by calculating the quantity $Q \times Y$, and then subtracting that from X. In other words, check the division by multiplication $(Q \times Y)$ and see how much it missed X by subtraction. The quantity $X - (Q \times Y)$ is also called X MOD Y or, more simply, the remainder obtained after dividing X by Y. If your BASIC package has a modulus (MOD) function (as the Apple II BASIC does), you can simplify line 1040 to:

$$1040 \ X = 10(X \ MOD \ Y).$$

In long division, any remainder is handled by writing it down, and putting a 0 after it. Try performing a division and see. In the computer, multiplying by 10 puts a 0 after a number. Line 1040 imitates what you do

```
1020   Q=X/Y
1030   PRINT Q;".";
1040   X=(X−Q*Y)*10
1050   Q=X/Y
1060   PRINT Q;
1070   N=N−1
1080   IF N>0 THEN GOTO 1040
1090   END
```

Listing 1: The BASIC program for unlimited integer division is really quite simple. It is explained fully in the text.

by hand. Then, in line 1050, the remainder multiplied by 10 is divided by the original divisor, Y. This gives us the next digit, which is printed in line 1060. The next two lines merely count how many digits have been printed and stop the program after N digits. If you take lines 1070 and 1080 and replace them with:

1070 GOTO 1040

then you get truly unlimited precision.

As long as you keep the computer running, it will turn out digits and they will all be correct. In the Apple II this means that no calculation ever exceeds 32,767. This is most likely to happen in line 1040. If you are using the modulus function, this can happen without getting a message and an incorrect result can appear. With the original line 1040, either the answer is exactly correct or the program halts.

If you experiment with this program, you will find that most decimal expansions of fractions repeat rather quickly. 1411 divided by 999 is 1.412412412 with the expression 412 repeating forever. More interesting is the quotient of 437 divided by 463, shown in table 1. [Incidentally, 355 divided by 113 gives a good approximation of π....CM] While most decimal expansions repeat quickly, every decimal expansion of a fraction is a repeating decimal. It is not too hard to prove this, but the proof is a bit outside the realm of this article.

To make this into a demonstration, I use the program in listing 2. Lines:

1090 PRINT
1100 RETURN

are added to convert the routine into a subroutine, and the request for a new numerator appears on a new line, not just after the last quotient.

[Once you've been using this routine for a while, try dividing some prime numbers. Of particular interest is the quotient of 99991 divided by 99989. So far we have generated 2500 decimal digits for this value at the BYTE offices without encountering a repetition....RGAC]∎

1	0	0	2	2	9	3	5	7	7	9	8	1	6	5	1	3	7	6	1	4	6	7	8
8	9	9	0	8	2	5	6	8	8	0	7	3	3	9	4	4	9	5	4	1	2	8	4
4	0	3	6	6	9	7	2	4	7	7	0	6	4	2	2	0	1	8	3	4	8	6	2
3	8	5	3	2	1	1	0	0	9	1	7	4	3	1	1	9	2	6	6	0	5	5	0
4	5	8	7	1	5	5	9	6	3	3	0	2	7	5	2	2	9						

Table 1: The result of dividing the number 437 by 436. The last three digits (229) begins the repetition sequence. Quite often, dividing two numbers which are very close to each other produces interesting repetition patterns with very long periods.

```
0100    PRINT "THIS PROGRAM DOES A VERY LONG, LONG DIVI-
        SION"
0110    INPUT "WHAT IS THE NUMBER TO BE DIVIDED? (THE
        NUMERATOR)" ,X
0120    INPUT "WHAT IS IT TO BE DIVIDED BY? (THE DENOMI-
        NATOR)" ,Y
0130    PRINT "HOW MANY DECIMAL PLACES SHOULD THE AN-
        SWER (THE QUOTIENT)"
0135    INPUT "BE CARRIED OUT TO" ,N
0140    GOSUB 1020
0150    GOTO 110
```

Listing 2: This is a demonstration program which will allow you to input any two integer values and have the result printed on an arbitrary precision.

COMPUTATIONAL METHODS

About This Section

Now that you are familiar with the fundamentals of computer mathematics, either through previous experience or through having read the preceding articles, it's time to move on to weightier things.

If you have a formal computer science background, you may recall with some trepidation courses with titles such as "Elementary Numerical Analysis" or "Numerical Methods for Scientists and Engineers." These courses acquired a reputation surpassed only by the "killer" physics course all colleges seem to have. And yet the reputation was largely undeserved since the courses often only pulled together information from many disciplines (mathematics, engineering, statistics) which the student already possessed. The details of the course were not particularly new to the student, but only rearranged or emphasized in a different light.

So it is with this section. A background in numerical methods would certainly be of help in understanding the articles included here, but it is hardly mandatory. Anyone with a firm grounding in higher mathematics should have no difficulty. Anyway, let's take a look at what is included in this section.

When working with trigonometric quantities, it is not always necessary to arrive at the precise value. Often a relationship between the desired value and the entire range of allowable values is sufficient. Robert Grappel discusses such an implementation in "An Easy Way to Calculate Sines and Cosines."

Many people use their computers as number crunchers and want quick, accurate algorithms for determining some fairly involved mathematical functions. Typical examples are trigonometric functions, hyperbolic functions, and exponentiation. In "Simple Algorithms for Calculating Elementary Functions," John Rheinstein details several algorithms to calculate these functions quickly.

In "Elements of Statistical Computation," Alan Forsythe covers the *dos* and *don'ts* of determining the mean and standard deviation of a set of data.

Taylor series expansions are not necessarily the best polynomial approximations for many functions. Fred R Ruckdeschel describes several minimax and rational polynomial approximations for some common functions in "Functional Approximations." A method for creating polynomial approximations for microcomputers using mathematical tables and large system statistical routines is also discussed.

Finally, Mark Zimmermann takes a look at recreational computing, "Recmath", in "Continued Fractions, or Pieces of Pi." In it he presents several methods for calculating accurate fractional parts of real numbers, and includes listings of his routines along with sample runs.

An Easy Way to Calculate Sines and Cosines

Robert Grappel

The instruction set of a typical 8 bit processor can be quite confining at times. Any task requiring more than simple integer addition and subtraction can become a nuisance. There are reference books from which multiplication and division routines can be obtained, and square root and other functions can be built by using expansion, iteration, or other well-known methods. Implementing these algorithms on a microprocessor uses much space and programming time. Trigonometric functions are among this class of difficult functions. However, if one can tolerate accuracy of one part in 100, and allow about 1 ms per computation, the routine described in this article will provide sine and cosine values in a very simple 40 byte routine. I have coded it for a Motorola M6800 processor but it could easily be converted to any other processor.

Theory

The algorithm is based on two trigonometric identities:

$$sine(\theta+s) = sin(\theta)cos(s) + cos(\theta)sin(s)$$
$$cos(\theta+s) = cos(\theta)cos(s) - sin(\theta)sin(s)$$

where θ is the angle we are interested in and s is a small step in angle added to θ. If we make the step small enough, we can approximate $sin(s)$ and $cos(s)$ as follows:

$$sin(s) = s$$
$$cos(s) = 1$$

Combining these four equations we get:

$$sin(\theta+s) = sin(\theta) + s\ cos(\theta)$$
$$cos(\theta+s) = cos(\theta) - s\ sin(\theta)$$

Solving for sine and substituting into the cosine formula:

$$cos(\theta+s) = (1+s^2)cos(\theta) - s\ sin(\theta+s)$$

Since s is very small, we can neglect s^2 and write:

$$cos(\theta+s) = cos(\theta) - s\ sin(\theta+s)$$

Given that we have values for $sin(\theta)$ and $cos(\theta)$ at some point, we can get to any

Location	Op Code	Operand	Label	Assembly Code
				* SUBROUTINE TO COMPUTE SINE AND COSINE
				* AS SINGLE-BYTE INTEGERS (SIGNED)
				* STEP SIZE OF 1/16 RADIAN, OR 3.58 DEGREES
				* ACCURACY OF ABOUT 1% FOR RANGE 0
				THROUGH 90 DEGREES
				*
0000			THETA	RMB 1 *ARGUMENT TO FUNCTION
0001			SINE	RMB 1 *SINE OF THETA
0002			COSINE	RMB 1 *COSINE OF THETA
0003	86	7E	START	LDA A #126 *BEGIN INITIALIZATION
0005	B7	0002		STA A COSINE
0008	7F	0001		CLR SINE
000B	B6	0000		LDA A THETA
000E	F6	0002		LDA B COSINE *COMPUTE NEW SINE
0011	57		CYCLE	ASR B
0012	57			ASR B
0013	57			ASR B
0014	57			ASR B
0015	FB	0001		ADD B SINE
0018	F7	0001		STA B SINE
001B	57			ASR B *COMPUTE NEW COSINE
001C	57			ASR B
001D	57			ASR B
001E	57			ASR B
001F	F0	0002		SUB B COSINE
0022	50			NEG B
0023	F7	0002		STA B COSINE
0026	4A			DEC A
0027	2C	E8		BGE CYCLE *LOOP UNTIL DONE
0029	39			RTS

Listing 1: 6800 routine for computing sines and cosines over the range 0 to $\pi/2$ radians (0 to 90 degrees).

other angle by stepping through the two approximations, first computing $\sin(\theta+s)$ and then using that to compute $\cos(\theta+s)$. We choose to start at θ equal to zero, and set $\cos(\theta)$ to the largest positive value that can be stored as a signed byte without causing overflow when negated and decremented. Hence $\cos(0) = 126$. Similarly the $\sin(0) = 0$. The step size is chosen to be 0.0625 radian or about 3.58°. The step size must be a binary fraction so that all the multiplication involved in the equations can be performed by arithmetic shifts. If more accuracy is needed, the step size is easily reduced by introducing more shifts into the algorithm.

Program

The assembly code program for the Motorola 6800 version of the routine is shown in listing 1. When called with the angle stored in variable THETA, it returns the sine and cosine of that angle. The accuracy is quite good for angles less than $\pi/2$ radians (90 degrees). For angles larger than $\pi/2$ radians, other trigonometric identities can be used:

$$\sin(\theta) = \cos(\pi/2-\theta) = \sin(\pi-\theta)$$
$$\cos(\theta) = \sin(\pi/2-\theta) = (-\cos(\pi-\theta))$$

Thus, the sine and cosine of any angle can be computed from the values over the range 0 to $\pi/2$ radians. These identities can be coded quite easily.

All the other trigonometric functions can be computed from the values of sine and cosine. All that is needed is an integer division routine such as the following:

$$\csc(\theta) = 126/\sin(\theta)$$
$$\sec(\theta) = 126/\cos(\theta)$$
$$\tan(\theta) = \sin(\theta)/\cos(\theta)$$
$$\cot(\theta) = \cos(\theta)/\sin(\theta)$$

Be careful of overflows and division by zero problems.

This algorithm can perform other tricks. It can generate continuous sine waves of any desired amplitude, period, or phase. Coupled with a digital to analog converter, it could form part of a modem or synthesizer. It could simulate mixers, AM or FM modulators, keyers, etc.

The maximum frequency it can generate depends on the processor cycle time. A 6800 processor running with a 1 MHz clock could generate a 200 Hz sine wave since there are about 50 machine cycles per step, and about 100 steps per wave. Increasing the step size to 0.125 radians would increase the maximum frequency to about 500 Hz. A step size of 0.25 radians would yield a maximum frequency of nearly 1050 Hz.

I hope that this algorithm will help programmers solve problems involving trigonometric functions, and that applications for microcomputers will expand into new areas where these functions are useful.■

Simple Algorithms for Calculating Elementary Functions

John Rheinstein

Several years ago, shortly after obtaining an HP-35 calculator, I became interested in the algorithm utilized by Hewlett-Packard to calculate the sine and cosine functions. Upon looking through the literature I found that the simple elegant algorithm employed is based upon the CORDIC technique developed by Volder. The basic algorithm was first described by Henry Briggs in 1624 in *Arithmetica Logarithmica*. This algorithm, which does not seem to be widely known, should be easily implemented in a microcomputer. Further, a simple variation of the algorithm, described by Walther in "A Unified Algorithm for Elementary Functions" (see references), allows the calculation of the hyperbolic functions and, more interestingly, the exponential function. Inverting the procedure allows the calculation of the inverse trigonometric and hyperbolic functions and the logarithm. These algorithms are generalizations of the well known add and shift algorithm used for multiplication.

Trigonometric Functions

The flowchart for calculating the tangent of an angle is given in figure 1. The algorithm may be carried out in any radix, R, generally the decimal ($R = 10$) or the binary ($R = 2$). The radix should be chosen so that the multiplication indicated in the iterative calculation of X_{i+1} and Y_{i+1} may be performed by shift operations only. Thus no multiplication or division is required until the final step of the algorithm is reached. The calculation may be in either degrees or radians, as long as either one is used consistently. α_j and δ_j should be prestored in memory and called as a look up table. It is not required that the calculation be per-

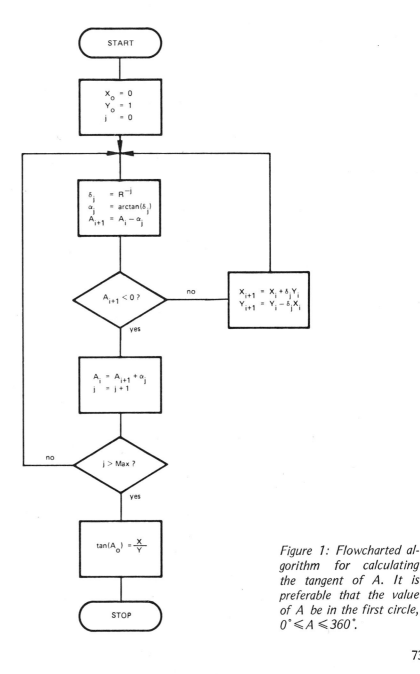

Figure 1: Flowcharted algorithm for calculating the tangent of A. It is preferable that the value of A be in the first circle, $0° \leqslant A \leqslant 360°$.

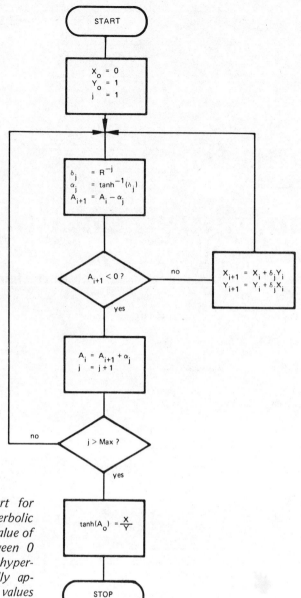

$$\sin(A_O) = \frac{(\text{sgn}X)(\tan(A_O))}{\sqrt{1 + \tan^2(A_O)}}$$

$$\cos(A_O) = \frac{\sin(A_O)}{\tan(A_O)}$$

where sgnX is the algebraic sign of X.

Hyperbolic Functions

A strikingly similar algorithm may be used to calculate the hyperbolic tangent of a number. For most of us this does not seem to be a very useful function, and the need for calculating it may not be clear. Having $\tanh(A_O)$ we can calculate $\sinh(A_O)$ and $\cosh(A_O)$.

$$\sinh(A_O) = \frac{\tanh(A_O)}{\sqrt{(1 - \tanh^2(A_O))}}$$

$$\cosh(A_O) = \frac{1}{\sqrt{(1 - \tanh^2(A_O))}}$$

Having the capability to calculate the hyperbolic sine and cosine is something that most of us could get along without.

The next step provides the exponential function, which is often of interest.

$$\exp(A_O) = \sinh(A_O) + \cosh(A_O)$$

Using the identities

$$\sinh(-x) = -\sinh(x)$$
$$\cosh(-x) = \cosh(x)$$

we also obtain

$$\exp(-A_O) = -\sinh(A_O) + \cosh(A_O).$$

The hyperbolic tangent approaches unity rapidly for arguments greater than about 5, causing a loss of accuracy in the algorithm. Thus it is best to prescale A_O to the range $0 \leqslant A_O \leqslant 1$. For prescaling, the following identity may be used.

$$\exp(Q\log_e(R) + D) = R^Q\exp(D).$$

Powers to any base may now be calculated. Setting D to zero above gives

$$\exp(Q\log_e(R)) = R^Q$$

from which we can obtain, for example

$$10^Q = \exp(2.3025851Q)$$
$$2^Q = \exp(0.69314718Q)$$

Figure 2 shows the flowchart for calculating

Figure 2: Flowchart for calculating the hyperbolic tangent of A. The value of A should be between 0 and 5 because the hyperbolic tangent rapidly approaches unity for values greater than 5.

formed in the first circle ($0° \leqslant A_O \leqslant 360°$); however, this is generally to be preferred. Care must be exercised if the final value of Y is very close to zero (A_O is close to 90° or 270°) since division by a very small number, or zero, is apt to blow up. A separate test for this condition should be included. Max indicates the number of iterations through the major loop and should be at least one larger than the accuracy desired. For example, if an accuracy of about one part in R^{-5} is desired, then Max should be about 6.

The final value of X obtained after exiting the major loop is proportional to the sine of A_O, and the final value of Y is proportional to the cosine of A_O, the proper signs being maintained. Thus having obtained the tangent of A_O, the sine and cosine may be obtained.

the hyperbolic tangent. Again α_j and δ_j should be prestored in memory and called by means of a look up table. It is relatively easy to combine these two algorithms into one. This saves some memory, but at the expense of control instructions. For this algorithm we again find that the multiplications carried out within the loop may be performed by shift operations only.

The Inverse Functions

Having implemented these two algorithms utilizing table look up procedures for the αs and δs, the inverse tangent and inverse hyperbolic tangent can easily be calculated with the same look up tables. Flowcharts are shown in figures 3 and 4. The arcsine and arccosine as well as the inverse hyperbolic sine and cosine may also be easily obtained. Another function of more general

interest, the logarithm, is obtained from the inverse hyperbolic tangent $(\tanh^{-1})$ by making use of the identity

$$\log_e (x) = 2 \tanh^{-1} \left(\frac{x-1}{x+1}\right).$$

The logarithm to any base, b, may be obtained

$$\log_b(x) = \log_e(x)/(\log_e(b)).$$

When calculating logarithms, prescaling should be carried out so that only the mantissa is calculated.

Given the arctangent, the arcsine and arccosine may be calculated from

$$\arcsin(x) = \arctan \left(\frac{x}{\sqrt{1-x^2}}\right)$$

$$\arccos(x) = \arctan \left(\frac{\sqrt{1-x^2}}{x}\right)$$

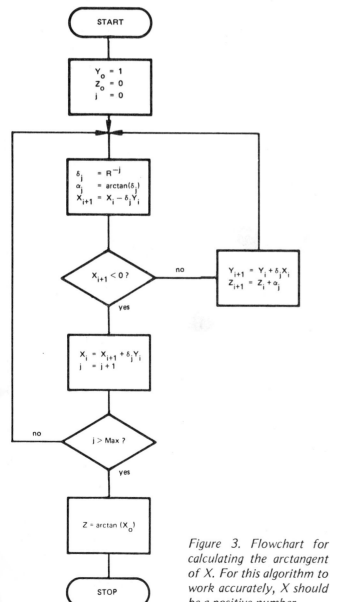

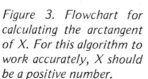

Figure 3. Flowchart for calculating the arctangent of X. For this algorithm to work accurately, X should be a positive number.

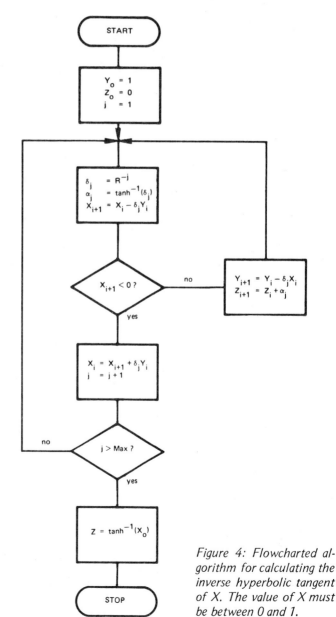

Figure 4: Flowcharted algorithm for calculating the inverse hyperbolic tangent of X. The value of X must be between 0 and 1.

If the argument of the arccosine is negative, 180° should be added to the result obtained from the above equation.

Given the inverse hyperbolic tangent, or logarithm, the inverse hyperbolic sine and cosine may be found.

$$\sinh^{-1}(x) = \log_e (x + \sqrt{(1 + x^2)})$$

$$\cosh^{-1}(x) = \log_e (x + \sqrt{(x^2 - 1)})$$

Basic Program

A listing of a BASIC program which uses these algorithms to calculate the tangent and arctangent is shown in listing 1 to indicate the manner in which these algorithms can be used. The program was written in MaxiBASIC for the Digital Group Z-80 system but it should run on almost any BASIC with only minor modifications, if any. This program operates in radix 10 ($R = 10$). I also tested a version in radix 2 ($R = 2$) changing only statements 10 and 20 and the DATA statements.

This program will operate well in BASIC as listed, but the real power of the algorithms can best be obtained if a machine language version is utilized. The multiplication indicated in statements 220, 230, 380 and 400 consume much of the time. In a machine language version these may be replaced by shift operations which take considerably less time.

Comments

These algorithms could easily be used to augment the set of available functions written in BASIC as subroutines or they could be added as machine language subroutines for high speed operation. The accuracy can be made quite high. For the sample program seven significant digits will be obtained.

I do not know whether Hewlett-Packard uses algorithms similar to these for all of the functions described. Walther reports that Hewlett-Packard did construct a hardware floating point processor of a generalized version of these algorithms, and reports excellent performance.■

```
5     REM** PROGRAM TO CALCULATE TAN OR ARCTAN OF
6     REM AN ANGLE (IN DEGREES)

10    LET R = 10
20    LET M = 8
30    FOR J = 0 TO M
35    REM** D(J) = DELTA SUB J
40    LET D(J) = R↑(−J)
45    REM** A1(J) = ALPHA SUB J
50    READ A1(J)
60    NEXT J
70    PRINT "DO YOU WANT TAN (ENTER 1) OR ARCTAN (ENTER 0)";
80    INPUT B
90    IF B = 1 THEN 120
100   IF B = 0 THEN 300
110   GOTO 70
120   PRINT "INPUT A(0)";
130   INPUT A
140   LET W = A
150   LET X = 0
160   LET Y = 1
170   FOR J = 0 TO M
180   LET A = A − A1(J)
190   IF A <0 THEN 250
200   LET X1 = X
210   LET Y1 = Y
220   LET Y = Y1 − D(J)*X1
230   LET X = X1 + D(J)*Y1
240   GOTO 180
250   LET A = A + A1(J)
260   NEXT J
270   LET T = X/Y
280   PRINT "TAN(";W;") = ";T
290   GOTO 70
300   PRINT "INPUT X(0)>0";
310   INPUT X
320   LET W = X
330   LET Y = 1
340   LET Z = 0
350   FOR J = 0 TO M
360   LET X1 = X
370   LET Y1 = Y
380   LET X = X1 − D(J)*Y1
390   IF X < 0 THEN 430
400   LET Y = Y1 + D(J)*X1
410   LET Z = Z + A1(J)
420   GOTO 360
430   LET X = X1
440   NEXT J
450   PRINT "ARCTAN(";W;") = ";Z
460   GOTO 70
470   DATA 45, 5.7105931, 5.729387E-1, 5.729576E-2, 5.7295779E-3
480   DATA 5.729578E-4, 5.729578E-5, 5.729578E-6, 5.729578E-7
999   END
```

Sample Runs:

```
DO YOU WANT TAN (ENTER1) OR ARCTAN (ENTER 0)? 1
INPUT A(0)? 26.3
TAN(26.3) = .49423074
DO YOU WANT TAN (ENTER1) OR ARCTAN (ENTER 0)? 0
INPUT X(0) > 0? .49423074
TAN( .49423074) = 26.300001
ARCTAN (.49423074) = 26.300001
```

Listing 1: A BASIC program for determining the tangent or arctangent of an angle. The program was written using the flowcharts of figures 1 and 3. The sample run gives a demonstration of the accuracy attained with these algorithms.

REFERENCES

1. Volder, Jack E, "The CORDIC Trigonometric Computing Technique," *IRE Transactions on Electronic Computers*, September 1959, page 330.

2. Walther, J S, "A Unified Algorithm for Elementary Functions," *Proceeding, Spring Joint Computer Conference*, 1971, page 379.

Elements of Statistical Computation

Alan Forsythe

The *mean* (average) is a frequently used statistic to summarize a set of data. It is used to report a *typical* value. For example, suppose we surveyed five automobile dealers and asked the price of the super luxury model car. The prices quoted for the car are:

Dealer	Price
1	$48,499
2	$48,503
3	$48,500
4	$48,498
5	$48,500

We could report the average price as:

$$\frac{(48499+48503+48500+48498+48500)}{5}$$

The sample mean price is $48,500.

The mean is defined as the sum of the values divided by the number of values. This can be written using the symbol Σ (the Greek capital sigma) to stand for the result of summation. The average of N values is:

$$\text{mean} = \frac{1}{N}\Sigma X$$

The sigma indicates a *sum* over all the data points.

Let's look at two algorithmic flowcharts for the calculation of the mean. The first, figure 1, reads all the data and stores it in array X. Next, it sums the values and performs the division. The second flowchart, figure 2, takes advantage of the fact that we really do not need to keep the values in memory to form the average. Each value is added to the total sum as it is entered. The program loops through the data once rather than twice. The second method is more efficient because it uses less memory, is faster, and uses fewer instructions. This difference

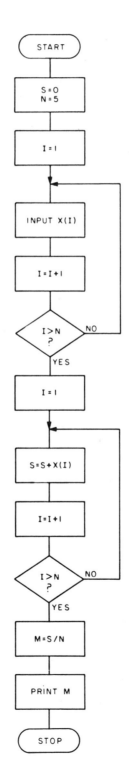

Figure 1: Calculation of the mean of a set of data. Using this method, the data values are used twice: once for input and the second time for summation. The method is wasteful of both time and memory.

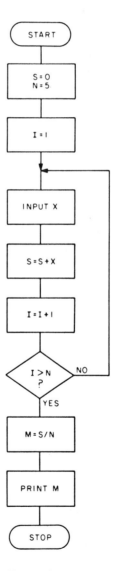

Figure 2: Second method of calculating the mean of a set of data. The data is examined only once and it does not need to be stored.

in efficiency may not be critical when only five values are being averaged, but when many observations are involved, the importance increases.

There is another difference worth mentioning. A noticeable pause between the entry of the last value and the printing of the average may result when the program in listing 1 is run, since the calculations are concentrated at this point in the program. Since the program in listing 2 does the summing after each data entry, the effect is a quick final response. Of these two methods, one is more efficient even though both would give the same answer.

There is another statistical calculation in which we can easily obtain the wrong answer unless we are careful. The average of a set of values gives only part of the picture. You may have heard of the man who drowned in a river that had an average depth of two feet. He happened to be in a section that was 12 feet deep. The moral is that we often want to know how much the values vary from the mean. This is commonly reported as the standard deviation. The usual symbol for the mean is $\overline{X}$ (read this as "X bar") and the standard deviation is abbreviated as the letter s. It is also convenient to have a name for s^2. It is called the variance, and its definition is:

$$s^2 = \frac{1}{N-1} \Sigma \, (X-\overline{X})^2$$

where N is the total number of samples taken. It follows, then, that the standard deviation is:

$$s = \sqrt{\frac{1}{N-1} \Sigma \, (X-\overline{X})^2}$$

The sigma (Σ) once again tells us that we are to perform a sum. This time we sum the deviations from the mean after we have squared them. That is, for each value we first subtract the mean. Next, we multiply the

difference by itself to form its square. We add these squared differences for all the values and then divide by N−1. The last step to obtain the standard deviation is to take the square root of s^2. It is calculations like these that make statisticians appreciate computers.

Before we move on to programs for the calculation of the standard deviation, let us work through these calculations for our example automobile prices. Remember that the average price was $48,500. The price from the first dealer was $48,499. The first dealer deviates from the mean by (48,499−48,500) or −1 dollar. The square of this deviation is 1. That is the first part of our sum. The squared deviation from the average for the second dealer is 9, and so on. The sum for all five dealers is 14. When we divide by 4 and then take the square root, we obtain a standard deviation of 1.87. The smaller this value, the closer the set of observations are to their mean. A large standard deviation tells us the data varied greatly from observation to observation. A standard deviation of zero says that all the observed values were equal to each other.

If you were to go to a statistics book you would probably find another formula for this calculation which is sometimes called the computing formula. This method of calculation uses the fact that $\Sigma \, (X-\overline{X})^2$ is algebraically identical to $\Sigma X^2 - N\overline{X}^2$. This tells us that we can calculate the sum of the squares of the individual values without subtracting the mean each time. We can multiply the square of the mean by N and subtract.

Mathematically these two formulas give the same answer. *Numerically* they are different. Why? They differ because our computers do not store or calculate numbers perfectly. If each number is stored in our computer in four 8 bit bytes, or 32 bits, we have about 7 digit accuracy for any single step in our calculation. The second formula lets the errors accumulate. This fact is not

```
10    REM FIRST PROGRAM TO CALCULATE THE MEAN
20    DIM X(5)
30    LET N=5
40    LET S=0
50    FOR I=1 TO N
60    INPUT X(I)
70    NEXT I
80    FOR I=1 TO N
90    LET S=S+X(I)
100   NEXT I
110   LET M=S/N
120   PRINT "THE MEAN IS "; M
130   STOP

*RUN
?48499
?48503
?48503
?48498
?48500
THE MEAN IS 48500
```

Listing 1: BASIC program to perform the algorithm given in figure 1. Note the storage of data in array X.

```
10    REM SECOND PROGRAM TO CALCULATE THE MEAN
30    LET N = 5
40    LET S = 0
50    FOR I=1 TO N
60    INPUT X
65    LET S = S+X
70    NEXT I
110   LET M = S/N
120   PRINT "THE MEAN IS "; M
130   STOP

*RUN
?48499
?48503
?48500
?48498
?48500
THE MEAN IS 48500
```

Listing 2: BASIC program to perform the algorithm given in figure 2. It is faster than the program in listing 1, since it uses the data only once. It also uses less memory space since the data is not stored.

considered in the mathematical proof.

Why is this second form given in books? First of all, some calculators work with more digits than many personal computers. Secondly, it is much easier and faster than using the formula for the definition. The Hewlett-Packard HP-21 calculator shows 10 decimal digits, as does the Texas Instruments SR-52. They can afford the luxury of round-off error that seriously hurts those with 32 bits. Before we show how we can almost get the best of both worlds, let us look at the numerical results of using this calculating formula on computers in which each number is kept in four bytes. (The IBM 370 single precision and many microcomputer BASICs are just two common examples.)

The program in listing 3 correctly gives the mean as 48,500. The standard deviation is computed to be 0. This is incorrect. All the prices are not equal to 48,500. Several books of BASIC programs include the calculation of the standard deviation. Those I checked out give the wrong answer for this set of data.

We know that we get accurate results if we first calculate the mean and use the differences from it in our calculation of the standard deviation. But we would like to avoid keeping all the data values in memory. Another alternative is to enter the data twice, but this seems unreasonable. A compromise between the two calculating forms that is not very sensitive to the accumulation of roundoff errors is available. The principle is to calculate a provisional mean as each value is entered, and to square the deviations from this mean.

The program in listing 4 reports the standard deviation for this set of data correctly as 1.87. This program is not as obvious as it may look. Notice that line 70 has a division by I and not N in the calculation of the mean. Line 80 also has a little trick. The product of D and $X-S$ is not $D*D$, because S has been changed since D was last calculated. If you have trouble working through the algebra, put print statements after lines 65, 70 and 80.

While writing statistical programs for microcomputers, I have been reminded of several important facts I hope you will keep in mind. Good programming takes thought.

```
10   REM POOR PROGRAM FOR CALCULATING THE
15   REM MEAN AND STANDARD DEVIATION
20   LET N=5
30   LET S=0
40   LET S2=0
50   FOR I=1 TO N
60   INPUT X
70   LET S=S+X
80   LET S2=S2+X*X
90   NEXT I
100  LET M=S/N
110  PRINT "THE MEAN IS "; M
120  LET D=N*M*M
130  LET V=(S2-D)/(N-1)
140  LET S=SQRT(V)
150  PRINT "THE STANDARD DEVIATION IS "; S
160  STOP

*RUN
?48499
?48503
?48500
?48498
?48500
THE MEAN IS 48500
THE STANDARD DEVIATION IS 0
```

Listing 3: Incorrect program for calculating the mean and standard deviation of a set of data. This program correctly calculates the mean but arrives at an incorrect value for the standard deviation.

```
10   REM REASONABLE PROGRAM TO CALCULATE
15   REM MEAN AND STANDARD DEVIATION
20   LET N=5
30   LET S=0
40   LET S2=0
50   FOR I=1 TO N
60   INPUT X
65   LET D=X-S
70   LET S=S+D/I
80   LET S2=S2+D*(X-S)
90   NEXT I
110  PRINT "THE MEAN IS" ; S
130  LET V=S2/(N-1)
140  LET S=SQRT(V)
150  PRINT "THE STANDARD DEVIATION IS "; S
160  STOP
*RUN
?48499
?48503
?48500
?48498
?48500
THE MEAN IS 48500
THE STANDARD DEVIATION IS 1.87083
```

Listing 4: Accurate program for calculating the mean and standard deviation.

We must balance several factors: speed, accuracy and memory requirements. Algebra is an essential tool, but we must remember that our machines have finite precision and adjust our program accordingly. A small machine can be quite potent, given adequate software.■

Functional Approximations

Fred Ruckdeschel

Many BASIC interpreters presently in use have limited function calculation capability. Almost all interpreters larger than 4 K bytes have built-in routines for determining square roots, logarithms and exponentials, as well as some trigonometric functions like sine and cosine. Several interpreters also provide inverse trigonometric functions via the arctangent function.

However, many minicomputer and microcomputer systems do not have such software. Also, some of the newer microprocessors presently do not have much support software. I have recently been developing software for use with the North Star Micro-Disk system; specifically, working with North Star BASIC, version 6, release 2. The North Star software contains sine and cosine functions but no inverse trigonometric routines. This deficiency led to a cursory investigation of series approximations which very quickly showed that Taylor series expansions are *not* generally optimum for computer use.

Taylor Series Expansion

In general, any real, continuous function f(x) having defined derivatives may be expressed as a polynomial expansion about a reference point x_o with the longhand representation:

$$f(x) = f(x_o) + f^{(1)}(x_o)(x-x_o) +$$
$$f^{(2)}(x_o)(x-x_o)^2/2! + \ldots$$
$$\text{(1a)}$$

Observe that $f^{(n)}(x_o)$ is defined to be the nth order derivative of $f(x)$ evaluated at x equal to x_o. The shorthand equivalent of equation (1a) is:

$$f(x) = \sum_{n=0}^{\infty} f^{(n)}(x_o)(x-x_o)^n/n!$$

or:

$$f(x) = \lim_{n \to \infty} f_n(x) \qquad \text{(1b)}$$

where:

$$0! \equiv 1$$

$$f^{(0)}(x_o) \equiv f(x_o)$$

$$f_n(x) \equiv \sum_{m=0}^{n} f^{(m)}(x_o)(x-x_o)^m/m!$$

Equation (1b) is in a form which is convenient in terms of BASIC's FOR-NEXT loop evaluation, which may account for its popularity with computer programmers.

Many programmers who are faced with approximating a function use a Taylor series expansion along with a convergence test such as:

$$|f_n(x) - f_{n-1}(x)| < \epsilon. \qquad \text{(2)}$$

Presumably when the difference between the approximation using n terms and that using n−1 terms is less than ϵ, the accuracy of $f_n(x)$ in approximating $f(x)$ is better than ϵ. This assumption can be grossly in error depending on the function being evaluated. Slowly converging series often present problems in this respect.

The reasons for not indiscriminately using equations (1) or (2) may be demonstrated by considering the sine and arctangent functions. The Taylor series expansion around the zero reference point (known as the MacLaurin series) for the sine function is:

$$\sin(x) = x - x^3/3! + x^5/5! - \ldots \quad (3a)$$

or:

$$\sin(x) = \sum_{n=0}^{\infty} (-1)^n x^{(2n+1)}/(2n+1)! . \quad (3b)$$

If we apply equation (2) as the test for accuracy, we have

$$\frac{x^{(2n+1)}}{(2n+1)!} < \epsilon. \quad (4)$$

If x is one radian (approximately 57°) and the required accuracy is 10^{-8}, then equation (4) indicates that seven terms are required in the series for the specified accuracy. The test for residual may be done more correctly in principle by noting that the series is uniformly convergent, having terms alternating in sign. Thus the absolute error of the approximation is less than the absolute value of the last term included. Therefore we again conclude that seven terms are needed for 10^{-8} accuracy in approximately calculating the sine of one radian. In the case of alternating series having terms which monotonically decrease in absolute value, equation (2) is applicable.

If, instead, we are interested in the sine of −1, the accuracy test would again call for seven terms. However, this time, because the signs of the terms do not alternate, a ratio test would have to be applied to correctly examine the residual, yielding the same result for the required number of terms. In general, if the series is rapidly converging, equation (2) is an adequate test for accuracy.

So far we have assumed that the computer is perfect in terms of roundoff error. In some eight decimal place accuracy interpreters and compilers, the computer rounds off to the eighth decimal place by consistently rounding down or up. Quite often the direction is down, since this corresponds to simple truncation. In those cases the en-

suing error in calculating n terms in a series expansion is on the order of $\pm (n/2) \times 10^{-8}$. (If the software is sophisticated enough to round to the nearest value, the error becomes $\sqrt{n} \times 10^{-8}$ for eight bits.) For the sine expansion example given above, the expected truncated series accuracy of 10^{-8} would be reduced to approximately 10^{-7} because of roundoff error. It is shown in the next section that a different series expansion for sine can be used which contains only five terms and which gives an error of less than 10^{-8} before roundoff, along with a generally better answer when roundoff is considered.

So far the observation is that the error test, equation (2), leads to a correct estimate for the required number of terms in the case of the Taylor series approximation for sine. There is an approximation in which only five terms are sufficient, which is described later. These are not very exciting conclusions, largely because the Taylor series expansion for sine in the first quadrant is very rapidly convergent and thus quite adequate. Another important function, arctangent, is not nearly as quickly convergent in some regions of its limited convergence interval. The MacLaurin series expansion for arctangent is

$$\arctan(x) = x - \frac{x^3}{3} + \frac{x^5}{5} - \frac{x^7}{7} + \ldots$$

$$= \sum_{n=0}^{\infty} (-1)^n x^{(2n+1)}/(2n+1)$$

$$(-1 < x \leqslant 1). \quad (5)$$

This expansion has difficulty converging near x equal to positive or negative one. When x equals negative one the series diverges, although a finite answer $(\pi/4)$ exists, whereas at x equal to one the series converges very slowly to $\pi/4$, or 45°. Only the region between 0° and 45° (0 and $\pi/4$ radians) need be used for the expansion, since trigonometric identities exist for extending the inversion to other regions (eg: $\arctan(x) = \pi/2 - \arctan(1/x)$ for $x \geqslant 0$). The technique of *range* reduction for improving accuracy will be considered in a later section.

Consider the use of equation (5) near an x value of one. Using equation (2) to determine the number of terms required for 10^{-8} accuracy, we get a value of 5×10^7 for n. Applying the alternating sign convergence test also leads to an n value of 5×10^7. In either case, this series expansion for arctangent is unusable. Even if the computer were fast enough so that the approximation could be calculated in an acceptable length of time, the ensuing roundoff error would be prohibitive. It is shown in the next section that there exist other series expansions which are better than (in terms of relative error) 4×10^{-8} and which have only eight terms. The series presented are operable either over the range $1 \leqslant |x|$ (note the equality sign) or over the range $0 \leqslant x < \infty$.

We observe that the error test, equation (2), would fail dismally for the Taylor series arctangent expansion near an x value of negative one. The test would again predict that on the order of 5×10^{-7} terms would be required for 10^{-8} accuracy, while in actuality the series diverged. In this case the Taylor series expansion is not rapidly converging, thus leading to a failure in equation (2). In general, equation (2) is practical only if:

- The series has decreasing alternating sign terms.
- The series has decreasing terms in which the absolute value of the ratio of neighboring terms is greater than 10 for all pairs of terms past the termination point. That is, if:

$$f(x) = \sum_{n=0}^{\infty} c_n x^n,$$

then beyond the termination point it is required that:

$$\left| \frac{c_n x^n}{c_{n+1} x^{n+1}} \right| = \left| \frac{c_n}{c_{n+1} x} \right| > 10.$$

Observe that this latter restriction is valid only for MacLaurin series expansions. For Taylor series expansions, replace x with $(x-x_o)$. Observe that small values of $(x-x_o)$ are very conducive to rapid convergence, but are not sufficient.

Approximate Series Expansions

Taylor series expansions have many nice properties. However, one of their less desirable properties is that they are not the optimal expansions for a given argument interval when a truncated series is to be used. This may be easily seen by a simple example.

Consider the single term approximation to sin(x) over the interval $0 \leqslant x \leqslant \pi/2$ (see figures 1 and 2). Although the accuracy of approximating the value of sin(x) with x is good for small values of x, it leads to an error of 0.57 at $\pi/2$. If instead we wish to minimize the maximum absolute error over that interval, then approximating sin(x) by 0.73x is better. The maximum absolute error is in this case less than 0.15, with two error maxima.

If our criterion is to minimize the relative error (percent deviation), the MacLaurin series single term truncation leads to 57 percent error at $\pi/2$, while the previous minimized (relative to maximum absolute error) approximation is off by less than 27 percent, with the maximum relative error occurring at zero. The maximum relative error can be further reduced to about 22 percent by using 0.78x as the approximation for sin(x). The maximum relative errors in this case occur at x values of 0 and $\pi/2$. This series is considered to be the *minimax* or optimal series expansion for sin(x) over the range $-\pi/2 \leqslant x \leqslant \pi/2$, given that one term is allowed.

The above example illustrates the fact that either by the criterion of absolute error or the criterion of relative error, the truncated MacLaurin series for the sine function is not optimal for approximation. Also observe that the coefficient (0.73 for absolute

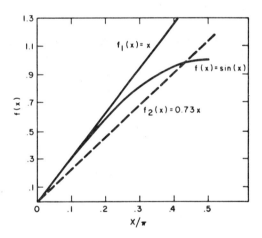

Figure 1: Single term approximations to sin(x) over the range $0 \leqslant x \leqslant \pi/2$. $f_1(x)$ is the truncated MacLaurin series expansion; $f_2(x)$ is the single term fit minimizing the maximum error.

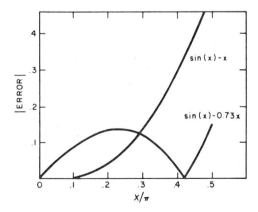

Figure 2: Graph of the errors due to single term approximations for the sine function.

Term	MacLaurin Coefficients	Optimal Coefficients
X	+ 1.00000000	+ 1.00000000
X^3	− 0.16666667	− 0.41123328
X^5	+ 0.00083333333	+ 0.050732026
X^7	− 0.00019841270	− 0.0029754116
X^9	+ 2.755732×10^{-6}	+ 0.000096437832
X^{11}	− 2.5052109×10^{-8}	
X^{13}	+ $1.6059045 \times 10^{-10}$	

Table 1: Coefficients for the MacLaurin and optimal series expansions for sin(x). The optimized interval is $-\pi/2 \leqslant x \leqslant \pi/2$. In this interval, the optimal (relative error) series is accurate to better than 5×10^{-9} when more accurate coefficients are used.

error or 0.78 for relative error) in the optimal approximation is dependent on the interval chosen. The more the interval is restricted to that region surrounding zero, the closer the coefficient is to unity. In general, the more the interval is restricted to the region immediately surrounding the Taylor series expansion point, the more the coefficients in the optimal series approximate those of the Taylor series expansion. This is because the highest convergence rate occurs near the expansion point, and it is hard to do better than that.

Continuing with the sine example, table 1 shows the series coefficients that would be used in the MacLaurin and optimal series expansions to give a desired accuracy (excluding roundoff) of approximately 10^{-8}. Observe that because the *relative* error is the criterion, the first coefficient in the optimal series is the same (to eight places) as that in the MacLaurin series. This is required because for very small x, sin(x) is approximately equal to x. Note, however, that all the other coefficients are drastically different, though the signs of the coefficients are preserved. The sign preservation is expected from a consideration of the derivatives.

A corresponding series expansion comparison for the arctangent is shown in table 2. Observe that about 10^7 terms are required in

the MacLaurin series for x equal to 1 to give the same order of accuracy as the optimal series evaluated at that point. The situation for the MacLaurin series is even worse in the vicinity of negative one.

It is interesting to note that in the series expansion comparison shown in table 2 the signs of the coefficients are conserved, and the coefficients themselves bear some semblance to one another up to the fifth term. After that the coefficients look quite different.

Variations

The optimal series coefficients given in table 2 for the arctangent approximation were stipulated to be optimal over the interval $-1 \leqslant x \leqslant 1$. This restricts us to the angular range of $\pm45°$ about $0°$ ($\pm\pi/4$ radians around 0 radians). A trigonometric identity was given earlier which allowed continuation through $90°$ ($\pi/2$ radians). However, this extra range changing step is not necessary, since another series expansion exists which is optimized over the interval $0 \leqslant x \leqslant \infty$. However, it does not have a simple x^n dependence:

$$\arctan(x) = \pi/4 + \sum_{n=0}^{7} C_n \left(\frac{x-1}{x+1}\right)^{(2n+1)}$$

(6)

This series is interesting in that it uses the same coefficients as given in table 2, and also gives the same order of relative accuracy. To execute this series on a computer one need only define x to be $(x-1)/(x+1)$ and proceed as before.

Hasting's book *Approximations for Digital Computers* (see references) presents several such optimal expansions, three of which are presented in table 3. Some alterations have been made to put this information into a form readily usable with typical microcomputer software.

Polynomial expansions are not the only forms useful for function approximations. Another important type is the *rational polynomial*. Table 4 shows a rational polynomial approximation for cos(x). The rational polynomial approximation to the cosine is slightly more accurate than the minimax approximation given earlier for the sine. However, the argument range of this cosine approximation is inconveniently restricted. In cases such as this it is the user's choice as to which approximation to apply.

There is a class of series expansions in which an improved approximation is not insured by including more terms. This class of series approximations is called *asymptotic*. An example of such a series is shown in table 5 for the error function. The reason this

Term	MacLaurin Coefficients	Optimal Coefficients
X	+ 1.00000000	+ 0.99999933
X^3	− 0.33333333	− 0.33329856
X^5	+ 0.20000000	+ 0.19946536
X^7	− 0.1428571	− 0.13908534
X^9	+ 0.11111111	+ 0.096420044
X^{11}	− 0.090909090	− 0.055909886
X^{13}	+ 0.07692308	+ 0.021861229
X^{15}	− 0.066666667	− 0.0040540580

Table 2: Coefficients for the MacLaurin and optimal series expansions for the arctangent. Accuracy (relative error) is better than 4×10^{-8}. The interval of convergence for the MacLaurin series is $-1 < x \leqslant 1$. The interval of convergence for the optimal series is $-1 \leqslant x \leqslant 1$.

(a)

Form:

$$\text{Log}_{10}\, X = \frac{1}{2} + \sum_{n=0}^{4} C_n\, \gamma^{(2n+1)}$$

where $\gamma = (X - \sqrt{10})/(X + \sqrt{10})$

Coefficients:

$$C_0 = 0.86859172$$
$$C_1 = 0.28933552$$
$$C_2 = 0.17752207$$
$$C_3 = 0.094376476$$
$$C_4 = 0.19133771$$

(b)

Form:

$$10^x = 1 + \sum_{n=1}^{6} C_n\, x^n$$

Coefficients:

$$C_1 = 1.15128759$$
$$C_2 = 0.66284315$$
$$C_3 = 0.25360332$$
$$C_4 = 0.075467547$$
$$C_5 = 0.013420940$$
$$C_6 = 0.005654902$$

(c)

Form:

$$e^{-x} \doteq \left[\sum_{n=0}^{6} C_n\, x^n \right]^{(-4)}$$

Coefficients:

$$C_0 = 1.00000000$$
$$C_1 = 0.24999868$$
$$C_2 = 0.031257583$$
$$C_3 = 0.0025913712$$
$$C_4 = 0.0001715620$$
$$C_5 = 0.0000054302$$
$$C_6 = 0.0000006906$$

Table 3: Several minimax polynomial expansions. Table 3a is for the case of the base 10 logarithm function. This expansion is applicable over the range $1 \leqslant x \leqslant 10$ with a relative error of better than 1.5×10^{-7}. Table 3b is the inverse of the base 10 logarithm function. The applicable range is $0 \leqslant x \leqslant 1$ with a relative error of better than 1.5×10^{-7}. Table 3c is the expansion for the negative powers of e. This expansion is applicable over the range $0 \leqslant x < \infty$ with a relative accuracy of better than 3×10^{-7}.

series approximation has problems when too many terms are included may be seen by examining the ratio of a general pair of terms:

$$R = \left| \frac{f_{n+1} - f_n}{f_n - f_{n-1}} \right| = \frac{2n-1}{2x^2}. \quad (7)$$

It is apparent that one can always go out far enough in the series expansion to find a value of n such that R is greater than 1. It is also possible that if we define a sufficiently small error limit, ϵ, for use in the accuracy test, equation (2), the computer may never find a condition satisfying that relation. In such a situation the computer may continue the calculation of terms until an overflow occurs. A way to avoid this problem is to also test whether or not the minimum term (smallest in absolute value) has been passed, and if so, stop the calculation on that term. The accuracy of the thus truncated series is approximated by the value of that last term.

Quite often the series or rational polynomial approximation approach may be surpassed in accuracy and possibly speed by an iterative technique. In fact, such iterative techniques can often also be put in a form in which roundoff error has a minimal impact on final accuracy.

Tables 6 and 7 show iterative approximations to $f(x) = \sqrt{x}$ and $f(x) = \sqrt[3]{x}$. These forms were derived from the Newton method for finding the zeroes of functions (see reference 2). The relations have been algebraically written such that the previous approximation in the iteration is improved upon by the subtraction of a correction term

Form:

$$\cos(x) \doteq \frac{1 + A_1\, x^2 + A_2\, x^4 + A_3\, x^6}{1 + B_1\, x^2 + B_2\, x^4 + B_3\, x^6}$$

Coefficients:

$$A_1 = -0.47059579$$
$$A_2 = 0.027388290$$
$$A_3 = -0.00037234227$$
$$B_1 = 0.029404212$$
$$B_2 = 0.00042372881$$
$$B_3 = 0.000003235543$$

Table 4: Rational polynomial approximation for cosine which is applicable over the range $-1 \leqslant x \leqslant 1$. The maximum relative error over this range is better than 10^{-8}.

$$\text{erf}(x) = 1 - \text{erfc}(x) = 1 - \frac{2}{\sqrt{\pi}} e^{-x^2} \times \frac{1}{2x} \times$$

$$\left\{ 1 - \frac{1}{(2x^2)} + \frac{1 \times 3}{(2x^2)^2} - \frac{1 \times 3 \times 5}{(2x^2)^3} + \frac{1 \times 3 \times 5 \times 7}{(2x^2)^4} - \cdots \right\}$$

Table 5: An asymptotic series approximation to the error function. Range and accuracy are dependent on the smallest term in the series (before it diverges). The series is truncated at the smallest term, which represents the error. Including more terms increases the error.

$$y_{n+1} = y_n - \frac{1}{2}\left(y_n - x/y_n\right)$$

$$y_0 = \frac{0.154116 + 1.893872\,X}{1 + 1.047988\,X}$$

$$n = 0, 1, 2 \ldots$$

Table 6: Iterative technique for determining the square root of x. The accepted range is from zero to infinity. The y_0 term is an approximation for the starting value over the interval $1/16 \leqslant x \leqslant 1$. The y_0 relative error is better than 0.025.

$$y_{n+1} = y_n - \left\{ \frac{y_n^2 - x/y_n}{2y_n + x/y_n^2} \right\}$$

$$n = 0, 1, 2 \ldots$$

Table 7: Iteration technique for determining the cubic root of x over the range zero to infinity. The y_0 term is the same as that used for the square root.

$$y_{n+1} = y_n - \left\{ \frac{y_n^m - x}{m\, y_n^{m-1}} \right\}$$

$$m = 2, 3, 4 \ldots$$
$$n = 0, 1, 2, 3 \ldots$$

Table 8: Iteration technique for determining the mth root of x. In this case, x is allowed to vary from zero to infinity. The convergence of this formula is quadratic.

Define: $\quad a_0 = (1+x^2)^{-1/2}$
$\qquad\qquad b_0 = 1$

Iterate: $\quad a_{n+1} = \frac{1}{2}(a_n + b_n)$
$\qquad\qquad b_{n+1} = \sqrt{a_{n+1} + b_n}$

Convergence Test: compare a_n and b_n (they approach one another)

Final Calculation: $\arctan(x) \doteq \dfrac{x}{\sqrt{a_n b_n}\,(1+x^2)}$

Table 9: Gauss iteration technique for approximating the arctangent function. This formula has been modified from a formula in the book Numerical Methods That Work (see references) to improve the accuracy in the final calculation. The variable a_n has been replaced by the expression $\sqrt{a_n b_n}$.

(which may be either positive or negative). Convergence is generally very good and can be significantly improved upon by using a *predictor* for the correction, though the price paid is a more complicated routine. The reader is referred to standard texts on numerical methods for descriptions of predictor-corrector techniques.

Table 8 gives a general iterative formula for determining the mth root of any nonnegative real number. Although it is potentially more accurate than using the logarithm-antilogarithm approximation routines, it suffers from speed limitations for large values of m, since many multiplications may be required (what would one do with $x^{1/137}$?).

As a final but very important example of an iterative approximation to a common function, arctangent, see table 9. This technique is due to Gauss and is a sure way to obtain accuracy limited only by the number of digits carried by your software; there is no cumulative roundoff error. Note that implementation of this method requires the use of a square root function, which we can have as another subroutine. Although the author has no literature information regarding the convergence of this iteration, the form looks fast in convergence but slow in calculation.

For example, listing 1 shows sample runs for x = 0.1, 1, 100 and 10^{30}. It seems that only 12 iterations maximum are required to attain a relative accuracy of 10^{-7}. However, the execution time for the BASIC program shown runs between 3 (x = 0.1) and 4 (x = 10^{30}) seconds, which is not very fast. Use of the optimal series, shown in table 2, cuts the execution time down to 90 ms with the same level of accuracy. However, a numerical overflow occurs when x = 10^{30}. The conclusion is that for 10^{-7} relative accuracy, the optimal series approximation is preferred over the iteration technique since it is about 40 times faster in execution. There is probably some hidden physical law which states that the elegance versus execution time product is a constant.

Some of the approximations we have discussed are not applicable over the entire possible range of arguments. The approximations requiring range reduction are:

Function	Range
$\sin(x)$	$(-\pi/2 \leqslant x \leqslant \pi/2)$
$\log_{10}(x)$	$(1 \leqslant x \leqslant 10)$
10^x	$(0 \leqslant x \leqslant 1)$

Table 10 outlines techniques that might be used in reducing the range to that required by the approximation.

Conclusions

Several approximation methods have been presented for use in software systems lacking particular function subroutines. These methods may be implemented in either machine language or in a higher level language. It is likely that the majority of readers will use the resulting subroutines in a BASIC interpreter unless they have an assembler with macroinstructions for multiplication and division, or something equivalent (such as floating point multiplication and division hardware).

The particular approximations given above can be used to evaluate many other functions by using identity or recursion relations. In cases where such relations do not exist, it may be possible to use statistical software packages on larger computers to find adequate functional approximations for use in microcomputers. For example, one might take a polynomial having coefficients to be determined and regress the coefficients against handbook tables representing the desired function. With some ingenuity in transforming variables, such as:

$$f(x) = \sum_{n=0}^{N} a_n \, y^n \, (x)$$

$$y(x) = \frac{x-1}{x+1}$$

it may be possible to obtain very accurate expansions having only a few terms. For example, if the function to be approximated goes to infinity at $x = 0$ and to zero at $x = a$, a transformation one might try is $y(x) = (x - a)/x$. Those electrical engineers familiar with pole analysis would probably be somewhat at ease with forming such expressions. However, these same people would probably have little experience with the available statistics routines.

The general conclusion is that relatively

```
10    REM ***ARCTAN(X) VIA GAUSS***
20    DIM A(20),B(20)
30    INPUT X
40    A(1)=1/SQRT(1+X*X)
50    B(1)=1
60    N=0
70    E=.0000001
80    N=N+1
90    A(N+1)=(A(N)+B(N))/2
100   B(N+1)=SQRT(A(N+1)*B(N))
110   T=X*A(1)/SQRT(A(N+1)*B(N+1))
120   PRINT N,"   ",T
130   D=(A(N+1)−B(N+1))/B(N+1)
140   IF ABS(D)>E THEN GOTO 80

?.1
1     9.9689307E−02
2     9.9673813E−02
3     9.9669946E−02
4     9.9668978E−02
5     9.9668736E−02
6     9.9668677E−02
7     9.9668662E−02
8     9.9668659E−02

?1
1     .79627295
2     .78796829
3     .78603187
4     .78555605
5     .7854376
6     .78540801
7     .78540062
8     .78539879
9     .78539831
10    .78539817
11    .78539813

?100
1     1.6692059
2     1.582113
3     1.5658381
4     1.5620399
5     1.5611064
6     1.560874
7     1.560816
8     1.5608014
9     1.5607978
10    1.5607969
11    1.5607967
12    1.5607966

?1E30
1     1.6817928
2     1.592546
3     1.5759366
4     1.5720637
5     1.5711121
6     1.5708751
7     1.5708159
8     1.5708012
9     1.5707975
10    1.5707966
11    1.5707963
12    1.5707962
```

Listing 1: The arctangent approximation shown in table 9 implemented in BASIC. Four sample runs are shown.

Table 10: Range reduction methods for the approximations we have considered so far.

---

sin (x) $(-\pi/2 < x < \pi/2)$

- Reduce range to first four quadrants:
  $$y = x - (INT \, (x/2\pi) \times 2\pi)$$
  (Note: It is assumed that the integer function returns next lower integer for positive and negative numbers.)
- If $|x| \geq \pi/2$, then $y = y - \pi$ and desired result is $(- \sin (y))$: otherwise the desired result is $\sin(y)$.

$\log_{10}$ (x) $(1 \leq x \leq 10)$

- Find range reduction factor (characteristic of logarithm): Divide (or multiply) by 10, I times until result is in range.
- Reduce range:
  $$y = x/10^I$$
- Desired result is:
  $$\log_{10} (x) = I + \log_{10} (y)$$
  Note: I may be negative.

10^x $(0 \leq x \leq 1)$

- Determine power of 10:
  $$I = INT \, (x)$$
- Reduce range:
  $$y = x - I$$
- Result
  $$10^x = 10^y \times 10^I$$

fast executing expansions exist for functional approximations. They tend not to be truncated Taylor series, but rather special (and sometimes ingenious) forms whose coefficients depend on the number of terms to be used as well as the argument interval desired. The minimax polynomials and rational polynomials are powerful examples of such approximations, and should be considered for use on small systems. Elegant iteration routines may also be very powerful, but there are situations, such as the nth root iterative technique (see table 8), and the Gauss technique (see table 9), in which the approach has intrinsically greater accuracy, but the execution time of the subroutine is prohibitive.

Function approximation is a creative art; I hope readers will try some of the techniques described herein.■

REFERENCES

1. Abramowitz, M, and Stegun, A, *Handbook of Mathematical Functions,* Dover, New York, 1964.

2. Acton, F S, *Numerical Methods That Work,* Harper and Row, New York, 1970.

3. Fike, C T, *Computer Evaluation of Mathematical Functions,* Prentice-Hall Inc, Englewood Cliffs NJ, 1968.

4. Hastings, C, *Approximations for Digital Computers,* Princeton University Press, Princeton NJ, 1955.

5. Smith, J M, *Scientific Analysis on the Pocket Calculator,* John Wiley and Sons, New York, 1975.

6. Weast, R C, *Handbook of Tables for Mathematics,* Chemical Rubber Co, Cleveland OH, 1967.

Continued Fractions,
or Pieces or Pi

Mark Zimmermann

"So what good is it?" Anybody who owns even the smallest microcomputer must get asked this question more often than any other. There are a thousand answers, of course, ranging from the commercial ("I can make money programming") to the artistic ("Just watch this pattern develop.") to the playful ("Here come the Klingons!"). I'd like to introduce the possibility of one more answer — a mathematical one. In the sixteenth and seventeenth centuries, talented amateurs (including, most of all, the famous Pierre Fermat) led the way in the development of modern mathematics. Today, support for mathematicians in the colleges and universities is shrinking. There has never been much opportunity in industry. But a literally infinite number of significant unsolved mathematical problems remain. I think that it's time for a new renaissance in mathematics, a renaissance in which microcomputers must surely play a major role.

"RecMath" means recreational mathematics. It includes the field of "games", but not so much in their playing as in their analysis. It also includes codes, ciphers, data encryption, parts of number theory, and the theory of computing itself — efficiency of algorithms, the "knapsack" and "traveling salesman" problems, prime, perfect, and amicable numbers. . . . What all these things have in common is that they can be a lot of fun, especially if you have a tool to do the difficult parts and to calculate special cases

to get the imagination started. Moreover, considering how fast recreational mathematics is growing, if even a small fraction of computing amateurs get involved with RecMath, the impact could be staggering.

Fractions

One of the first things that many people do when they get personal computers is to calculate PI (π). (I did nine years ago, but I didn't do a very good job.) Another popular pursuit, when learning about program loops, is to start looking for "good" fractions to represent PI. The Hebrews believed that π was equal to 3 (in the Old Testament); the early Greeks and most people today know π is approximately equal to 22/7, and a few may recall that π is also approximately equal to 355/113. (Try that last one — it's good to 8 decimal places.) But what is it that makes 22/7 a "good" approximation, and 314/100 = 157/50 a "poor" one?

Before going any further, let's define PI = 3.14159265358979. . . . , a decimal fraction that never terminates and never repeats (if it did either one, we could write an exact fraction for it by application of the continued fraction method described below), and also define what is meant by "good". If we try to approximate PI by a fraction A/B, we expect that as B gets larger, our error E = ABS(PI−(A/B)) will shrink. For instance, if B=100000 and A=314159, then E=2.65E−6.

Listing 1: An exhaustive search method for calculating π. The inputs to the program are the limits of A and B, the numerator and denominator of the fraction used to calculate π. The outputs are A and B, the value of π calculated by the program, and the "goodness" factor for the calculation.

```
10  REM PROGRAM A
20  REM STUPID SEARCH FOR CLOSE APPROXIMATIONS TO PI
30  REM SEEK A/B NEAR PI
100 LET P1=3.141592653
109 REM INITIALIZE GOODNESS G
110 G=1000
118 REM INPUT LIMITS OF SEARCH
119 REM 1<=A<=L, 1<=B<=M
120 INPUT L,M
129 REM BEGIN LOOPS OVER POSSIBILITIES
130 FOR A=1 TO L
140 FOR B=1 TO M
149 REM T IS TEMPORARY STORAGE OF GOODNESS
150 T=ABS(P1*B-A)
158 REM COMPARE AND OUTPUT IF GOODNESS
159 REM IS BETTER THAN BEST PREVIOUS VALUE FOUND
160 IF T>=G THEN 190
170 PRINT A,B,A/B,T
180 G=T
190 NEXT B
200 NEXT A
210 END

READY
RUN
```

?100			
?100			
1	1	1	2.14159
2	1	2	1.14159
3	1	3	0.141593
22	7	3.14286	8.85177E-3

Figure 1: A plot of the line A/B, with slope π.

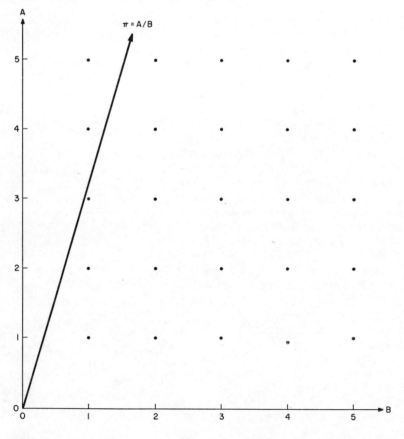

One might reasonably rate the "goodness" of a fraction A/B by the product ExB. This way, a premium is placed on economy; "goodness" G=ExB will be a small number if we find a close approximation with a small B for the denominator. Thus, since G=ABS (BxPI−A), G=8.85E−3 for 22/7; but for 157/50, G=7.96E−2. So, 22/7 is very good compared to 157/50, since the larger numbers in the latter fraction don't give a comparable payoff in improved accuracy.

Now that "goodness" is defined, we can begin to look for the "best" approximations to π (or any other number) systematically. The program in listing 1 was my first effort. The exhaustive search I used is both slow and inefficient. As can be seen by the list of values (A, B, A/B, "goodness" factor) at the bottom of listing 1, the best value for both numerator and denominator less than 100 is the old standby 22/7... a lot of computer time wasted for small return. We can do much better.

More Fractions

Look at the problem from a geometric point of view. If we plot B horizontally and A vertically, then PI=A/B defines a line in the B−A plane with slope PI, as shown in figure 1. The allowable values of A and B in the fraction are represented by the points at all the pairs of integers (A,B).

One quickly sees that the line PI passes very near the point B=1, A=3, then near B=2, A=6, etc. For any value of B, the only numbers A that we should spend time checking are those that the line passes between. ("Goodness" in figure 1 turns out to be the vertical distance by which the line misses any given point.) The program given in listing 2 does just that.

The improvement of this program over the program in listing 1 is obvious. It zooms past 22/7 to 333/106 to 355/113, an approximation so good that many machines won't ever find a better one without resorting to multiple precision arithmetic. (The next "best" approximation has B > 33000.)

Fractions, Continued

But there's still a better way. It's called the "continued fraction algorithm", and it's guaranteed to give precisely the "best" rational approximations to any number. (The proof of the guarantee is a bit complicated and unnecessary here; see, for example Stark's An Introduction to Number Theory for details.) The algorithm itself is simple enough to enter into almost any programmable calculator, and can be done by hand on a simple 4 function calculator.

The algorithm is as follows: to approximate a number X, make the fraction:

$$a_0 + \cfrac{1}{a_1 + \cfrac{1}{a_2 + \cfrac{1}{a_3 + \cdot}}} =$$

$$a_0 + 1/(a_1 + 1/(a_2 + 1/(a_3 + \ldots))))$$

where

$a_0 = INT(X)$
$a_1 = INT(1/FRC(X))$
$a_2 = INT(1/(FRC(1/FRC(X))))$, etc.

(INT is the integer portion of a number, FRC the fractional portion.)

This looks quite messy, but BASIC makes it simpler. The program shown in listing 3 produces the values $a_0, a_1, \ldots, a_N$ for any X input.

Now, applying one or the other of these routines to PI, we get $a_0=3$, $a_1=7$, $a_2=15$, $a_3=1$, $a_4=292$, ... Cutting the fraction off at a_0 means PI $\approx$ 3. Moving the cutoff to a_1 says PI $\approx 3 + 1/7 = 22/7$. With cutoff at a_2, PI $\approx 3 + 1/(7 + 1/15)=333/106$, etc. If you try to evaluate the approximation from cutting off at a_4, you may have noticed that it took a lot of work. There is, again, a better way, which doesn't require starting all over again at the bottom to go from 22/7 to 333/106.

The program for calculating continued fractions is given in listing 4. The method works by keeping track of the two previously calculated fractions, P/R and Q/S; after getting started with the "values" 0/1 and 1/0, at each stage the next fraction is given by $(X/Y) = (A*Q+P)/(A*S+R)$ if the next term in the continued fraction expansion is A. Try it for PI!

One word of caution: since the input value of π (or whatever number is being approximated) is given only to finite accuracy in the machine, the fractions that we get out to represent π cannot be infinitely accurate. In fact, it may only take a few terms in the expansion before all the precision we have put in is exhausted. After that point, the numbers in the "expansion" that the program of listing 3 cranks out are meaningless. They are pseudorandom positive integers, biased somewhat toward the smaller numbers; interesting in themselves, but a rather different subject. To get increasingly better fractional approximations, one must start out with more decimal places and do higher precision calculations along the way, or else try a completely different approach.

Further Fractions

Once you've got the program of listing 3 set up, try taking the continued fraction expansion of some "quadratic" numbers such as SQRT(2), SQRT(3), or the golden ratio (1+SQRT(5))/2. You'll get a pleasant surprise. Looking for patterns in these expansions is not only fun, but it has applica-

Listing 2: A better approach to calculating π using fractions. The input is the limit for B (A needs no limit since its value is determined by B), and the outputs are the same as described for listing 1.

```
10  REM PROGRAM B
20  REM SLIGHTLY SMARTER SEARCH FOR FRACTIONS A/B
30  REM NEAR PI . . . SEE PROGRAM A FOR DEFINITIONS . . .
100 P1=3.141592653
110 G=1000
119 REM ONLY NEED LIMIT ON B, SINCE A IS DETERMINED BY B
120 INPUT M
130 FOR B=1 TO M
140 A=INT(B*P1)
149 REM CALCULATE GOODNESS FOR A AND A+1 IN T AND U
150 T=ABS(P1*B-A)
160 U=1-T
169 REM OUTPUT ANY VALUE OF G BETTER THAN PREVIOUS ONES
170 IF T>=G THEN 210
180 PRINT A,B,A/B,T
190 G=T
200 GO TO 240
210 IF U>=G THEN 240
220 PRINT A+1,B,(A+1)/B,U
230 G=U
240 NEXT B
250 END

READY
RUN

?1000
3           1          3            0.141593
22          7          3.14286      8.85177E-3
333         106        3.14151      8.81577E-3
355         113        3.14159      3.81470E-5
```

Listing 3: The continued fraction method for calculating π. The output values must be summed as described in the text to calculate the value of π.

```
10  REM PROGRAM C
20  REM CONTINUED FRACTION EXPANSION OF X
30  REM ALGORITHM DESCRIBED IN TEXT
40  REM PROGRAM CALCULATES FIRST N+1 TERMS
100 INPUT N
110 INPUT X
119 REM I IS JUST A COUNTER
120 FOR I=0 TO N
130 PRINT INT(X)
140 X=1/(X-INT(X))
150 NEXT I
160 END

READY
RUN

?10
?3.141592653
3
7
15
1
237
2
1
2
11
1
1
```

```
10  REM PROGRAM D
20  REM PRODUCES CONTINUED FRACTION, GIVEN COEFFICIENTS
30  REM A(0),A(1),A(2), . . . AS INPUT
40  REM SEE TEXT FOR DEFINITIONS
100  P=0
110  Q=1
120  R=1
130  S=0
140  INPUT A
150  IF A=0 THEN 240
151  REM END IF INPUT ZERO
160  X=A*Q+P
170  Y=A*S+R
180  PRINT X;"/";Y,X/Y
190  P=Q
200  Q=X
210  R=S
220  S=Y
230  GO TO 140
240  END

READY
RUN


?3
3/1                     3
?7
22/7                    3.14286
?15
333/106                 3.14151
?1
355/113                 3.14159
?237
84468/26887             3.14159
?0
```

tions in the solution of certain quadratic equations using integers. For example, if you can determine the expansion of SQRT(3) you can find all the solutions of the equation $X^2 - 3Y^2 = 1$ for X and Y integers. While expansions of square roots of numbers have been largely explored, there are still many open problems concerning cube roots, etc.

Finally, an extremely practical and profitable application of the continued fraction idea exists in approximating not just numbers, but functions. Do you evaluate EXP(X) by multiplying and adding up the power series $1 + X/1 + X^2/1 \cdot 2 + X^3/1 \cdot 2 \cdot 3 + \ldots$? You may be able to save a lot of time by converting the series to a computationally efficient continued fraction form.∎

Listing 4: A program which produces the continued fractions for π, given the coefficients calculated in the program of listing 3.

RANDOMIZING

About This Section

Anyone who has implemented any sophisticated computer game or simulation understands the need for random numbers (some insist on qualifying "random" with "pseudo", since there is no true infinitely random sequence of numbers). The authors of this section have chosen traditional as well as unique methods for calculating random sequences. No one way is necessarily correct, but the use of one or another method may be inappropriate in certain situations. To help you decide on which generator to use when, read "Testing a Random Number Generator" by Fred Ruckdeschel. The analysis of your chosen generator could eliminate a potential source for errors in your program.

Random Number Generation in Microcomputers

George Atkinson

The traditional approaches to random number generation in large-scale computers have proven unsuitable for use in a microcomputer environment. Up to now, most algorithms for the production of random numbers have been based on multiplication, a primitive instruction on large-scale computers. Since this operation must generally be simulated in software on microcomputers (microcomputers usually don't have a built-in multiplication instruction), a number of alternative methods of generating random numbers are being investigated. These investigations have underscored the importance of tailoring each generation algorithm to its proposed application.

Random numbers are used extensively in large-scale computers for problems involving simulation and modelling. In the Monte Carlo approach to the solution of mathematically "intractable" problems, certain basic events, for example collisions between nuclear particles, are assumed to occur at random within some framework of problem-specific constraints. From the statistical analysis of the effects of a number of random events, it is possible to infer the global behavior of the system being modelled, e.g., the rate of nuclear fission. Although it is not likely that a microcomputer user will attempt a complex simulation problem, there are numerous applications for random numbers in a microcomputer environment. In the area of data collection it is often desirable to sample given inputs at random times. So-called "nondeterministic" algorithms rely heavily on random numbers for their efficiency. To the personal computer experimenter, the most important use

of random numbers is in the area of game playing. Beyond the obvious random throwing of dice and shuffling of card decks, many optimal strategies defined in game theory require weighted random selection among alternatives. For each of these applications, an understanding of what is meant by the notion "random" is of central importance.

What is a Random Number?

According to popular intuition, a random number is the result of a selection of one of a number of alternatives by some chance process. The throw of a die, for example, will result in the selection of one of six alternatives. If a four is rolled, one would tend to consider this a random result. But there is no way of telling if a single, isolated event is random. If a four were obtained each time on a dozen successive rolls, one might well conclude that the die was loaded and that the result was definitely non-random. The notion of "randomness" is relative, for the randomness of an observed event depends on its similarity to other like events, yet at the same time on its independence of these events.

Thus, the key question is: Can a sequence of numbers be produced that appears to be random, that is, exhibits the same lack of pattern one would expect to find in successive rolls of a die? Such a sequence will be considered random if it satisfies all statistical tests for randomness. These tests involve the examination of a sufficiently large number (the celebrated "statistical sample") of elements of the sequence in order to verify (1) its uniform distribution, which in the case of a thrown die means that each of the possible numbers 1 through 6 occurs with about the same frequency, and (2) the independence of the elements; that is, even with complete information about the outcome of previous "rolls", one is not able to predict the next element any more successfully than without this information. One should like to embody a random number generator in software or hardware in such a way that a reasonably efficient routine may be invoked on demand to produce the next element of the sequence.

Basic Approaches to Random Number Generation

In a microcomputer environment, several fundamental methods of generating random numbers are employed, sometimes in combination. Among the most common are (1) a "random box" external to the microprocessor, (2) an internal counter which is "read" upon occurrence of an external event, and (3) a pseudorandom number generator. A brief examination of these approaches will illuminate their advantages and drawbacks.

A random box consists of a hardware register with ever changing contents external to the microprocessor. Whenever a new random number is required, the current value of the register is transmitted to the microprocessor. This register might consist of a free-running counter, i.e., one not connected to the system clock. The values read from such a register easily satisfy the uniform distribution requirement: each of the 256 bit combinations of an 8 bit register is equally likely to be chosen. If, however, random numbers are requested periodically, for example in a loop, the phenomenon of "harmonic coupling" becomes apparent. Successive requests might result in a sequence such as:

```
10111000
00010011
01101110
11001010
00100101
10000001
```

which appears random to the untrained eye. But closer examination reveals that each number in the sequence differs from its predecessor by either 91 or 92: The independence requirement has thus been violated. One can infer that between accesses, the register has been incremented about 91 times plus some multiple of 256, and hence the next number is very likely 11011100. To avoid harmonic coupling, the random box register is usually not implemented as a counter, but as a hardware version of the *feedback shift register* algorithm. Regardless

of the exact implementation of the random box, additional hardware is required and, since hardware costs are always more conspicuous than software costs, relatively few microcomputer designers opt for this solution.

Another method of generating random numbers uses an internal register which is periodically altered by software and is accessed upon occurrence of some asynchronous external event such as the mechanical actuation of a switch. Such a register can even be a simple counter if it is incremented sufficiently often. Harmonic coupling is hardly a problem when electronic speeds are matched with mechanical actions: a human finger stabbing on a push button simply cannot stop a kilohertz clock with any precision. The chief disadvantage of this approach to random number generation is the requirement that a separate mechanical action be performed for each number generated. To circumvent this restriction, the internal register is often updated by a pseudorandom algorithm to permit the generation of a number of values for each mechanical action.

In large-scale computers, the most popular approach to random number generation is the implementation of a pseudorandom algorithm. Given a starting value (the "seed"), such an algorithm produces a sequence of numbers that appears to be haphazard, yet is completely deterministic. An important feature of such algorithms is their repeatability, i.e., when started with a given seed, the same sequence of numbers will always be generated. This is particularly useful during program testing: if two successive test runs produce different outputs, one can be certain this was due to alterations in the program and is not a result of using a different set of random numbers. The inherent determinism of a pseudorandom algorithm, however, causes some headaches in the specification of a random number generator. Since each number *does* depend on its predecessor, the independence constraint is technically violated and a good pseudorandom algorithm must be so cunningly designed that the dependency is subtle enough to escape detection by statistical methods. Perhaps the most important design consideration (and certainly one not sufficiently emphasized in the literature) is the selection of a suitable value range.

Range of a Pseudorandom Element

If, say, 3 bit pseudorandom numbers are to be generated to simulate throws of a die, the first major decision is the choice of element size. For example, suppose that each element of the sequence consists of three bits. A pseudorandom algorithm which transforms 3 bit combinations into other 3 bit combinations might produce a sequence such as:

000 101 010 111 100 001 110 011 000 101 ...

The cyclic nature of this sequence is immediately apparent and is a feature of every pseudorandom algorithm. Since each element depends entirely on its predecessor, repetition must set in as soon as any combination reoccurs. As there are only eight possible 3 bit combinations, the sequence already has the longest possible period and, worse, is perfectly predictable rather than random (a "001" always follows a "100", a "011" never follows a "001"). For the generation of 3 bit values, an element size of three bits is clearly inadequate.

Suppose the range of the pseudorandom register is doubled. A 6 bit register permits the generation of a sequence with a period as large as 64. An easily generated sequence is (in octal):

```
01 14 23 21 11 56 15 37 02 30
47 43 22 35 32 77 04 61 17 07
45 73 65 76 10 42 36 16 13 66
52 74 20 05 75 34 26 54 25 70
41 12 72 71 55 31 53 60 03 24
64 62 33 63 27 40 06 51 50 44
67 46 57 01 ...
```

If the last octal digit of each sequential element is taken as the random number, this pseudorandom number generator appears much more promising: every possible successor of, say, a "1" will occur somewhere in the sequence and the order of elements now appears to be unpredictable. The knowledge that a 3 has just been 'rolled" is of little help in predicting the following number in the sequence.

But, alas, even this pseudorandom number generator is not perfect. It is quite possible when rolling a die to come up with three identical results in three rolls of a die, but nowhere in the sequence of final digits is such a combination to be found. A close examination of the final digits reveals a further defect: if the last two generated final digits are known, the next is easily predicted. Even if the range of the psuedorandom register were to be extended further to permit all possible combinations of three successive digits to be included in the sequence, it is certain that there will be some combinations of four consecutive final digits which will not occur. In fact, no finite extension of the element range will suffice. In order to produce a truly patternless sequence of pseudorandom numbers, all patterns (i.e., subsequences) must be at least possible.

Thus, the answer to the question "How does one choose the range of a pseudorandom element?" can only be "It depends on the application." If cards are being dealt (6 bit quantities are generated) and a poker hand of five cards is to be produced, a pseudorandom register of at least 30 bits must be implemented if every combination is to be possible. If a shorter register is used, some combinations will be excluded, and even though the sequence may appear quite random, one can be certain that specific combinations, for example a royal flush in spades, are either not possible at all or will occur more frequently than in "real life."

Pseudorandom Algorithms

Once a suitable element range has been chosen, an appropriate algorithm for the generation of the sequential elements must be selected. One of the earliest pseudorandom algorithms (suggested by von Neumann) is the center-square method: An n-bit element is multiplied with itself and the middle n bits of the product serve as the next element. This method has fallen into disfavor, for it was soon recognized that, depending on the initial seed, the sequence produced tended to degenerate rapidly into a sequence with a relatively short period.

A more recent algorithm is the linear congruential method proposed by D.H. Lehmer. The previous element of the sequence is multiplied by a factor, a constant is added to the product, and the remainder after division by a modulus is taken as the next element. With a suitable choice of factor, constant, and modulus, pseudorandom sequences of maximal period can easily be generated. While this method is fine for large computers with adequate hardware for multiplication, its implementation on a microcomputer generally requires that multiple precision multiplications be simulated in software at considerable cost in memory and execution time.

In microprocessors, a cheaper method of generating pseudorandom sequences is the feedback shift register technique. The fundamental generation operation consists of an "end-around" shift of the previous sequential element in conjunction with an exclusive OR operation to produce the next element. Provided certain elementary precautions are observed, a feedback shift register algorithm can produce a pseudorandom sequence that not only passes all simple statistical tests for randomness, but is also easily implemented on a microcomputer. The realization of such an algorithm in a microcomputer program is based on two rather simple ideas.

A Feedback Shift Register Algorithm

The basic idea behind all feedback shift register algorithms is the generation of a sequence of bits in which each bit can be derived from a limited number of its predecessors (the so-called feedback bits). The derivation operation chosen for this purpose is usually the exclusive OR (XOR), a "balanced" primitive instruction that produces approximately equal numbers of zeroes and ones when applied to random inputs. A glance at a truth table confirms that most other logical operations are "unbalanced". The AND and NOR, for example, tend to produce three times as many 0s as 1s when applied to two arbitrary bits, while the OR and NAND generate too many 1s.

Suppose for simplicity that each bit in the sequence is the exclusive OR of exactly two of its predecessors, and that the two feedback bits are five and six positions behind the bit being generated. If six bits (not all zero) are arbitrarily selected as a seed, say 011101, one can repeatedly carry out the derivation operation:

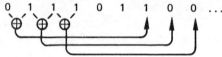

to generate the pseudorandom bit sequence:

```
0111011001101010111111000001000011000
0101001111010001110010010110011101 . . .
```

which repeats with a period of 63. This sequence contains every possible combination of six adjacent bits except six zeroes

and satisfies most statistical tests for randomness of bits. This bit derivation operation can be easily implemented on a microcomputer. If the predecessor bits are stored in a one byte register, the exclusive OR of the feedback bits is carried out and then a rotate operation performed. If the microprocessor doesn't have a rotate (end-around shift) instruction, the order of operations can be inverted: an end-off shift is performed first and then the newly derived bit inserted.

Although the bits generated by this technique are individually quite random, Knuth has pointed out that one should not fall into the trap of believing that the sequential values of the register(s) containing the predecessor bits will be random. To understand this pitfall, suppose the last three bits of the predecessor register just defined are taken as the values of a pseudo-random sequence. The first few values are:

```
00011101
00111011
01110110
11101100
```

and the corresponding sequence

```
5 3 6 4 1 3 6 5 2 5 2
5 3 7 7 7 7 6 4 0 . . .
```

fails the test of element independence. The reason lies in the generation procedure itself: each iteration of the bit derivation operation results in the "creation" of only one "new" bit; the other bits are not altered, but merely shifted. Thus, a 6 can follow only a 3 or a 7 and can be followed only by a 4 or a 5.

The second fundamental idea behind a successful feedback shift register algorithm (and one largely ignored in the literature) remedies this defect: if n-bit values are required, simply perform the bit derivation operation n or more times to generate each value. In the case of the bit sequence above, eight iterations of the bit derivation operation between values will result in the sequence of 6 bit values given earlier. The repetition of the bit derivation operation need not even result in a longer running program, since multiple iterations can often be carried out in parallel with the same computational effort as a single operation.

In byte oriented microprocessors, it is usually convenient to perform eight such operations in parallel. Consider, for example a 16 bit feedback shift register generator with feedback bits 15 and 8. A single iteration would modify the two byte register as shown in figure 1.

As it has become a tradition in the microprocessor literature for each author to supply samples of code tailored to his own

Figure 1.

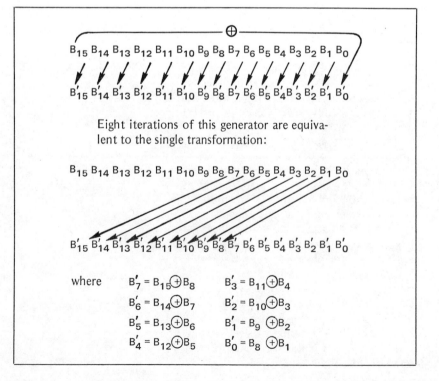

Eight iterations of this generator are equivalent to the single transformation:

where

$$B'_7 = B_{15} \oplus B_8 \qquad B'_3 = B_{11} \oplus B_4$$
$$B'_6 = B_{14} \oplus B_7 \qquad B'_2 = B_{10} \oplus B_3$$
$$B'_5 = B_{13} \oplus B_6 \qquad B'_1 = B_9 \oplus B_2$$
$$B'_4 = B_{12} \oplus B_5 \qquad B'_0 = B_8 \oplus B_1$$

favorite microprocessor, a coded version of this algorithm in the symbolic assembly language of the Intel 8035 is included here (see listing 1). Addresses have been omitted from the listing as the code is fully relocatable. The least and most significant bytes of the 16 bit Feedback Shift Register were arbitrarily assigned to registers 20 and 21, respectively. If the initial seed is one (r20=1, r21=0), the period of the pseudorandom sequence is 63457. The generated sequence passes all statistical tests for two adjacent values if random values of less than eight bits are required; every combination of two 6 bit values, for example, will occur either 15 or 16 times during a single period.

Any desired degree of randomness can be obtained by selecting a sufficiently long feedback shift register. Although the 16 bit feedback shift register is inadequate for the generation of "truly random" poker hands, the basic ideas of the feedback shift register technique can easily be applied to longer registers. If a 32 bit feedback shift register is initialized with a seed of 1, and bits 35 and 26 are selected as feedback bits, the period of the bit generator will be 3758096350. If, further, seven iterations of the bit generation operation are performed in parallel to generate the next sequential element (seven is not a factor of the period), the pseudorandom sequence of six-bit quantities that is obtained will have the same period.

Conclusion

Pseudorandom sequences of arbitrarily long periods can be efficiently produced in microcomputers by simple, easily implemented algorithms. Personal computer

Hex Code	Op Code	Operand	Comment
B8 20	MOV	R0,#20H	;LET R0 POINT TO LS BYTE
B9 21	MOV	R1,#21H	;LET R1 POINT TO MS BYTE
F1	MOV	A,@R1	;AC = $B_{15} B_{14} B_{13} B_{12} B_{11} B_{10} B_9 B_8$
67	RRC	A	;CARRY = B_8
F0	MOV	A,@R0	;FETCH LS BYTE
67	RRC	A	;AC = $B_8 B_7 B_6 B_5 B_4 B_3 B_2 B_1$
D1	XRL	A,@R1	;XOR WITH MS BYTE
20	XCH	A,@R0	;STORE $B_7' B_6' B_5' B_4' B_3' B_2' B_1' B_0'$ AND ; FETCH $B_7 B_6 B_5 B_4 B_3 B_2 B_1 B_0$
A1	MOV	@R1,A	;STORE $B_{15}' B_{14}' B_{13}' B_{12}' B_{11}' B_{10}' B_9' B_8'$

Listing 1: An 8 bit pseudorandom number generator using a 16 bit feedback shift register in the symbolic assembly language of the Intel 8035 processor.

enthusiasts in need of a random number generator are no longer limited to a choice between the cumbersome linear congruential algorithm and simpler, but far "less random" methods. The improved techniques of generating random numbers are likely to play a significant role in a number of exciting new developments ranging from the construction of "unbreakable" ciphers to the non-deterministic control of robots.■

REFERENCES

1. Grappel, R, "Randomize Your Programming." BYTE, v. 2 #1. Sep 1976. pp. 36-38.

2. Knuth, D E, *The Art of Computer Programming*, v. 2 Addison-Wesley, 1969. pp. 1-160.

3. Lewis, T G and Payne, W H, "Generalized Feedback Shift Register Pseudorandom Number Algorithm", *Journal of the ACM*, v. 20 #3. July, 1973. pp. 456-468.

4. Martin, B, "Need a Better Random Number Generator?", *Interface Age*, v. 2 #3. Feb 1977. pp. 94-100.

A Pseudorandom Number Generator

Richard Mickelsen

A convenient source for random numbers in computer programming is the *pseudorandom sequence*, a sequence that appears to be random but which technically is not.

A pseudorandom number generator should be economical in both execution time and storage; should be logical; and should produce what appears to be statistically random output. These desiderata need not be abandoned for small computer applications. One of the best methods currently available is well suited to small computers.

In 1973, Lewis and Payne (see references) presented a general feedback shift register random number generator for which:

- The algorithm is simple and entails no multiplication or division.
- Operation is independent of the number of bits per word.
- Statistical properties are generally good.
- Storage requirements can be selected by the user.

Operation of the generator requires three ingredients: two numbers (p and q) and a table, t, of length p. To illustrate the algorithm, assume p, q, and t are given. Let $j = p-q + 1$ and k=1 initially. Then, the procedure in listing 1 returns a pseudorandom number.

This procedure is coded in listing 2 in 8080 assembler language for a p value of 10, a q value of 3, and a particular table. The total execution time averages $146+14/p$ states exclusive of the call and saving and restoring registers. The number of bytes used is 33 plus the length of the table.

Selecting p and q

The theoretical basis for the successful operation of the generator depends on the properties of primitive trinomials of the form: x^p+x^q+1: The list of p and q forming

```
INTEGER PROCEDURE rand;
  BEGIN
    j:=j−1; IF j=0 THEN j:=p;
    k:=k−1; IF k=0 THEN k:=p;
    t(j):=t(j) XOR t(k);
    RETURN (t(j))
  END;
```

Listing 1: High level procedure to generate a random number by using an exclusive OR function between two variables.

Label	Op Code	Operand	Commentary
RAND:	XRA	A	
	MOV	B,A	
	MOV	D,A	
	LXI	H,J0	;address of j
	MOV	C,M	;load j
	DCR	C	;j:=j−1
	JNZ	S1	;if j=0 then
	MVI	C,0A	; j:=p
S1:	MOV	M,C	;store j
	INX	H	;address of k
	MOV	E,M	;load k
	DCR	E	;k:=k−1
	JNZ	S2	;if k=0 then
	MVI	E,0A	; k:=p
S2:	MOV	M,E	;store k
	XCHG		
	DAD	D	;address of t(k)
	MOV	A,M	;load t(k)
	XCHG		
	DAD	B	;address of t(j)
	XRA	M	;t(j) xor t(k)
	MOV	M,A	;store new t(j)
	RET		;return random number in ACC,
			; and its address in M
J0:	08		;j=p−q+1 initially
	01		;k=1 initially
	5F		;t(1)
	22		;t(2)
	CD		
	66		
	6A		; .
	52		; .
	CC		; .
	02		
	F4		
	C5		;t(10)

Listing 2: The high level random number generator given in listing 1 converted into 8080 code to increase the execution speed.

p	q	p	q	p	q
10	3	21	2	31	3,6,7,13
11	2	22	1	33	13
15	1,4,7	23	5,9	35	2
17	3,5,6	25	3,7	36	11
18	7,9	28	3,9,13	39	4,8,14
20	3	29	2	41	3,20

Table 1: Collection of all primitive trinomials for a value of p between 10 and 46, with q values ranging from 1 to p/2.

```
PROCEDURE setup;
   BEGIN
      INTEGER ii,jj,kk,dummy;
      FOR ii:=1 THRU p DO t(ii):=0;
      FOR kk:=1 THRU b DO
      BEGIN
         FOR ii:=1 THRU p DO t(ii):=t(ii)*2+1;
         FOR jj:=1 THRU delay DO dummy:=rand
      END;
   END;
```

Listing 3: Routine to construct a table of random values using the techniques previously developed in listing 1.

p=10,q=3	p=17,q=5	p=31,q=6	p=36,q=11
5F05C68F	19E440CB	FEDD4BB2	4F5959FF
22D594DD	16ED0DCC	AE673132	48458869
CD73EA11	D92FE2D9	E649BBD0	55404347
66C82713	C7551DD0	BA6B798E	A4D13595
6A5818E7	7F8EEC75	670779F4	174B1122
52B11522	61023B6B	3140C9C2	CFC30EA2
CCB4427F	32B9DF81	C4084813	57457E10
02380AA9	FE1EFABA	549E5190	61D478FE
F42C7DA1	7F493399	22521CE6	3FC396CA
C501B69A	42822A67	C08F9D97	561A8A8C
	DA9AE2FA	A32496A7	E2002618
	16C474E4	A30F65A8	6EA84CC4
	BE6C5637	9192C86D	B538F265
	A38E2BAA	FCD3A7BC	A7E884B9
	4E21BB7A	15A75CA1	17688193
	D651FCBC	B0068033	3DF94489
	AAF62034	05392E12	5EA78ADC
		C15DEAA5	5793EF10
		C29CF748	C97F4496
		51ED2EA8	6A7F85B6
		A5B57A64	2F095D35
		030CDE2B	A4030FFA
		D15CB542	7F33237D
		DEB718BC	BC88A65C
		2A5B5CBB	D33619ED
		BEF60C3A	87290B2B
		9ACDCCE6	C461EC1A
		53D55F0C	8A908991
		4C26EECD	8A708FED
		AA01D6A3	E5C9E614
		CD86A9E9	AA0F4CBD
			9BA7F0B4
			7B01C4CA
			57ACC8B7
			8CDDD075
			D3FB1432

Table 2: Pseudorandom numbers for various values of p and q. Notice that the pseudorandom numbers are hexadecimal.

primitive trinomials given in table 1 is taken from Zierler and Brillhart, who present such a table for values of p from 2 thru 607.

The period of the random sequence produced by the algorithm using p and q from a primitive trinomial and a suitable table is 2^p-1. Every possible bit pattern except all zeros will occur in a p bit word. Every possible bit pattern will also appear in a b bit word (where b is less than p). Hence, p should be chosen to be greater than or equal to the number of bits in the required random number.

If successive random numbers are to be used to form a random point in n-dimensional space, p should be greater than or equal to n times b. Thus, if two 8 bit numbers (b equal to 8) are to be used to form a random point in a plane (n=2 for the two-dimensional case), then p should be no less than 16.

For good statistical properties it is known that q should be neither too small nor too near p/2. Finally, as a crude generalization, statistical goodness increases with p, though, as will be shown, small p generators appear to be reasonably good.

Tables

Suppose values for p and q have been chosen. Then a suitable table can be constructed as follows. First, select a positive value called the delay which is either:

- Relatively prime to the period (2^p-1).
- Less than (period)/b.

For example, for a value of p at 10, the period 1023 has factors 3, 11, and 31. If b is set equal to 8, then a delay which is not a multiple of these factors or is less than 127 will suffice. Note that for p values of 17 or 31, the period is prime. In general, large values of the delay are preferable (Lewis and Payne use $100 \cdot p$).

One method of constructing the table is shown in listing 3. The idea is to shift left a partially filled table and introduce a column of 1s, mix it up by invoking the procedure *rand*, and repeat the process until all b columns are filled.

A slightly different method is presented in Lewis and Payne's set up algorithm. This latter method was employed on a 32 bit machine to produce table 2 for selected values of p and q.

For a chosen pair (p,q) and a word of b random bits, any b contiguous columns of the appropriate table given here may be chosen to form a new table. For example, the table of the sample program was chosen as the first eight columns from the (10,3 table. However, it could have been any eight contiguous columns. Based on the 32 bit tables, many different tables for small values of b may easily be created.

Various obvious modifications can be employed to normalize the resulting random number. If the leftmost (high) bit is to be the sign bit, the high bit column of the table entries should all be zero. For floating point applications, the table may be used directly and the random number considered the mantissa to be adjoined to a normalizing exponent.

Tests

Since the properties of this generator for small p are not reported, 1000 32 bit random numbers normalized to the interval -0.5 to 0.5 were generated for each p, q, t combination presented here. The following statistics were computed: the average of the sum of the numbers (sample mean), the average of the sum of each number squared (sample variance), and the first and second lagged sample *autocovariance*. The first and second lagged autocovariance is the average of the sum of products of each random number and the number preceding it in the

sequence by one or two, respectively.

All the generators pass these simple tests according to traditional statistical criteria. A (28,9) and a (31,13) generator were also constructed and tested. Both looked suspiciously poor in the tests and are not reported. The reported generators all have sample statistics within 1.5 standard deviation units of the expected values. These particular results can be generalized to a generator using bit columns consecutively from the high bit position of the tables given here.

More thorough testing is, of course, necessary for certification. Sophisticated tests may uncover problems inherent in these short table generators, but so far they appear to be quite suitable for small machine use.■

REFERENCES

1. Lewis, T G, and Payne, W H, "Generalized Feedback Shift Register Pseudorandom Number Generator," *Journal of the ACM,* volume 20, number 3, July 1973, pages 456 thru 468.

2. Zierler, N, and Brillhart, J, "On Primitive Trinomials (Mod 2)," *Information and Control,* volume 13, 1968, pages 541 thru 554.

Random Number Generation

Philip J Ferrell

When a personal computer experimenter elects to forego the blessings of BASIC, the need for a random number generator in assembly language becomes quickly apparent. How else does one stock the galaxy with Klingons, shuffle cards, or roll dice? A good place to start our search for random numbers is with large computers. The IBM Scientific Subroutine Package contains a pseudorandom number generator written in FORTRAN. This subroutine, called RANDU, is coded in five lines and employs the "power residue" method. A 32 bit odd integer is multiplied by a "seed" number (65539 for RANDU) and the least significant 32 bits of the product are retained. The resulting integer is floated and normalized, becoming a floating point quantity having a uniform distribution between 0 and 1.

The Association for Computing Machinery (ACM) has published a series of algorithms which include random number generators which may be found in *Collected Algorithms from the CACM* as numbers 133 and 266). They differ from RANDU in word length and multiplier (or seed), but the principle is the same. We could continue in this vein, but we already have a problem in that multiplication at this level of programming is a non-trivial task.

The power residue method outlined above may be regarded as a linear transform of one computer word into another, and is closely related to another method of generating pseudorandom sequences using a shift register. On a large computer having long word length and a multiply instruction, the power residue method is efficient, but using this method on a microprocessor is another matter entirely. Communication

engineers use shift registers to generate pseudorandom sequences, and it is this approach that we shall follow.

A shift register may be connected with its input determined by the modulo 2 sum of the last stage and one or more intermediate stages. Under certain conditions this feedback shift register (FSR) can generate a pseudorandom sequence which is quite long compared to the number of shift register stages. It is the feedback connections which determine the length of the resulting sequence. A single shift of our register may be regarded as a transformation of one word into another which is conveniently represented in matrix form. This shifting matrix has a characteristic polynomial (see MacLane and Birkhoff's *Algebra*, p. 310) which has a profound effect on the resulting pseudorandom sequence. Indeed, for each shift register length N, there exist two or more maximal or M-sequences which include every binary number of length N except a number consisting only of 0 bits. Thus a maximal sequence will run $2^N - 1$ shifts before repeating.

Are these sequences really random? No, since they are of finite length and are periodic, but they certainly possess many random-like qualities.

Characteristic polynomials which result in shift register maximal sequences may be found in tables of irreducible polynomials such as those appearing in the works of Peterson and Marsh. The relationship between polynomial and shift register connection is straightforward. The degree of the polynomial equals the number of shift register stages, represented by N. Each non-zero coefficient corresponds to a "tap" or stage which is connected to the input of a modulo 2 adder. The output of this adder is connected to the input stage of the shift register, thus completing the loop.

A modulo 2 adder may be thought of as a binary adder with no carry. An even number of 1s in the input results in a 0 output, while an odd number of 1s gives a 1 output. It is variously known as a half adder and an exclusive OR gate.

The example in figure 1 should clarify the above. A degree 12 polynomial is realized as a feedback shift register with 12 stages. Since polynomial coefficients are binary (0 or 1), a neat way of writing the polynomial is to write the coefficients in descending order, left to right, then express the resulting binary sequence in hexadecimal or octal. The polynomial in the example is thus written in hexadecimal as 1053. Note that shifting is assumed to be left to right.

The tables of irreducible polynomials previously referenced are not widely available, so table 1 is included, which gives a selection of maximal irreducible polynomials through degree 32 which are suitable for use in microprocessor random number generators. Shift registers and modulo 2 adders are easily implemented in software, and the steps required to produce a simulation of a feedback shift register random number generator are given in table 2.

The conceptual scheme for a feedback shift register as it may be realized in software is shown in figure 2. The carry bit (CY) is shown in several places for the sake of clarity. Note that shifting is from right to left, as opposed to the example in figure 1, and the feedback inputs are reflected accordingly. The characteristic polynomial is of degree 24 (hexadecimal 1000087) which has all four feedback positions in one register byte. This eliminates step 5 of part C in the procedure in table 2. The feedback mask is hexadecimal E1 (the reverse of 87 due to reversal of direction of shift) which identifies the four feedback positions specified by the polynomial. Four bytes of variable storage are required; three simulate the 24 stage shift register, and the fourth is used to calculate the feedback bit.

If all three register bytes initially contain zero, an all-zero sequence is generated which is not likely to prove useful. Any other initial condition causes the maximal sequence to run. The length of this maximal sequence is 16,777,215.

Table 1: Maximal-irreducible polynomials in hexadecimal notation. The asterisk (*) indicates all feedback positions are within a single byte.

Degree	Polynomial in Hexadecimal	Sequence Length
8	11D*	255
12	1069*	4095
16	1002D*	65535
18	4004D*	262,143
24	1000087*	1.678×10^7
28	10000009*	2.684×10^8
31	80000009*	2.147×10^9
32	100400007	4.295×10^9

A. Select a maximal irreducible polynomial of the degree yielding the desired sequence length from table 1.

B. Identify those stages (ie. bit positions) marked by the polynomial as feedback inputs.

C. Calculate the feedback bit (the modulo 2 sum of feedback inputs), in the following manner:
 1. Zero the feedback byte.
 2. Load the accumulator with a byte containing feedback inputs.
 3. Mask the accumulator, clearing all positions except feedback bits.
 4. One bit at a time, shift the accumulator into the carry bit and add 1 to the feedback byte if the carry is set to 1.
 5. Repeat steps 2, 3, and 4 if other feedback bits must be collected from other shift register bytes.
 6. (The feedback byte now contains the sum of all 1s in the feedback positions, and the least significant bit of this byte is our desired modulo 2 sum, that is, the feedback bit.) Shift the least significant bit into the carry bit.

D. Rotate through the carry bit all the bytes representing the shift register (be careful of the order of operations) which simulates a single feedback shift register shifting operation.

Table 2: The steps required to produce a simulation of a feedback shift register random number generator.

Figure 1: An example of a characteristic polynomial which results in shift register maximal sequences.

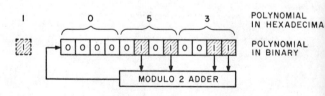

Figure 2: A feedback shift register which may be realized in software.

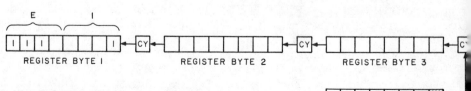

A Typical Implementation

This example has been programmed as a subroutine for a 6502 microprocessor and is presented here as listing 1. Eight shifts per subroutine call give eight new bits in register byte 3, and keep the old random numbers available for two calls in register bytes 2 and 1.

Successive calls to this subroutine yield a sequence of pseudorandom bytes having a uniform distribution between hexadecimal 00 and FF. It is helpful to imagine a decimal point to the left of this quantity. The quantity will now become a binary fraction between 0 and 1.

This number may then be used in a variety of ways. For example, to represent the roll of a die, the number may be multiplied by 6 and the product truncated. The resulting integer will have an equal probability of value between 0 and 5. Adding 1 to this integer yields the desired result, which in this case is a number having equal probability of value from 1 to 6.■

REFERENCES

1. MacLane and Birkhoff, *Algebra*, MacMillan Co., 1967, pp. 310-318.

2. Marsh, R.W., *A Table of Irreducible Polynomials Over GF$_2$ Through Degree 19*, National Security Agency, 1960.

3. Peterson, W.W., *Error Correcting Codes*, MIT/John Wiley, 1961, Appendix C.

```
0000   A2  08        LDX  #08    ;INITIALIZE NMBR OF SHIFTS PER CALL
0002   A0  00    X1  LDY  #00    ;
0004   84  03        STY  ?03    ;ZERO FEEDBACK BYTE
0006   A0  08        LDY  #08    ;
0008   A5  02        LDA  ?02    ;LOAD ACC WITH BYTE CONTAINING ALL
                                 ;FEEDBACK BITS
000A   29  E1        AND  #E1    ;MASK ALL BIT POSITIONS EXCEPT
                                 ;FEEDBACK BITS
000C   0A        X2  ASL  A      ;SHIFT ACC INTO CARRY
000D   90  02        BCC  X3     ;SKIP IF CY CLEAR
000F   E6  03        INC  ?03    ;INCREMENT FEEDBACK BYTE IF CY SET
0011   88        X3  DEY         ;
0012   D0  F8        BNE  X2     ;GET ALL 8 BIT POSITIONS
0014   46  03        LSR  ?03    ;SHIFT LEAST SIGNIFICANT BIT OF
                                 ;FEEDBACK BYTE INTO CY
0016   26  00        ROL  ?00    ;ROTATE FEEDBACK SHIFT-REGISTER THRU
0018   26  01        ROL  ?01    ;CY TO SIMULATE REGISTER SHIFT
001A   26  02        ROL  ?02    ;
001C   CA            DEX         ;
001D   D0  E3        BNE  X1     ;PERFORM ALL 8 SHIFTS
001F   A5  00        LDA  ?00    ;LOAD PSEUDO-RANDOM BYTE IN ACC
0021   60            RTS         ;RETURN
```

Listing 1: An implementation of the random number generator written in 6502 assembly language.

Three Types of

Pseudorandom Sequences

C Brian Honess

Random numbers are extensively used in virtually all areas of data processing, from the simplest games for a hobby microprocessor, up to the most complex business and scientific applications. Deterministic games programmed without the benefit of some random parameter soon become boring and easy to "beat," so it would seem that random number generation and testing should be of interest to even the neophyte programmer or computer hacker when trying to get a simple game up and running. Random numbers are used extensively in various business applications. For example, random numbers would be used by an auditor faced with a large number of transactions to audit, and using a sampling technique to only look at a certain percentage of representative transactions. The number of checkout stations at your local discount department store may have been determined by using a mathematical model of the store, wherein the arrival and departure of "customers" was simulated using random numbers. Market research makes extensive use of random numbers, in selecting the people, streets, blocks, households, etc, to interview or to mail questionnaires. A mathematical model can also be "built" of an element, molecule or compound, and a particle introduced at random and collisions counted. Suppose further that you had a photograph of some obscure planet, covered in an extremely irregular way with areas

you assumed to be water. You could divide the photograph into small squares, or maybe overlay with a piece of graph paper, and then "take shots" at the grid with a random number generator, wherein the random number would determine the coordinates of the "shot" and you could then tally the number of "hits" and "misses" and thereby determine the number of hits out of the total number of shots, and get an approximation of the percentage of the surface covered by water.

Before reading on, let me suggest that you try a short experiment. Consider the set of integers from 0 to 99, and quickly write down a list of random 2 digit numbers. Use whatever your current idea of random is, and make a list of 100 numbers. Later we'll see several methods for determining how random your numbers are, but I'll hasten to guess that they won't be very random. Psychologists repeatedly show that the average human just cannot think up random numbers. Upon inspection, there might be too many 4s compared with 6s, or maybe very few 0s and an abundance of 5s.

While it's true that a machine can produce a much better selection of truly random numbers than a human, the problem is that the numbers produced by the machine aren't really random either. If you could build a perfect roulette wheel, you'd get truly random numbers, but the mechanical considerations of such a device are, of course, impossible, to say nothing of the costs, speed, maintenance, testing, and so forth. There is really not much need to strive for such a device for the usual application of random numbers, because there are some mathematical methods which produce what are called pseudorandom numbers. Implemented on a computer, they are quite fast, easy to implement, and just as much fun to play with as a roulette wheel!

Before looking at some of these methods, I might mention that there are a couple of other ways to get random numbers for your games, experiments, or business applications. You could always punch or key into your system as many numbers as you want from the Rand table. This is a formal table used by statisticians entitled *A Million Random Digits* and published by Rand Corporation. There are a million of them, so this could take quite a while. Of course, you're assured that these numbers are thoroughly tested and as unbiased as possible, but assuming you have the time and perseverance to do the job, unless you work out some scheme for using different parts of the table or different orderings, you'll always get the same string of digits. You might find an abbreviated table in the back of some statistics book and use the numbers therein, but the problem here is that you'll probably need more numbers than appear in the table. Of course you could always go through the table more than once, but this doesn't multiply the size of the table. In some applications it might be desirable to be able to use the same random numbers, in the same order, more than once. For example, you may want to duplicate the results of an experiment, an audit, a market research test, or a game. But usually, you'll want a new string of numbers, and this can be secured by selecting starting values or other parameters in the mathematical algorithms that follow.

The Center Squared Method

The earliest computer oriented method for producing pseudorandom numbers was probably the center squared method. In this method we begin with a *2n* digit number, square it, and then extract the center *2n* digits from the *4n* digit result, and this becomes the next random number, and also becomes the number which is squared in the next iteration. For example, suppose you want some 4 digit random numbers. In this case, of course, $n = 2$, and let's assume we start off with the number 4321 as our "seed" value. Figure 1 shows the process through three iterations.

This method makes a good little program to assign to a beginning programming class because it is easy to explain, easy to determine what the answers "should be," but it has several problems which arise as you get deeper into the problem. In FORTRAN or BASIC, lacking any specific digit manipulation instructions, the hard part comes when you try to strip off the digits either side of the center. Listing 1 shows a simple BASIC program which will generate one random number. *[This program assumes an interpreter with greater than eight digits of arithmetic precision].* Here, we see that we desire four digits, and enter the seed 4321. Squared this becomes an 8 digit number in line 120. Line 130 divides by 100 in the first step of

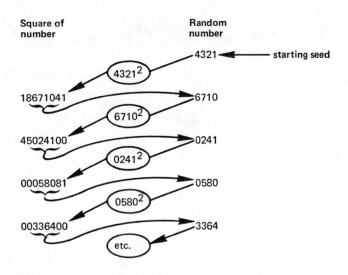

Figure 1: Operation of the center squared method of random number generation can be illustrated by this example. Here we use 8 digit decimal numbers, and assume the ability to extract the center four digits as the 4 digit random number for each cycle. [In principle this algorithm could be done on a binary basis by picking the middle 16 bits of a 32 bit product, or the middle 32 bits of a 64 bit product ... CH] *All versions of this algorithm are subject to the problem of degeneration, since if the middle digits happen to become 0, the square will continue to be 0 through successive generations of the algorithm.*

BASIC Program	Sample Results
100 PRINT "INPUT A 4-DIGIT SEED";	
110 INPUT N	4321
120 LET N = N * N	18671041
130 LET N = N / 100	186710.41
140 LET N = INT(N)	186710
150 LET A = A / 10000	18.6710
160 LET A = INT(A)	18
170 LET A = A * 10000	180000
180 LET N = N − A	6710
190 PRINT N	6710
200 END	

Listing 1: A BASIC program which accomplishes one generation of the center squared method of calculation. Note that this program assumes an interpreter with at least eight decimal digits of accuracy.

several necessary to get out the four center digits. Of course if you wanted 2 digit random numbers your seed would have been a 2 digit number; you'd have a 4 digit square, and you would change line 130 to divide by 10. For 6 digit numbers, you'd change it to divide by 1000, etc. Line 140 completes the removal of the right-hand two digits by integerizing the number. This resulting 6 digit number is then set aside, and you start removing the front two digits. This is done by dividing by 10000, integerizing the result and then multiplying by 10000. In line 180 you subtract this number from the one previously set aside and out come the center four digits, the new random number. If you are working with 2 digit random numbers, the divisor in line 150 would be changed to 100 and you'd then multiply by 100 in line 170.

One number isn't going to be enough for most applications, so let's put in a loop and get "n" numbers. Listing 2 shows the modifications necessary. Also, we'll combine lines 120 to 140, and lines 160 to 170 in listing 1.

I remember when I first coded this method in a beginning FORTRAN class. I've forgotten what 4 digit seed the instructor used at the time, but it was a revelation when I found out about something he called "degeneration." I'm sure a simple program can be written to discover any and all of the 4 digit seeds which will cause this program to degenerate to zero, but let's assume that there is at least one, and that Murphy's Law will guarantee that this particular one is the seed you choose for your first run. It is not difficult to imagine that there is a 4 digit number, which, when squared, will have four zeros in the middle. Maybe your number squared will be 12000034, or 65000025, etc. This being the case, you'll get 0000 as your next random number until you discover what is going on and get out of the loop. Listing 3 shows how we'll test for that problem and perform an ad hoc fix; we'll just call for another seed when a random number of zero is obtained.

Our final try at the center square program still doesn't solve one of the worst problems with this method. The method doesn't give very long periods for many seeds, and you really can't predict what the results will be until you try it. The method starts repeating numbers, and even the place where it starts repeating can't be determined without trying it. For example, you may print out 722 different numbers, and then it will start repeating the last 34 of them. The method is easy, and it is fun, and it may just produce all the pseudorandom numbers you need for your application.

Fibonacci Series Technique

A second method for generating random numbers makes use of the Fibonacci series, so named for its discoverer Leonardo of Pisa, known as Fibonacci (meaning son of Bonaccio). Leonardo was perhaps the greatest European mathematician of the Middle Ages, and if not for him you might be programming your machine using Roman numerals, because it was Leonardo who recognized the enormous superiority of the Hindu-Arabic decimal system with its positional notation and the zero symbol, over the much clumsier Roman system. Table 1 shows several numbers in the Fibonacci series, and you'll notice that each number is simply the sum of the previous two numbers. Actually, we could make up any number of series by starting with any two numbers and letting their sum be a new random number, and repeating this for our desired number of iterations. The reason that we'll use the Fibonacci series specifically, and not any other series, is that the characteristics of the Fibonacci series have

```
100     PRINT "HOW MANY NUMBERS DO YOU WANT?";
110     INPUT J
120     PRINT "INPUT A 4-DIGIT SEED";
130     INPUT N
140     FOR I = 1 TO J
150     LET N = INT(N*N/100)
160     LET A = INT(N/10000)*10000
170     LET N = N – A
180     PRINT N
190     NEXT I
200     END
```

Listing 2: A BASIC program which will generate a list of random numbers using the center squared method. The program embeds a revised form of the calculation of listing 1 within a FOR-NEXT loop.

```
100     PRINT "HOW MANY NUMBERS DO YOU WANT?";
110     INPUT J
120     PRINT "INPUT A 4-DIGIT SEED";
130     INPUT N
140     FOR I = 1 TO J
150     LET N = INT(N*N/100)
160     LET A = INT(N/10000)*10000
170     LET N = N – A
180     PRINT N
190     IF N < > 0 THEN 230
200     PRINT "DEGENERATION AFTER"; N ; "NUMBERS"
210     PRINT "ENTER ANOTHER 4-DIGIT SEED";
220     INPUT N
230     NEXT I
240     END
```

Listing 3: The program of listing 2 will occasionally produce examples of degenerate cases. The center squared method is prone to such degeneration with an unpredictable frequency, so for purposes of illustration this version incorporates an ad hoc fix to ask for a new seed when degeneracy is detected, and report on how many cycles were required to reach degeneracy.

(a) The Fibonacci Series

n	F_n
1	1
2	1
3	2
4	3
5	5
6	8
7	13
.	.
.	.
.	.
19	4181
20	6765
21	10946
22	17711
.	.
.	.
.	.

(b) Some Characteristics of the Fibonacci Series

Final digit (LSD)	repeats	in	cycle	of	60
Last 2 digits	repeat	in	cycle	of	300
Last 3 digits	"	"	"	"	1500
Last 4 digits	"	"	"	"	15000
Last 5 digits	"	"	"	"	150000
etc.					

Every	3rd	F_n is	divisible by	2
"	4th	"	"	3
"	5th	"	"	5
"	6th	"	"	8
etc.				

} Note: this is also the Fibonacci series.

Table 1: The Fibonacci series is a numerological phenomenon which is generated by the following definition: the next term in the series is the sum of the previous two terms, with the first two terms defined to be a value of 1 as a starting point. At (a) are listed several representative sections of the Fibonacci series, and at (b) are shown several miscellaneous characteristics of the Fibonacci series abstracted from the mathematical literature. This series can be used as a basis for a random number generator, as described in the text.

been studied, and we know several facts about it that will be of interest. Table 1 for example shows that if we want more than 60 single digit random numbers, the Fibonacci series isn't going to work. Of course we could start extracting 2 digit numbers from different parts of the numbers produced, but here we're on our own as far as statistical characteristics are concerned.

Listing 4 shows a BASIC program for calculating and printing "n" random numbers of five digits each. Notice that the generator is seeded with two seeds from table 1. These could have been INPUT, of course, and in that way a different series of random numbers could be produced.

I've chosen the first two 5 digit numbers in the sequence, but there is nothing special about them. Also, you might consider having the generator run through the loop a number of times before it starts printing the output. This could be easily implemented with another INPUT statement and another FOR . . . NEXT loop, or maybe by just adding the number of unwanted numbers to J, and then putting in an IF to suppress printing of the first J-N numbers. Listing 4 is straightforward: after determining how many numbers you want, it takes the two seeds and calculates the first number. It is possible that the result will be over five digits when the two previous numbers are added, but it can never be greater than 199998 (99999 + 99999), so we check for this condition in line 160 and simply subtract 100000 if the number is larger than 99999. Lines 190 and 200 serve to shift the second number into the location previously holding the first number, and the new random number into the location previously holding the second number, and we're ready for a new iteration.

In order to find the nth Fibonacci number, you needn't go up to "n" one at a time. There is an easier method, although you might not think so when you see the formulas in figure 2. You might try to find the 20th Fibonacci number with your pocket calculator (or maybe your computer?) using formula a of figure 2. We know the answer is 6765, from table 1. This formula produces the exact answer, but we can get it with a little less calculation by using formula b in figure 2. The term $(1 + \sqrt{5}) / 2$ is known in the mathematical literature as the "Golden Ratio" and is often symbolized by the Greek letter Φ (phi)

```
100     PRINT "HOW MANY NUMBERS DO YOU WANT?";
110     INPUT J
120     LET A = 10946
130     LET B = 17711
140     FOR I = 1 TO J
150     LET N = A + B
160     IF N < 100000 THEN 180
170     LET N = N − 100000
180     PRINT N
190     LET A = B
200     LET B = N
210     NEXT I
220     END
```

Listing 4: A BASIC program which implements a Fibonacci series random number generation technique. The program works machines of finite precision (even though the Fibonacci numbers eventually get infinitely large) because only the low order digits are kept as part of the pseudorandom number. Since the high order portion of a Fibonacci number has no effect on the low order portion during calculation of the next number, it is possible to completely ignore the high order part.

If formula b is evaluated and then rounded to the nearest integer, it will produce F_n. You might try this, again, with n = 20.

The Golden Ratio assumes importance when using the Fibonacci series random number generator, because it is used as a "correction factor." The results of the generator, aside from being somewhat predictable as shown in table 1, fail many of the statistical tests usually applied to random number generators. A big improvement can be made in the results if we use only every k^{th} number, where k is almost any number which will make the Golden Ratio to the kth power relatively large. Figure 2c is the required formula. If this modification is implemented, and k is large, your calculating time for each random number that is to be used will greatly increase, but you'll have numbers that are about as good statistically as any other method.

Power Residue Calculations

A third general class of pseudorandom number generators is called the Power Residue Method. It is this method that is usually favored by hardware manufacturers, software writers and mathematicians, because long periods prior to repetition can be assured, and the numbers generated hold up well to statistical tests for randomness. The method is, however, machine dependent since it relies on the word size of the machine. The Power Residue Method is the method employed in RANDU, an extremely popular random number generator appearing in the "Scientific Subroutine Package" (IBM publication number H20-0205) for the IBM System 360 and 370 computers. The publication gives a FORTRAN listing of this subroutine and documentation on how to use it, and also delineates a FORTRAN listing and instructions for use of GAUSS, which is a program for producing a normal distribution of random numbers. The methods can easily be extended to distributions other than the normal. Background on the number theory aspects of the Power Residue Method can be obtained in another IBM booklet, Random Number Generation and Testing" IBM publication number C20-8011).

Listing 5 shows a BASIC version of a program to produce one random number on a 32 bit machine. The program can be easily modified, of course, along the lines we followed for the center squared and Fibonacci methods covered earlier. The multiplier in line 130 is 2^{-31} and of course you'll be rounding it to fit your particular BASIC compiler. Line 130 simply transforms our new random number X into a floating-point version between 0 and 1,

which is a more usual way of delineating random numbers. With a 32 bit machine (1 sign bit) we use 2^{-31}, and this would be changed to correspond to the particular machine upon which the method is implemented. The multiplier in line 120 is also machine dependent. It has the form: $8i \pm 3$, where i is any integer. The trick here is to choose i, such that the resultant multiplier is close to $2^{b/2}$. Since b = 32 for this example (b is the number of bits), then we want the multiplier to be close to 2^{16} = 65536. If i = 8192, then the multiplier will be 65536+3=65539. The seed multiplied by the multiplier produces a product which is $2b$ bits long and we discard the b high order bits, and the remaining b low order bits become the random number and the input seed for the routine for the next number. Using this method we will get 2^{b-2} terms before repeating. Actually, the sign bit doesn't count, so we'll have $2^{31} - 2$ or 2^{29}, or over half a billion numbers before repeating. I'm not about to try and prove this, but I will give it a "go" with a smaller machine assumed.

(a)
$$F_n = \frac{1}{\sqrt{5}} \left[\left(\frac{1+\sqrt{5}}{2} \right)^n - \frac{1-\sqrt{5}}{2}^n \right]$$

(b)
$$F_n = \frac{\Phi^n}{\sqrt{5}} = \frac{((1+\sqrt{5})/2)^n}{\sqrt{5}}$$
rounded to nearest integer.

(c)
$$(Golden\ ratio)^k = \left(\frac{1+\sqrt{5}}{2} \right)^k = \Phi^k = 1.61803^k \ldots$$

Figure 2: The program of listing 4 was an iterative calculation. It turns out that there are several ways to calculate Fibonacci numbers directly which do not involve iteration. Formula (a) is an exact calculation of the nth Fibonacci number. Formula (b) is also an exact calculation if the result is rounded to the nearest integer. Formula (c) defines a criterion for making the Fibonacci sequence pass various statistical tests which would otherwise fail: pick every k^{th} number where k is chosen so that the "golden ratio" to the kth power is relatively large compared to the low order portion of the Fibonacci numbers which is used as a random number output.

```
100   PRINT "INPUT ANY ODD INTEGER";
110   INPUT N
120   LET X = N * 65539
130   LET Y = X * 0.4656612873077392578125E-09
140   PRINT X ; Y
150   END
```

Listing 5: A BASIC program to calculate one cycle of a pseudorandom sequence using the power residue method. This particular program is the algorithm used for a 32 bit machine as found in the IBM System 360 and 370 "Scientific Subroutine Package," IBM publication number H20-0205. In the source document cited, this algorithm is given as a FORTRAN subprogram named RANDU.

Let's assume a 6 bit machine. This should produce 2^{b-2}, or $2^4 = 16$ numbers before repeating, and that shouldn't be too difficult to inspect manually. We want a multiplier of the form $8i \pm 3$ which is close to $2^{b/2} = 2^{6/2} = 2^3 = 8$. If $i = 1$, we'd have $8 \times 1 + 3 = 11$ and $8 \times 1 - 3 = 5$. Both of these possibilities are equally 3 away from our desired value of 8, so let's try both. Table 2a shows how we get started using 5 as the multiplier, and table 2b shows the whole cycle of all 16 numbers produced. Table 2 also shows that if we had chosen a multiplier of 11 the procedure would also have produced 16 numbers before repeating.

You've probably noticed that the two columns of numbers in table 2 just don't look too random. Both columns have numbers that always end in 1. For the 11 multiplier case, the 4th digit is always 0, and the 5th digit alternates between 0 and 1. For the 5 multiplier case, the 5th digit is always 0 and the 4th digit alternates between 0 and 1. Obviously the low order bits are far from random. If you wanted random digits, and not random numbers, it would obviously be to your advantage to choose high order bits, or possibly the bits you discarded when you cut the product from 12 to six bits. The usual scheme, after developing the numbers in table 2, would be to place the binary point at the beginning of the 6 bit numbers, and thereby transform the whole list to a distribution between 0 and 1.

Testing Randomness

Tests of the randomness of a series of numbers usually fall into one of two major categories, those that examine the digits appearing in the numbers and those that treat the numbers as points in the interval 0 to 1. Some tests can handle either case, of which the Chi-square test is one. It can be applied directly to the digits produced, or to groupings of the digits, or we can divide the interval 0 to 1 into subintervals and see how many of the random numbers fall into each of the subintervals and apply the Chi-square test to see if the distribution is biased.

The Chi-square (symbol X^2) statistic looks somewhat formidable, but in reality is easy to work with. The formula is:

$$X^2 = \sum_{i=1}^{k} \frac{(o_i - e_i)^2}{e_i}$$

$$= \frac{(o_1 - e_1)^2}{e_1} + \frac{(o_2 - e_2)^2}{e_2}$$

$$+ \dots + \frac{(o_k - e_k)^2}{e_k}$$

where e_i is each expected frequency, and o is the actual observed frequency. If we had generator which produced 250 digits w would expect each of the digits 0 through to appear 25 times, although the digits migh actually appear more or less than 25 times Assume that your random number generato has just produced a series of 500 digits. Yo count all the zeros, ones, etc, and tabulat these observed frequencies (as in table 3 along with the expected frequency in eac case of 50. You have counted 58 zero 28 ones, etc. You next put these observe and expected frequencies into the X formula and arrive at an answer of 46.45 shown. At this point we need to turn to Chi-square distribution table, which can b found in the back of almost any statisti book. Table 4 shows a portion of such table and will suffice for most of our nee for uses like this application of the Ch square statistic. The table is entered afte you calculate the "degrees of freedom" the column labeled "v" and after yo determine the level of significance yo

(a)

1. Choose an odd integer starting value. We'll choose the 6 bit number 100001 (simply because it'll be easy to multiply).
2. Choose the multiplier. (We've already decided on 5, binary 101.)
3. Compute the product. (100001) * (000101) = 000010100101
4. Cross out the first six bits, and you have the new number.
   000010100101 = 100101
5. (100101) * (000101) = 000010111001 = 111001
6. (111001) * (000101) = etc.

(b)

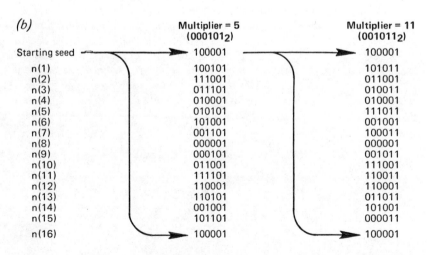

	Multiplier = 5 (000101_2)	Multiplier = 11 (001011_2)
Starting seed	100001	100001
n(1)	100101	101011
n(2)	111001	011001
n(3)	011101	010011
n(4)	010001	010001
n(5)	010101	111011
n(6)	101001	001001
n(7)	001101	100011
n(8)	000001	000001
n(9)	000101	001011
n(10)	011001	111001
n(11)	111101	110011
n(12)	110001	110001
n(13)	110101	011011
n(14)	001001	101001
n(15)	101101	000011
n(16)	100001	100001

Table 2: The power residue method, adapted to a 6 bit example with two possible multipliers. The algorithm is shown at (a), and the complete set of 16 pseudorandom output states is listed in this table at (b). Note the deviations from randomness apparent in the regular patterns seen in the two low order bits of each number.

Digit	0	1	2	3	4	5	6	7	8	9	Sum
Observed frequency	58	28	40	34	70	62	72	36	40	60	500
Expected frequency	50	50	50	50	50	50	50	50	50	50	500

$$X^2 = \frac{(58-50)^2}{50} + \frac{(28-50)^2}{50} + \frac{(40-50)^2}{50} + \ldots + \frac{(60-50)^2}{50} = \underline{46.56}$$

Table 3: A random number sequence can be tested with various statistical measures. One excellent test is the Chi-square test, here illustrated with a hypothetical single digit decimal random number generator with the observed frequencies shown in a trial of 500 cycles of calculation. If the result were truly random, of course, the expected frequencies of each digit would be uniform. The Chi-square test involves calculating the characteristic number shown by the formula here (using this table's data). This characteristic number is then used with a statistical reference table of the Chi-square distribution and the number of degrees of freedom allowed by the statistics (here v=9), to check the quality of the pseudorandom sequence.

v	$X^2_{.995}$	$X^2_{.99}$	$X^2_{.95}$	$X^2_{.90}$	$X^2_{.75}$
1	7.88	6.63	3.84	2.71	1.32
5	16.7	15.1	11.1	9.24	6.63
9	23.6	21.7	16.9	14.7	11.4
10	25.2	23.2	18.3	16.0	12.5
19	38.6	36.2	30.1	27.2	22.7
24	45.6	43.0	36.4	33.2	28.2

Table 4: An abbreviated portion of a standard Chi-square table used as described in the text to check the quality of a pseudorandom sequence.

want to test. The degrees of freedom in our case are $10 - 1 = 9$. This simply means that after we have determined nine of the observed frequencies, the 10th one is fixed. The frequencies have to add to 500, so we have "nine degrees of freedom." Traditionally, the Chi-square statistic is used to test the hypothesis that the numbers are randomly distributed. If the computed value of Chi-square is greater than the critical value read from the table, we would then conclude that the observed frequencies differ significantly from the expected frequencies and we would reject the hypothesis of randomness at whatever level of significance we select. The levels of significance often used are 0.05 and 0.01, corresponding to the $X^2_{.95}$ and $X^2_{.99}$ columns respectively, in the table. Going back to our example, we calculated a value of 45.56, but in the table for nine degrees of freedom and at the .01 level of significance, we see that the critical value of Chi-square is 21.7. Since $46.56 > 21.7$ we therefore conclude that the observed distribution of numbers produced by our generator differs significantly from the expected distribution at the 0.01 level of significance, and we therefore cast considerable suspicion on our random number generator. As previously mentioned, we could take our list of generated numbers in the 0 to 1 interval and set up some subdivisions of this interval. Next, we could see how many of the numbers fell into each subinterval, calculate the expected frequency for the subintervals, and apply the Chi-square test in the same fashion.

A second test frequently applied to random numbers is called the "poker test," but is in reality similar to the frequency test already considered. In the poker test we look for specific combinations of digits. For example, suppose we are generating 5 digit integer random numbers in the interval 00000 to 99999. Probability theory tells us the number of numbers we should have where all digits are the same, like 22222 or 66666 etc. We can also calculate the expected number of pairs, three-of-a-kind and full houses, etc. The Chi-square test can be applied to the analysis of the results.

A very similar test, called the "gap test," can be applied in like manner to the distances separating two like digits or two like groups of two or more digits. Again, Chi-square is a useful statistic in the analysis of these findings. The power residue method satisfactorily passes the poker test, the gap test and the usual frequency test; however it often fails to pass tests which consider runs of numbers. We've already seen how the power residue method produces certain predictable results, so this should not come as a surprise. However, if we are generating

Run length	Formula
1	$(5n + 1) / 12$
2	$(11n - 14) / 60$
k (for $k < n - 1$)	$2 \left\{ (k^2 + 3k + 1)n - (k^3 + 3k^2 - k - 4) \right\} / (k + 3)!$
$n - 1$	$2 / n!$

Figure 3: Several formulas for the run test of a pseudorandom sequence.

random *numbers* instead of random *digits*, this is not a big problem. A study of the runs up and down is often a good test to determine which multipliers are better than others when you use the power residue method, and the "run test" will also consistently prove that the Fibonacci series method will not produce the predicted number and lengths of runs. Taking, for example, a long string of random generator produced bits, we would count the number of strings of zeros bracketed by ones for each length, from one, on up to the longest string length. Number theory helps us determine the number of total runs we should have for both the ones and zeros. Figure 3 shows how to calculate these lengths, assuming "n" bits. There are several special tests similar to the run test, for example: "runs above and below the mean," etc. And, as usual, the Chi-square test is frequently applied to see if the actual results are reasonable.

I can't guarantee all of the above will help you program your computer to play interesting Star Trek or sophisticated One-Armed-Bandit games but at least you'll be able to come up with generators that are biased in your favor.■

Random Numbers and a New Way to Get Them

William L Colsher

Random numbers: what would we do without them? If we couldn't generate them in some way, think of all the things we would have to do without: computer solutions to probabilistic models by means of statistical sampling techniques, Monte Carlo, evaluation of definite integrals, Star Trek, blackjack, and roulette. Fortunately, there are many ways to generate random (actually pseudorandom) numbers using computers, including the power residue method (perhaps the best for most purposes), the center square method (which is slow), and the Fibonacci Series method (which tends to show lack of randomness). All these methods require carefully designed, extensive software, and unless they are initialized in some way, they will yield the same series of numbers every time you start them up. The ability to generate the same results every time is a useful property for some types of experimentation, statistical studies, etc, but it is unsuitable for games.

One way to prevent games from repeating is to use the time of day as an argument in a FOR/NEXT loop, calling the random number routine each time through. This method lacks elegance. For Z-80 users, however, there is a way around this problem. The Z-80 chip contains a memory refresh register called R, which contains a seven bit value that enables the Z-80 user to use dynamic memory as easily as static. The memory refresh register is automatically incremented after each instruction fetch, and while the processor is decoding the fetched instruction, the value in this register is sent out on

Hexadecimal Code	Op	Operand	Commentary
F5	PUSH	AF	SAVE THE A REGISTER
ED5F	LD	A, R	LOAD A REGISTER FROM R REGISTER
2600	LD	H, 00H	CLEAR THE H REGISTER
6F	LD	L, A	PUT RANDOM NUMBER IN L REG.
F1	POP	AF	RESTORE A REGISTER
C9	RET		RETURN TO CALLER

Listing 1: A Z-80 assembly language program designed to create random numbers by referencing the machine's R register. The routine makes use of the Z-80's memory refresh register, R, which increments automatically after each instruction fetch. When the user hits a key, a random value between 0 and 127 inclusive will be present in the register. This can be normalized for various applications.

```
10      LET X=CALL(1792,0)
20      INPUT "MODULUS?",M
30      LET A=INT(X/M)
40      LET A=A*M
50      LET N=X—A+1
60      PRINT "RANDOM NUMBER MODULO ";M;" IS";N
70      END
```

Listing 2: A Maxi-BASIC program that calls the program in listing 1, asks the user for the desired modulus, transforms the modulo 128 random number to the desired modulus, and prints out the result.

the low order portion of the address bus along with a signal telling the memories that this is a refresh. The processor never has to slow down. Keep in mind that R is incremented with every fetch.

Let's take a look at exactly what a random number is. The invaluable IBM publication *Random Number Generation and Testing* says, "Strictly speaking, a random number exists only as a result of a random process." The roll of a die, the toss of a coin and the fall of a ball into a compartment in a roulette wheel are all examples of random processes. Let's take a look at another example. Is not the exact moment that a person presses a key on a keyboard a sort of a random process? Most input routines sit and loop while waiting for a key to be pressed. That means that the computer is executing some series of instructions a number of times. There is no way to determine exactly how many times those instructions are executed. The memory refresh register is being incremented with every instruction fetch, in effect counting how long the computer is waiting for a key to be pressed. In fact, it has been counting modulo 128 ever since you turned on the processor. There are several random factors involved here: the time between turn on and starting the game, the time it takes a person to type in commands or moves, and the amount of work the machine has to do based on the user's moves. There is no way that you'll be able to tell what's in the register, so a random number is obtained. So

```
10    INPUT "HOW MANY SAMPLES?" ,A
20    LET X=0
30    FOR I=1 TO A
40    LET Y=CALL(1792,0)
50    LET X=X+Y
60    NEXT I
70    PRINT "THE AVERAGE IS" ;X/A
80    END
```

Listing 3: A Maxi-BASIC program which tests listing 2 by averaging a run of samples. The average of a random sampling in the range of 0 to 127 should fall on or near 63.5. This program does not give a fair test of this method because the test loop of lines 30 to 60 will take a fixed (but unknown) amount of time to execute, so there will be correlations between one test sample and the next.

```
10    INPUT "HOW MANY SAMPLES?" ,A
20    LET X=0
30    LET B=A/10
40    FOR I=1 TO 10
50    FOR J=1 TO B
60    LET Y=CALL(1792,0)
70    LET X=X+Y
80    NEXT J
90    INPUT Z$
100   NEXT I
110   PRINT "THE AVERAGE IS" ,X/A
120   END
```

Listing 4: A Maxi-BASIC program to improve the program in listing 2. This program stops at various times waiting to further insure that the R register is being examined at random. This eliminates the possibility that the numbers generated will be correlated in any way due to the arbitrary human timing input.

long as the time between references to the random number on the memory refresh register are long enough and not fixed, the number at the time of reference will be relatively uncorrelated, ie: random.

To implement this idea in BASIC, we need a BASIC package with the ability to call a machine language subroutine. This ability is useful for driving peripherals and the like. It also gives us access to the R register.

I use Digital Group Maxi-BASIC, so my example will use the register conventions of that language. You'll have to find out what registers your version of BASIC uses to talk to subroutines. In Maxi-BASIC the HL register pair contains the value returned from the subroutine. So the problem is to get the contents of the R register into HL and then get back to BASIC.

We can't load HL directly from the refresh register, so we first put the contents of R into the A register. We can then load the L register from A, clear the H register (otherwise we won't know the range of the numbers we are dealing with) and return to BASIC. Listing 1 contains the code needed to implement this procedure. Notice that the first instruction is a PUSH. In this way we save the contents of the A register, which we will alter in the next instruction. Whenever you intend to change the contents of a register in a subroutine, it's a good idea to first save the old contents and then restore them before returning to the calling program. This is so important that it is a standard in large installations to save all the computer's registers in a particular way on entry to every program. This enables each program to talk to others, and more important, to talk to the operating system which handles all IO in these systems. One of the most common causes of programs blowing up is the failure to properly save or restore the registers. The next three instructions get the random number into HL; then we POP the A register, and finally return to BASIC.

Now we have a number somewhere between 0 and 127, inclusive. But we often want random numbers to be in the range of some common gambling device. For example, between 1 and 52 for a deck of cards, 1 and 6 for a die, or 1 and 36 for a roulette wheel. It is easy to convert a modulo 128 random number to some other modulo N random number. We simply divide by N and use the remainder plus one as the random number. Getting access to the remainder in a floating point BASIC can be a little tricky, but an easy way to do it is shown in listing 2. This simple program calls the machine language random number routine, asks the user for the desired modulus, performs the calculation men tioned above, and outputs the calculated number.

The numbers generated by a random number generator should be evenly distributed over the entire range. If we generate a large number of random numbers using the scheme outlined above, their average should be close to 63½ (remember the range of the R register is from 0 to 127). This is a necessary but not sufficient condition for randomness. Listing 3 calculates such an average. When I ran this program, the average of 1000 random numbers from the refresh register routine was 64.736, which is not particularly bad. There are several possible problems with the routine as it is written. The major one is that the same sequence of instructions is being executed over and over again, which would cause the same series of numbers to be generated over and over. To remedy this, I changed the program to look like listing 4. I inserted logic to break the loop up ten times, each time accepting a user input. Since the machine loops while waiting for input, and since I varied the amount of time I took to type in a character, the average should have been a bit closer to the theoretical average of 63.5. Sure enough, the average this time was 63.818. Since that sounded suspiciously good, I ran it again, getting 59.533. A third run gave an average of 63.824. I decided to quit there with the conclusion that this technique produces reasonably good random numbers, at least for the purposes of most games.■

Testing a Random

Number Generator

Fred Ruckdeschel

Introduction

One of the most heavily used functions found in personal computer software and even large system software is the random number generator. In personal computer applications it has been largely employed as a means to add chance to games. However, there are also professional applications of great importance such as in the Monte Carlo analysis of semi-random processes or even deterministic systems involving complex interactions. The needs of game-oriented personal computer experimenters are often not very demanding. They hardly care if a random number generator sequence repeats every 10^5 or every 10^{39} numbers. The professional user is somewhat more concerned with the period of repetition of a generated sequence, since excessive nonrandomness can cause significant changes in the results of an analysis. However, in either case the user would feel more secure if the generator being exercised passed at least a few criteria of randomness. In this article we will discuss some simple tests which may be performed to get a preliminary idea of how good the generator being probed is. For more extensive information on the subject, the reader is referred to the books listed at the end of this article. Much of this material is complicated, however.

Computer software designers are usually careful in describing their particular random number generator as "pseudorandom"; there is no perfect generator, though some imple-

mentations come very close. Murphy's law of perversity precludes the possibility of a perfect generator.

There are two general approaches one may take in creating an adequate random number generator; hardware and software. The hardware method is generally based on the quasi-randomness of some physical effect, such as thermal noise. For example, a zener diode may be biased to the knee of its characteristic curve and the junction noise amplified and digitized to create a number sequence having a particular distribution function (a function which tells what the relative probability of observing a particular number interval is).

The software approach appears to be the more widely chosen path, probably because the results are more controlled and predictable (?). Many generators are discussed in the references given at the end of this article. The book references tend to be large computer oriented while the magazine articles are generally directed toward personal computer systems. These generators sometimes create sequences dependent on the computer used (e.g., dependent on integer word bit lengths). Which generator is the best? This is a very difficult question to answer completely. For example, look at the two sequences shown in table 1 which were created by two different generators. Can you tell which was made by the "better" generator? Remember your answer, because we will compare the two generators later in this article.

Table 1. Two 1000 number long sequences. One was derived from a generator which showed obvious flaws when tested. Which generator is "better"?

Sequence A

```
8 2 6 0 4 8 3 7 1 5 9 3 7 2 6 0 4 8 2 6 1 5 9 3 7
1 5 0 4 8 2 6 0 4 9 3 7 1 5 9 3 8 2 6 0 4 8 2 7 1
5 9 3 7 1 6 0 4 8 2 6 0 5 9 3 7 1 5 9 4 8 2 6 0 4
8 3 7 1 5 9 3 7 2 6 0 4 8 2 6 1 5 9 3 7 1 5 0 4 8
2 6 0 4 9 3 7 1 5 9 3 8 2 6 0 4 8 2 7 1 5 9 3 7 1
6 0 4 8 2 6 0 5 9 3 7 1 5 9 4 8 2 6 0 4 8 3 7 1 5
9 3 7 2 6 0 4 8 2 6 1 5 9 3 7 1 5 0 4 8 2 6 0 4 9
3 7 1 5 9 3 8 2 6 0 4 8 2 7 1 5 9 3 7 1 6 0 4 8 2
6 0 4 9 3 7 1 5 9 3 8 2 6 0 4 8 2 7 1 5 9 3 7 1 6
0 4 8 2 6 0 5 9 3 7 1 5 9 4 8 2 6 0 4 8 3 7 1 5 9
3 7 2 6 0 4 8 2 6 1 5 9 3 7 1 5 0 4 8 2 6 0 4 9 3
7 1 5 9 3 8 2 6 0 4 8 2 7 1 5 9 3 7 1 6 0 4 8 2 6
0 5 9 3 7 1 5 9 4 8 2 6 0 4 8 3 7 1 5 9 3 7 2 6 0
4 8 2 6 1 5 9 3 7 1 5 0 4 8 2 6 0 4 9 3 7 1 5 9 3
8 2 6 0 4 8 2 7 1 5 9 3 7 1 6 0 4 8 2 6 0 5 9 3 7
1 5 9 4 8 2 6 0 4 8 3 7 1 5 9 3 7 2 6 0 4 8 2 6 0
5 9 3 7 1 5 9 4 8 2 6 0 4 8 3 7 1 5 9 3 7 2 6 0 4
8 2 6 1 5 9 3 7 1 5 0 4 8 2 6 0 4 9 3 7 1 5 9 3 8
2 6 0 4 8 2 7 1 5 9 3 7 1 6 0 4 8 2 6 0 5 9 3 7 1
5 9 4 8 2 6 0 4 8 3 7 1 5 9 3 7 2 6 0 4 8 2 6 1 5
9 3 7 1 5 0 4 8 2 6 0 5 9 3 7 1 5 9 3 8 2 6 0 4 8
2 7 1 5 9 3 7 1 6 0 4 8 2 6 0 5 9 3 7 1 5 9 4 8 2
6 0 4 8 3 7 1 5 9 3 7 2 6 0 4 8 2 6 1 5 9 3 7 1 5
0 4 8 2 6 0 4 9 3 7 1 5 9 3 8 2 6 0 4 8 2 6 1 5 9
3 7 1 5 0 4 8 2 6 0 4 9 3 7 1 5 9 3 8 2 6 0 4 8 2
7 1 5 9 3 7 1 6 0 4 8 2 6 0 5 9 3 7 1 5 9 4 8 2 6
0 4 8 3 7 1 5 9 3 7 2 6 0 4 8 2 6 1 5 9 3 7 1 5 0
4 8 2 6 0 4 9 3 7 1 5 9 3 8 2 6 0 4 8 2 7 1 5 9 3
7 1 6 0 4 8 2 6 0 5 9 3 7 1 5 9 4 8 2 6 0 4 8 3 7
1 5 9 3 7 2 6 0 4 8 2 6 1 5 9 3 7 1 5 0 4 8 2 6 0
4 9 3 7 1 5 9 3 8 2 6 0 4 8 2 7 1 5 9 3 7 1 6 0 4
8 2 6 0 5 9 3 7 1 5 9 4 8 2 6 0 4 8 2 7 1 5 9 3 7
1 6 0 4 8 2 6 0 5 9 3 7 1 5 9 4 8 2 6 0 4 8 3 7 1
5 9 3 7 2 6 0 4 8 2 6 1 5 9 3 7 1 5 0 4 8 2 6 0 4
9 3 7 1 5 9 3 8 2 6 0 4 8 2 7 1 5 9 3 7 1 6 0 4 8
2 6 0 5 9 3 7 1 5 9 4 8 2 6 0 4 8 3 7 1 5 9 3 7 2
6 0 4 8 2 6 1 5 9 3 7 1 5 0 4 8 2 6 0 4 9 3 7 1 5
9 3 8 2 6 0 4 8 2 7 1 5 9 3 7 1 6 0 4 8 2 6 0 5 9
3 7 1 5 9 4 8 2 6 0 4 8 3 7 1 5 9 3 7 2 6 0 4 8 2
6 1 5 9 3 7 1 5 0 4 8 2 6 0 4 8 3 7 1 5 9 3 7 2 6
```

Sequence B

```
6 9 1 6 0 5 8 5 4 5 4 1 8 3 8 1 7 0 4 0 9 6 9 6
5 8 5 9 8 0 0 6 1 1 6 9 9 9 0 1 6 7 0 5 1 1 8 6
9 4 2 4 2 1 7 0 9 7 1 5 3 4 2 1 3 2 8 2 5 9 9 1
2 9 4 9 9 9 9 6 7 1 3 6 6 4 9 8 2 1 3 8 7 9 1 2
4 5 0 1 0 3 4 6 1 6 6 4 1 2 8 8 1 9 7 5 0 0 8 9
5 9 7 5 5 0 3 5 6 8 3 4 3 0 2 8 1 5 4 5 2 4 5 6
8 4 4 9 1 9 6 8 8 2 9 4 5 5 0 8 8 9 4 1 6 4 3 8
5 8 7 4 8 0 3 2 5 9 4 9 1 3 2 7 2 2 4 2 5 1 6 6
6 6 0 7 6 0 5 0 5 9 5 9 0 9 9 7 8 2 1 1 5 5 2 9
5 6 5 8 4 6 6 9 1 6 1 0 9 0 1 8 6 0 8 7 8 0 7
0 9 5 7 2 4 0 3 1 9 3 5 3 3 0 2 9 7 3 1 7 3 3 8
1 9 4 7 6 2 5 0 2 3 2 1 1 9 5 8 6 5 1 4 6 1 3 2
3 4 5 0 6 2 8 6 9 7 3 8 8 1 0 8 2 8 1 7 5 9 6 2
4 2 7 0 3 4 6 9 8 4 6 1 4 0 8 5 9 1 5 0 6 7 2 8
5 7 8 6 0 5 9 8 0 3 2 3 5 0 6 2 4 1 4 0 2 3 2 0
4 6 5 2 4 9 9 9 6 3 2 3 2 6 2 9 7 5 1 4 6 5 3 4 9
9 1 7 1 1 2 5 6 5 5 2 6 8 8 5 2 7 5 4 3 9 1 7 0 4
7 9 1 0 5 6 5 7 6 9 1 7 3 8 7 4 4 6 8 0 0 9 8 8
4 7 7 8 3 7 2 7 5 7 7 7 0 6 5 5 2 8 1 2 3 6 7 4
6 8 4 3 4 5 3 4 9 3 0 8 3 8 7 7 0 1 8 4 9 1 0 5
4 7 2 2 4 0 9 7 6 8 5 8 4 0 6 3 7 4 4 4 4 2 2 1
1 4 9 6 6 3 9 5 8 3 9 3 1 2 0 6 8 1 7 4 8 1 2 0
4 0 1 6 9 6 6 3 0 4 1 5 0 8 8 6 6 9 5 4 3 7 8 6
3 0 3 5 2 5 2 2 6 4 2 1 1 6 8 5 0 2 1 6 4 2 5 2
6 9 2 6 1 5 3 5 9 7 1 9 9 3 2 1 3 6 8 4 9 5 9 9
4 2 0 3 9 6 5 9 8 0 7 7 6 3 7 6 7 2 2 9 6 8 5 6
9 0 2 0 4 3 7 6 0 6 2 0 3 0 1 7 2 1 7 7 6 1 6 7
5 3 1 4 7 2 8 6 2 5 6 6 7 9 2 6 0 7 2 1 4 4 4 4
3 2 3 8 3 8 0 5 5 3 5 1 4 6 9 6 1 9 5 2 0 7 1 7
8 5 7 3 4 8 1 3 2 9 5 3 1 2 2 9 5 5 9 4 7 5 4 0
9 3 5 9 9 6 4 8 2 4 4 0 8 4 1 3 3 2 4 7 4 9 5 5
1 8 9 3 5 4 5 8 3 1 3 1 7 0 9 8 2 0 2 9 5 7 4 6 0
8 6 0 3 5 6 2 9 4 6 1 0 4 1 0 2 9 1 9 5 7 7 4 2
0 3 5 8 0 2 7 4 3 0 2 3 1 9 3 5 8 4 6 8 6 8 7 9
5 5 0 8 5 1 6 0 6 4 0 8 9 8 1 8 9 3 3 5 9 1 1 9
3 2 3 1 5 1 4 9 2 7 2 8 4 7 1 2 3 1 6 0 9 9 5 7
0 9 4 3 8 4 6 4 4 1 2 3 1 3 3 0 6 6 2 9 7 2 3 4 0
2 5 6 6 1 0 3 2 8 4 4 1 7 8 6 2 7 2 0 0 7 2 6 4
0 1 1 9 9 7 3 1 3 6 6 0 6 7 0 9 4 8 4 8 9 9 3 5
4 6 6 2 5 6 9 6 6 1 4 0 2 2 6 7 8 2 6 6 3 6 0 8
```

122

There are many types of exhaustive statistical tests that can be employed to partially determine how good a particular generator is. Unfortunately, as Knuth has observed (see *The Art of Computer Programming*), a random number generator can pass 50 tests with flying colors, only to be tripped up by test number 51. However, such extensive testing is not necessary in many cases if the intended use is factored in. For example, if all that is required is that the numbers be evenly spread out, then some nonrandomness in the ordering may not be important if enough numbers are used.

In this article we will discuss only fairly simple tests, including some dealing with frequency and gap statistics, with the Chi-Square statistic being the highest level discriminator employed. These tests will be applied to the random number generator contained in North Star BASIC, Version 6, Release 2; to a modification of the same; to a clearly nonrandom generator; and to generators based on doing things with irrational numbers. It will become apparent that even the simple tests demonstrated here are sufficiently stringent to identify some subtle generator weaknesses.

Although the discussion centers on the uniform distribution of numbers, it is not limited in utility to just that class of statistics. For example, it is shown in the accompanying text box on the following page how one may convert the uniform distribution to a normal distribution. If the uniform generator is found acceptable, then other acceptable non-uniform generators can be derived from it.

The software and analyses appearing in this article for testing a generator are given for the uniform distribution case. By using the techniques shown in the text box, a non-uniform generator can be transformed into the uniform one, and the tests shown in the following sections may then be directly applied.

The theory behind the tests to be discussed is reasonably elementary and will not be considered in great depth. The associated mathematics is simple as the uniform distribution function is easy to deal with in terms of integration and related procedures.

Number Frequency Distribution

Consider a continuous (as opposed to discrete) sequence of numbers, x_1, created by a random number generator to be tested. Let this sequence be of length N. If the generator were perfect by all criteria, the *population* (all numbers considered) would have the following statistical properties:

Distribution Function:

$$f(x) = 1 \qquad 0 \leqslant x \leqslant 1$$
$$f(x) = 0 \qquad \text{otherwise}$$

That is, every number in the interval 0 thru 1 is equally likely to occur. Observe that $f(x)$ behaves as a "weighting" function;

Mean:

$$\bar{x} = E\left\{x\right\} = \int_{-\infty}^{+\infty} x f(x) dx = \int_0^1 x dx = \frac{1}{2}$$

E is defined as the "expectation operator". Note that we integrate over all possible

---

The random number generator discussed in the main text is special in that its *probability density function*, $f(x)$, is uniform over the interval $x=0$ to $x=1$. That is:

$$f(x)=1 \qquad 0 \leqslant x \leqslant 1$$
$$f(x)=0 \qquad \text{elsewhere} \tag{1}$$

The random number sequence, $x_1\ x_2\ x_3 \ldots x_n$, which results from $f(x)$ may be one-to-one converted into a sequence, $y_1\ y_2\ y_3 \ldots y_n$, which corresponds to some other probability density function, $g(y)$, by observing that the chance of a number falling in the interval "dx" must equal that of falling in the converted interval "dy". The equivalent mathematical statement is:

$$f(x)dx = g(y)dy \tag{2}$$

The above equation is key to making probability transformations. If some care is taken in setting up the problem, the transformation can be performed relatively simply. For example, assume we wish to convert to a *Normal distribution*:

$$g(y) = \frac{1}{S\sqrt{2\pi}}\ \exp\left\{-(y-\bar{y})^2/2S^2\right\} \tag{3}$$

The first thing done in the name of simplicity is to linearly change variables to $w=(y-\bar{y})/S$. The basic probability distribution to be converted to is then:

$$g(w) = \frac{1}{\sqrt{2\pi}} \exp(-w^2/2) \tag{4}$$

By equation (2)

$$\int_0^x f(x')dx' = \int_{w=w(o)}^{w=w(x)} \frac{1}{\sqrt{2\pi}} \exp(-w^2/2)dw \tag{5}$$

Observe that $w(o)$ is the minimum value of w, negative infinity. $w(x)=w$ is the value which corresponds one to one with x according to the transformation rules given above. Also observe that $0 \leqslant x \leqslant 1$, but $-\infty < w < +\infty$. Thus equation (5) becomes:

$$x = \int_{-\infty}^w \frac{1}{\sqrt{2\pi}} \exp(-w^2/2)dw = \frac{1}{2} + \frac{1}{\sqrt{2\pi}} \int_0^w \exp(-w^2/2)dw \tag{6}$$

Converting to the *error function* notation:

$$\text{erf}(w) = (2/\sqrt{\pi}) \int_0^w e^{-t^2} dt$$

we get:

$$x - 1/2 = \text{erf}(w)/2 \tag{7}$$

Defining erf^{-1} as the inverse error function and going back through the linear transformation we have:

$$y = \bar{y} + S \text{ erf}^{-1}(2x - 1) \tag{8}$$

Equation (8), though not in a functional form immediately calculable by most microcomputer software, represents the transform for going from the linear probability distribution number sequence to a normally distributed sequence. The inverse error function may in practice be dealt with using an approximation to the error function itself (see *Handbook of Mathematical Functions*):

$$T = \text{erf}(t) = 1 - (a_1 u + a_2 u^2 + a_3 u^3) e^{-t^2} \qquad o \leqslant t < \infty$$

$$\text{where} \quad u = \frac{1}{(1+pt)}$$

$$\text{and} \quad \begin{aligned} p &= 0.47047 \\ a_1 &= 0.3480242 \\ a_2 &= 0.0958798 \\ a_3 &= 0.7478556 \end{aligned}$$

The associated error in calculating T is less than 2.5×10^{-5}. To approximate the t which goes with a given argument T in the inverse form $t = \text{erf}^{-1}(T)$, one can search for the zero of $h(t) = T - \text{erf}(t)$ by using one of the zero determining algorithms, e.g., interval halving/doubling; steepest descent; etc..

number values (minus infinity to plus infinity), but find elements only in the unit interval:

Second Moment:

$$\overline{(\overline{x} - x)^2} = E\left\{(\overline{x} - x)^2\right\} = \int_0^1 (\overline{x} - x)^2 dx = \frac{1}{12}$$

Third Moment:

$$\overline{(\overline{x} - x)^3} = \int_0^1 (\overline{x} - x)^3 dx = 0$$

Fourth Moment:

$$\overline{(\overline{x} - x)^4} = \int_0^1 (\overline{x} - x)^4 dx = \frac{1}{80}$$

The theoretical value of knowing the moments of the generator output is that if *all* the moments are known, then the distribution is uniquely determined. Since we know what the moments of the ideal uniform distribution are, we may compare them with those obtained from the generator being tested. If the ideal values are strongly in variance with the observed values, then there is an obvious problem. However, two caveats are in order. First, one cannot in a practical situation calculate and compare all the possible moments of the suspect generator. Second, only a *sample* of the entire population is available from the generator for study (unless it repeats), a sequence of finite length N. Using this sample we may estimate the population moment statistics as follows:

Mean:

$$\overline{x} = \frac{1}{N} \sum_{i=1}^{N} x_i$$

Second Moment:

$$\overline{(\overline{x} - x)^2} = \frac{1}{N} \sum_{i=1}^{N} (\overline{x} - x_i)^2$$

Third Moment:

$$\overline{(\overline{x} - x)^3} = \frac{1}{N} \sum_{i=1}^{N} (\overline{x} - x_i)^3$$

Fourth Moment:

$$\overline{(\overline{x} - x)^4} = \frac{1}{N} \sum_{i=1}^{N} (\overline{x} - x_i)^4$$

As estimates of the population statistics, the above four moments perform the following chores: The mean estimates the average value, which is of clear importance. However, the sequence $\{.1, .9, .1, .9, .1, \ldots\}$ has the expected mean value 0.5, but is definitely not a random sequence of numbers. The second moment partially tests for this. For this obviously non-random sample we

would get $\overline{(\overline{x} - x)^2} = 0.41$, which is much larger than the desired ideal value of 0.0833 (1/12).

It is possible to satisfy the mean and second moment tests, yet still have a statistical distribution which is nonsymmetrical, or skewed (the uniform distribution is symmetrical). If the population distribution is symmetrical, then the sample distribution third moment should be near zero.

The fourth moment can be pictured as a test for "flyers" which are far from the mean, but do not show up in the second moment test. The fourth power emphasizes their existence.

It is difficult to attach clear conceptual meaning to the higher moments, and this path is not pursued further than the fourth moment.

Since we have at our disposal only a sample from the complete population, some misinterpretations may occur when immediately making judgements using the sample estimates. For example, if the expected mean is 0.50, is a calculated mean of 0.48 an indication of a good or bad random number generator? To help deal with this, there is a statistical technique which may be used to get a handle on the *expected* error. For long enough sample sequences we can anticipate (by the Central Limit Theorem) that the estimated (from the samples) values for the mean will be normally distributed about the true (population) mean with the following standard deviation, which involves the second moment:

$$S = \left\{ \sum_{i=1}^{N} \frac{(\overline{x} - x_i)^2}{(N-1)} \right\}^{\frac{1}{2}} = \text{second moment} \times \sqrt{\frac{N}{N-1}}$$

The second moment may be further used to estimate the error in the mean value:

$$\text{standard error of the estimate} = \frac{S}{\sqrt{N}}$$

In the testing program shown in listing 1a, the individual sequence lengths examined are 1000 numbers in extent. The statistics we thus expect for the frequency of occurrence of sequence numbers are shown in table 2.

Table 2: Expected statistics for the frequency of occurrence for a 1000 number long sample sequence belonging to a population which has a uniform distribution.

Mean (and error estimate):	0.500 (±0.003)
Second moment (about mean):	0.0833
Third moment (about mean):	0.0000
Fourth moment (about mean):	0.0125

Text continued on page 130.

125

Listing 1a: Random number generator test program. In this particular version the seeds used are 0, 0.1, 0.2, . . ., 0.9. Repeated use of RND(0) follows RND(seed). Running time is about six hours on an IMSAI 8080/North Star computer combination.

```
10 REM RANTEST7 AS OF 1400 HOURS, 2/17/78
20 PRINT "RANDOM NUMBER TEST"
30 PRINT "WRITTEN BY F.R. RUCKDESCHEL"
40 PRINT "2/6/78"
50 PRINT\PRINT\PRINT
60 DIM X(1001),M(10),S(10),C(10,10),B(10),T(10),C1(10)
70 DIM F(10),B1(10),D1(10,10),D2(10,10),D3(10,10),D4(10,10)
80 DIM P1(13),C3(13),P2(13)
90 REM P1(N) ARE THE CHI-SQUARE EXPECTED VALUES
100 P1(1)=.21\P1(2)=.25\P1(3)=.33\P1(4)=.42\P1(5)=.54
110 P1(6)=.64\P1(7)=.83\P1(8)=1.07\P1(9)=1.22\P1(10)=1.47
120 P1(11)=1.69\P1(12)=1.97\P1(13)=2.17
130 REM P2(N) ARE THE CHI-SQUARE PERCENTILES
140 P2(1)=99\P2(2)=98\P2(3)=95\P2(4)=90\P2(5)=80\P2(6)=70\P2(7)=50
150 P2(8)=30\P2(9)=20\P2(10)=10\P2(11)=5\P2(12)=2\P2(13)=1
160 REM INITIALIZE FREQUENCY MOMENTS
170 FOR J=1 TO 10
180 M(J)=0
190 S(J)=0
200 T(J)=0
210 F(J)=0
220 REM C1(J) IS USED FOR CHI-SQUARE TEST OF GAP DISTRIBUTION
230 C1(J)=0
240 X(1)=(J-1)/10
250 REM CREATE RANDOM NUMBERS AND MEAN
255 X(2)=RND(X(1))
260 FOR I=2 TO 1001
270 X(I)=RND(0)
280 M(J)=M(J)+X(I)
290 NEXT I
300 M(J)=M(J)/1000
310 REM GENERATE MOMENTS FOR EACH SEED SET
320 FOR I=2 TO 1001
330 H=M(J)-X(I)
340 S(J)=S(J)+H*H
350 T(J)=T(J)+H*H*H
360 F(J)=F(J)+H*H*H*H
370 NEXT I
380 S(J)=S(J)/1000
390 T(J)=T(J)/1000
400 F(J)=F(J)/1000
410 REM PRINT FREQUENCY RESULTS
420 PRINT "NUMBER RECURSION FREQUENCY"
430 PRINT "--------------------------"
440 PRINT
450 PRINT "SEED: ",(J-1)/10
460 PRINT "MEAN: ",%8F4,M(J)
470 PRINT "SECOND MOMENT: ",%8F4,S(J)
480 PRINT "THIRD MOMENT: ",%8F4,T(J)
490 PRINT "FOURTH MOMENT: ",%8F4,F(J)
500 PRINT
510 REM FOR EACH SEED SET, CALC. CUMULATIVE DIST.
520 FOR N=1 TO 10
530 C(J,N)=0
540 FOR I=2 TO 1001
550 IF X(I)<=N/10 THEN C(J,N)=C(J,N)+1
560 NEXT I
570 C(J,N)=C(J,N)/10
580 PRINT "PER CENT BELOW ",N/10," IS ",C(J,N)
590 NEXT N
600 PRINT\PRINT
610 REM START NUMBER GAP DISTRIBUTION CALC.
620 PRINT "NUMBER SPACING DECTILE DISTRIBUTIONS"
630 PRINT "------------------------------------"
640 PRINT\PRINT "DECTILE/MOMENT (1,2,3,4)"
650 FOR L=1 TO 10
```

```
660 REM GOTO SUBROUTINE FOR NUMBER GAPS
670 GOSUB 1930
680 REM FOR A GIVEN DECTILE, RETURN WITH GAP MOMENTS
690 PRINT "   ",L,%8F2,D1,%8F2,D2,%8F2,D3,%8F2,D4,"    (",%3I,D5,")"
700 REM STORE GAP MOMENT INFORMATION FOR EACH DECTILE AND SEED SET
710 D1(J,L)=D1
720 D2(J,L)=D2
730 D3(J,L)=D3
740 D4(J,L)=D4
750 REM FORM CHI-SQUARE STATISTIC FOR THIS SEED
760 C1(J)=C1(J)+(100-D5)*(100-D5)
770 NEXT L
780 PRINT
790 REM SCALE STATISTIC
800 C1(J)=C1(J)/1000
810 PRINT
820 REM GOTO CHI-SQUARE STATISTIC PRINTOUT
830 GOSUB 2360
840 PRINT
850 NEXT J
860 REM END OF TEN PASSES THROUGH THE 1000 NUMBER SEQUENCE
870 REM NOW COMPILE STATISTICS ON THE TEN SETS
880 REM CALCULATE MEAN CUMULATIVE DISTRIBUTION
890 PRINT\PRINT "---------------------------------------"
900 PRINT "CUMULATIVE DISTRIBUTION RESULTS"
910 PRINT
920 PRINT "NUMBER FREQUENCY DISTRIBUTION"\PRINT
930 FOR N=1 TO 10
940 C2=0
950 C3=0
960 FOR J=1 TO 10
970 C2=C2+C(J,N)/10
980 NEXT J
990 REM CALCULCTE DEVIATION
1000 FOR J=1 TO 10
1010 C3=C3+(C2-C(J,N))*(C2-C(J,N))
1020 NEXT J
1030 C3=SQRT(C3)/3
1040 PRINT "PERCENT BELOW ",N/10," IS ",%6F2,C2," WITH DEV. ",%6F2,C3
1050 NEXT N
1060 REM Z=0 STANDS FOR FREQUENCY STATISTICS
1070 REM Z>=1 STANDS FOR GAP STATISTICS
1080 Z=0
1090 REM CALCULATE MEAN MOMENTS
1100 M=0
1110 S=0
1120 T=0
1130 F=0
1140 FOR J=1 TO 10
1150 M=M+M(J)
1160 S=S+S(J)
1170 T=T+T(J)
1180 F=F+F(J)
1190 NEXT J
1200 M=M/10
1210 S=S/10
1220 T=T/10
1230 F=F/10
1240 REM CALCULATE DEVIATIONS OF MOMENTS
1250 M1=0
1260 S1=0
1270 T1=0
1280 F1=0
1290 FOR J=1 TO 10
1300 M1=M1+(M-M(J))*(M-M(J))
1310 S1=S1+(S-S(J))*(S-S(J))
1320 T1=T1+(T-T(J))*(T-T(J))
1330 F1=F1+(F-F(J))*(F-F(J))
1340 NEXT J
1350 PRINT\PRINT
```

```
1360 REM CALCULATE STANDARD DEVIATION
1370 M1=SQRT(M1)/3
1380 S1=SQRT(S1)/3
1390 T1=SQRT(T1)/3
1400 F1=SQRT(F1)/3
1410 IF Z=0 THEN PRINT "NUMBER RECURSION FREQ. RESULTS"
1420 IF Z<>0 THEN PRINT "NUMBER GAP RECURSION RESULTS"
1430 PRINT
1440 PRINT "GRAND AVERAGE MEAN: ",%8F4,M,
1450 PRINT "    DEVIATION: ",%8F4,M1
1460 PRINT "GRAND AVERAGE SECOND MOMENT: ",%8F4,S,
1470 PRINT "    DEVIATION: ",%8F4,S1
1480 PRINT "GRAND AVERAGE THIRD MOMENT: ",%8F4,T,
1490 PRINT "    DEVIATION: ",%8F4,T1
1500 PRINT "GRAND AVERAGE FOURTH MOMENT: ",%8F4,F,
1510 PRINT "    DEVIATION: ",%8F4,F1
1520 REM Z=0 DENOTES FREQUENCY STATISTICS ROUTINE
1530 IF Z>=10 THEN GOTO 1870
1540 Z=Z+1
1550 REM GOTO RENOTATION SUBROUTINE
1560 GOSUB 2470
1570 PRINT\PRINT
1580 PRINT "-------------------------------------------"
1590 IF Z=1 THEN PRINT "GAP CUMULATIVE DISTRIBUTION RESULTS"
1600 PRINT
1610 REM RETURN WITH DECTILE Z MOMENTS FOR EACH SET
1620 PRINT "STATISTICS FOR DECTILE ",Z
1630 REM JUMP TO MEAN AND DEVIATION CALC.
1640 GOTO 1100
1650 REM CUM. DIST. STATISTICS
1660 REM CALCULATE AVERAGE FOR EACH FREQ. DECTILE
1670 FOR N=1 TO 10
1680 B(N)=0
1690 FOR J=1 TO 10
1700 B(N)=B(N)+C(J,N)/10
1710 NEXT J
1720 NEXT N
1730 REM CALCULATE DEVIATION FOR EACH FREQ. DECTILE
1740 FOR N=1 TO 10
1750 B1(N)=0
1760 FOR J=1 TO 10
1770 B1(N)=B1(N)+(B(N)-C(J,N))*(B(N)-C(J,N))
1780 NEXT J
1790 B1(N)=SQRT(B1(N))/3
1800 NEXT N
1810 FOR N=1 TO 10
1820 PRINT "TOTAL PERCENT BELOW ",N/10," IS ",%8F3,B(N),
1830 PRINT " WITH DEV. ",%8F3,B1(N)
1840 NEXT N
1850 GOTO 1530
1860 REM COMPARE GAP DISTRIBUTION RESULTS WITH EXPECTED
1870 GOSUB 2560
1880 END
1890 REM ********************
1900 REM SUBROUTINE TO CALCULATE GAPS
1910 REM THIS CALCULATION IS DONE FOR EACH DECTILE
1920 REM L DENOTES THE NUMBER DECTILE
1930 I=2
1940 D=-5
1950 REM D1 THROUGH D4 ARE GAP MOMENTS
1960 D1=0
1970 D2=0
1980 D3=0
1990 D4=0
2000 REM D5 IS THE NUMBER OF ELEMENTS IN A DECTILE
2010 D5=0
2020 REM CHECK TO SEE IF THE NUMBER IS A SPECIFIC ONE OF 10
2030 IF INT(10*X(I)+1)<>L THEN GOTO 2100
2040 REM IF SO, COUNT IT AND BEGIN TO FORM MEAN GAP
2050 REM IF NOT, CHECK NEXT NUMBER IN SEQUENCE
```

```
2060 G=(I-D)/10
2070 D1=D1+G
2080 D5=D5+1
2090 D=I
2100 I=I+1
2110 REM TEST TO SEE IF END OF SEQUENCE REACHED
2120 IF I>=1001 THEN GOTO 2180
2130 REM IF NOT, CHECK NEXT NUMBER IN SEQUENCE
2140 GOTO 2030
2150 REM MEAN GAP TOTAL GAP MEASURED/NUMBER OF EQUAL NUMBERS
2160 REM THIS GIVES MEAN FOR USE IN OBTAINING MOMENTS
2170 REM SEPARATING THE MEAN FROM THE OTHER MOMENTS IS FOR DEBUG
2180 D1=D1/D5
2190 REM RECALCULATE AS ABOVE, BUT FOR MOMENTS ABOUT MEAN
2200 I=2
2210 D=-5
2220 IF INT(10*X(I))+1<>L THEN GOTO 2280
2230 G=(I-D)/10-D1
2240 D2=D2+G*G
2250 D3=D3+G*G*G
2260 D4=D4+G*G*G*G
2270 D=I
2280 I=I+1
2290 IF I>=1001 THEN GOTO 2310
2300 GOTO 2220
2310 D2=D2/D5
2320 D3=D3/D5
2330 D4=D4/D5
2340 RETURN
2350 REM ********************
2360 REM CHI-SQUARE TEST
2370 PRINT "CHI-SQUARE TEST"
2380 PRINT "PROBABILITY:   99%  98%  95%  90%  80%  70% ",
2390 PRINT "50%  30% 20%  10%   5%   2%   1%"
2400 PRINT "               ---  ---  ---  ---  ---  ---  --- ",
2410 PRINT "--- --- --- --- --- --- "
2420 PRINT "DISTRIBUTION: .21  .25  .33  .42  .54  .64 .83 ",
2430 PRINT "1.07 1.22 1.47 1.69 1.97 2.17"
2440 PRINT\PRINT "CHI-SQUARE RESULT: ",%6F2,C1(J)
2450 RETURN
2460 REM ********************
2470 REM RENOTATION SUBROUTINE FOR GAPS
2480 FOR N=1 TO 10
2490 M(N)=D1(Z,N)
2500 S(N)=D2(Z,N)
2510 T(N)=D3(Z,N)
2520 F(N)=D4(Z,N)
2530 NEXT N
2540 RETURN
2550 REM ********************
2560 REM CHI-SQUARE COMPARISON FOR GAP RESULTS
2570 REM C1(N) ARE THE CHI-SQUARE STATISTICS
2580 REM P1(N) ARE THE EXPECTED STATISTICS
2590 REM CALCULATE THE OBSERVED DISTRIBUTION, C3(N)
2600 FOR N=1 TO 13
2610 C3(N)=0
2620 FOR J=1 TO 10
2630 IF C1(J)>=P1(N) THEN C3(N)=C3(N)+.1
2640 NEXT J
2650 NEXT N
2660 REM PRINT COMPARITIVE DISTRIBUTIONS
2670 PRINT\PRINT
2680 PRINT "-----------------------------------------------"
2690 FOR I=1 TO 13
2700 PRINT %6F2,P1(I)," :",TAB(P2(I)/2),"*"
2710 PRINT %6F2,C3(I)," :",TAB(C3(I)*50),"+"
2720 NEXT I
2730 PRINT "-----------------------------------------------"
2740 RETURN
```

continued from page 125.

In later sections we will use table 2 as a comparison test for whether or not the sequences observed fit what we expect from an ideal uniform random number generator.

Number Gap Distribution

In the previous section we discussed the statistics associated with the frequency of occurrence of numbers in a sequence. This led to the comparison chart (table 2). However, we have thus far neglected one very important aspect of number sequences — order. For example, we could take a well behaved thousand number random sequence and order it with the smallest numbers first, largest last, and still not affect the moments calculated earlier. However, the sequence would certainly be nonrandom.

There are at least two paths to choose from in developing a test for order. One approach is to deal with the sequences as continuous distributions and use a complicated (to me) test such as the Smirnov-Kolmolgorov (see *Analytical Decision Making in Engineering Design*). This involves calculations based on the differences between two continuous distributions, the expected and the observed.

Another approach is to divide the continuous distribution into segments (0 to 0.1, 0.1 to 0.2, etc.), assign a simple number to each element which occurs within a segment (if 0.157 appears, call it 1), and look at the statistics associated with such a discrete number distribution. In particular, one could examine the expected and observed mean

Mean (and error estimate):	10 (±3)
Second moment (about mean):	90
Third moment (about mean):	1710
Fourth moment (about mean):	72990

Table 3a. Expected statistics for the distribution of gaps between like numbers in a 1000 number long sample sequence belonging to the same uniform distribution as referred to in table 2.

Scaled mean (and error estimate):	1.0 (±0.3)
Scaled second moment (about mean):	0.90
Scaled third moment (about mean):	1.7
Scaled fourth moment (about mean):	7.3

Table 3b: Same as table 3a, but with scaling for convenience. This table is to be compared with the computer printouts.

gaps between all 1's, all 2's, and so on. Note that, whereas in the previous section the mean had to be between 0 and 1, now it may be between 1 and N−1. Suffice it to say that the statistics are quite different between the frequency and gap distributions. The former is uniformly distributed, while the latter is binomially distributed (Poisson in the limit).

If we choose to divide the number range (or domain) into 10 equal segments such that a sequence like those shown on table 1 results, then the average sequence gap between like values (e.g., the 3's) should be 10. The probability of the occurrence of that number at any one location is P = 1/10. Using P as the probability factor, the ith moment may be calculated from the following equation:

$$i\text{th moment} = \sum_{n=1}^{\infty} (n-1/P)^i \, P(1-P)^{n-1}$$

The moments thus calculated are:

(Mean: $\bar{n} = 1/P$)

Second Moment: $\overline{(n-\bar{n})^2} = \dfrac{1-P}{P^2}$

Third Moment: $\overline{(n-\bar{n})^3} = \dfrac{2-3P+P^2}{P^3}$

Fourth Moment: $\overline{(n-\bar{n})^4} = \dfrac{9-18P+10P^2-P^3}{P^4}$

For P=0.1 (i.e., ten equal segments numbered 0 through 9), we get the values shown in table 3.

Again it is assumed that the means calculated from the samples are normally distributed about the population mean. Thus the second moment is used (divided by $\sqrt{N-1}$) to give an estimate of the expected error, as shown in table 3a. Note that this time the third moment is not 0; the binomial distribution is far from being symmetrical. There is a long, but diminishing tail to the distribution, corresponding to big (but improbable) gaps between the recurrence of like numbers, and this leads to high values for the moments. However, as before we can still compare the expected and observed moments to examine how well a particular random number generator is doing in this respect.

For convenience in comparison (and printout), a scaled down version of table 3 is actually printed by the program. See table 3b.

Once the continuous random number range has been broken up into equal segments, one can consider the observed frequency of occurrence of numbers falling into a particular segment (or slot) and cor pare this against the expected. The Chi-Square test developed by Karl Pearson provides a statistical means for performing this comparison quantitatively. If the expected (from the hypothesized generator) frequency of occurrence for a particular discrete number (or segment) is F_i, and the observed frequency is f_i, then one may form the following statistic:

$$\chi^2 = \sum_{i=1}^{M} \left(\frac{F_i - f_i}{F_i} \right)^2$$

The index M stands for the number of segments, in our case 10. If the generator is truly random, we may expect any particular number (say 5) to appear 100 times in a sequence of 1000. Thus $F_i = 100$ for all 10 segments. If the f_i (observed frequencies) differ markedly from 100, then χ^2 becomes a large number (much greater than unity), indicating the *possibility* that the generator being tested is not behaving as expected. Further, if all the f_i are equal to 100, which is very unlikely, then $\chi^2 = 0$; very small and very large values of χ^2 strongly indicate the possibility that the actual generator is not ideal. Unfortunately, the test is not completely decisive. For ten segments, the distribution of χ^2 values *expected* is shown in table 4. In extreme cases (e.g., $\chi^2 = 0$), it is obvious that the sample does not fit our preconceived notions as to how the generator should perform. However, what does one do if $\chi^2 = 1$, which is likely, but yet not a conclusive proof of the generator validity? In this situation we may plot the observed *cumulative* distribution ($F(\chi^2)$) of χ^2 values and compare it with the cumulative distribution shown in table 4. For example, $F(.83)$ would be the fraction of χ^2 results observed having values greater than 0.83. If the generator is good, this fraction will be near 0.5, or 50%. The program shown in listing 1a also performs this comparison task.

A word of caution is in order when using the χ^2 statistic. It is a test of the hypothesis that the *sample* comes from a *population* which obeys the distribution statistics (the F_i) we have assumed. We have assumed $F_i = 100$. If the "true" distribution were really random, but not uniform, then the test might indicate failure. However, a non-uniform generator can be salvaged for use as a uniform generator by "bending" it the right way. Thus some promising random number generators may be passed over using the results of this test.

The Big Guns

If we were concerned about testing a random number generator in depth and wanted to use a simple-minded approach even though the technique might consume a semi-infinite amount of computer time, the following procedure might be followed:

(1) Create as long a sequence as possible within the memory bounds of the computer. Since the statistical calculations to be performed are of the cumulative or "running" type, the sequence length really need only be limited by the available external mass storage (e.g., disk or tape).

(2) Divide the continuous number set into segments as before. The sequence may now look like table 1.

(3) Calculate the frequency of occurrence of each discrete number (e.g., the number of 1's, 2's, 3's, etc.). Compare these results with the expected values for the ideal population and check to see if they compare within the error estimate (as done earlier). The Chi-Square test may be employed.

(4) Repeat Step (3), but for all *pairs* of neighbors (e.g., 12's, 27's, 91's, etc.) found when stepping two at a time through the sequence. Note there are only N/2 pairs to be checked (if N is even), not N.

(5) Repeat the above steps, but for triplets, quadruplets, etc.

(6) Repeat as above, but for *each* segment, where each segment is subdivided. Continue subdividing the segments.

CHI-SQUARE
TEST

PROBABILITY:	99%	98%	95%	90%	80%	70%	50%	30%	20%	10%	5%	2%	1%
DISTRIBUTION:	.21	.25	.33	.42	.54	.64	.83	1.07	1.22	1.47	1.69	1.97	2.17

Table 4: Expected χ^2 distribution for 10 segments. For example, statistically, if the generator is random, 99 times out of 100 the observed χ^2 value will be greater than 0.21. Thus $\chi^2 = 0.01$ is highly improbable and one would be immediately suspicious if such a value occurred. However, for a "reasonable" generator the χ^2 values observed should span the range, and one must then compare the expected and observed distributions for χ^2.

The above test is extensive. It not only checks the frequency of occurrence of the individual numbers, but also probes the ordering. The reason the required computing time is so extreme may be seen from the number of comparisons (IF or ON-GOTO statements) which are evaluated. For a 10 level discrete random variable, the number of comparisons performed in Step (3) above is 10N. In Step (4) the number of comparisons is approximately 100N/2. The maximum number of comparisons possible (the error in the associated statistics gets poor quickly as the i-tuple gets large) is roughly:

$$\sum_{i=1}^{N} 10^i \, (N/i).$$

For N=100,000 one *might* be tempted to go as far as i=100, or roughly 10^{103} comparisons. The computational weakness of this "big guns" approach is apparent. Thus the need for more limited tests, such as those discussed in the previous sections.

Specific Random Number Generator Tests

The program used for performing the tests as described in the previous section is shown in listing 1a. The listing is fairly well endowed with comment statements and so will not be described in detail here.

Generally, the program is set up to use a given generator to create a 1000 number sequence, and then to subsequently analyse its output. It does this ten times, with a different "seed" on each pass, and compiles cumulative statistics. The actual generation of the number sequences occurs between statements 240 and 290, inclusive. In statement 240 the seed, X(1), is generated. The loop between 260 and 290 creates the sequence, X(I).

North Star Random Number Generator Using RND(0)

Listing 1b shows the computer analysis printout for the first 1000 number sequence generated using the RND(0) generator in North Star BASIC, Version 6, Release 2 seed = 0.0. The number frequency mean calculated was 0.4944. From table 2 we expect 0.500 +/− 0.003. Although the sample mean

Listing 1b: First block of test information printed out using the program shown in listing 1a.

NUMBER RECURSION FREQUENCY

```
SEED:  0
MEAN:      .4944
SECOND MOMENT:     .0817
THIRD MOMENT:      .0004
FOURTH MOMENT:     .0120

PER CENT BELOW  .1 IS  10.2
PER CENT BELOW  .2 IS  20
PER CENT BELOW  .3 IS  31.1
PER CENT BELOW  .4 IS  40.3
PER CENT BELOW  .5 IS  49.7
PER CENT BELOW  .6 IS  61
PER CENT BELOW  .7 IS  69.9
PER CENT BELOW  .8 IS  80.8
PER CENT BELOW  .9 IS  92.2
PER CENT BELOW  1 IS  100
```

NUMBER SPACING DECTILE DISTRIBUTIONS

```
DECTILE/MOMENT (1,2,3,4)
    1     .98     .72     .84    2.36   (102)
    2    1.01     .79    1.00    3.15   ( 98)
    3     .90     .75    1.25    4.02   (111)
    4    1.10    1.00    1.84    7.94   ( 91)
    5    1.07    1.00    2.13    9.22   ( 94)
    6     .88     .81    1.86    7.60   (113)
    7    1.12    1.61    7.54   57.45   ( 89)
    8     .92     .67    1.04    3.47   (109)
    9     .87     .60    1.12    4.87   (114)
   10    1.24    1.39    2.86   13.88   ( 78)
```

CHI-SQUARE TEST

PROBABILITY:	99%	98%	95%	90%	80%	70%	50%	30%	20%	10%	5%	2%
DISTRIBUTION:	.21	.25	.33	.42	.54	.64	.83	1.07	1.22	1.47	1.69	1.97 2.1

CHI-SQUARE RESULT: 1.30

is a little further from 0.5 than expected, there is no immediate cause for concern. The other moments are near what is expected, which is encouraging.

Also listed is the cumulative distribution of numbers which is expected to go in 10% (10%, 20%, 30%, ...) steps, which it approximately does. This information is broken out more clearly in the number spacing (gap) information printout. The values in parentheses are the numbers of sequence elements which fell within each segment, or *dectile* (since there are ten segments). As discussed in the previous section, these data may be used to create the Chi-Square statistic which is shown at the bottom of the listing. The particular X^2 value calculated is a little off-beat (only about 15% of the observed values should be greater than this particular level), but not significantly so. That

is, it is not sufficient proof that the generator is not random. In fact, it will turn out that this generator is reasonably good.

The magnitudes calculated for each of the dectile means is also interesting. From table 3b the expected error (which should be exceeded 1/e of the time) in estimating the mean is 0.3. The worst discrepancy observed was 0.24; the sample means appear to be a little more closely clustered about the population mean than anticipated, but again the difference is not immediately significant. Curiously, a few people who have seen these results had the intuitive feeling that the observed scatter in the sample means was *more* than "normal"; they expected to see variations on the order of 0.1. It is apparent that the cool objectivity of statistics must be employed in such tests.

The average (scaled) value of the sample

CUMULATIVE DISTRIBUTION RESULTS

NUMBER FREQUENCY DISTRIBUTION

```
PERCENT BELOW  .1 IS   10.35 WITH DEV.   .78
PERCENT BELOW  .2 IS   20.05 WITH DEV.   .68
PERCENT BELOW  .3 IS   30.28 WITH DEV.  1.05
PERCENT BELOW  .4 IS   40.27 WITH DEV.   .86
PERCENT BELOW  .5 IS   50.38 WITH DEV.   .73
PERCENT BELOW  .6 IS   60.38 WITH DEV.   .70
PERCENT BELOW  .7 IS   70.61 WITH DEV.   .94
PERCENT BELOW  .8 IS   80.45 WITH DEV.   .72
PERCENT BELOW  .9 IS   90.41 WITH DEV.   .85
PERCENT BELOW  1 IS  100.00 WITH DEV.   .00
```

NUMBER RECURSION FREQ. RESULTS

```
GRAND AVERAGE MEAN:         .4965   DEVIATION:     .0038
GRAND AVERAGE SECOND MOMENT:    .0826   DEVIATION:    .0018
GRAND AVERAGE THIRD MOMENT:    -.0002   DEVIATION:    .0003
GRAND AVERAGE FOURTH MOMENT:    .0123   DEVIATION:    .0004
```

Listing 1c: Cumulative distribution results for the frequency of occurrence. These were compiled from the listings similar to (and including) listing 1b. The standard deviations were calculated from these data. Assuming that somehow the individual values used for calculating the cumulative distribution are normally distributed about the population value, an estimate of the error may be derived from the standard deviation by dividing by $\sqrt{10}$.

AP CUMULATIVE DISTRIBUTION RESULTS

STATISTICS FOR DECTILE 1

NUMBER GAP RECURSION RESULTS

```
GRAND AVERAGE MEAN:       1.0098   DEVIATION:     .1229
GRAND AVERAGE SECOND MOMENT:    .9341   DEVIATION:    .3265
GRAND AVERAGE THIRD MOMENT:   2.1460   DEVIATION:   1.9972
GRAND AVERAGE FOURTH MOMENT:  11.3967   DEVIATION:  16.5569
```

Listing 1d: Printout of cumulative gap distribution results for the first dectile. The same comments regarding expected error estimates apply here as were given with listing 1c.

second moment is observed to be 0.93, which is in excellent agreement with table 3b. The observed sample third and fourth scaled moments are 2.1 and 11.4 respectively. These data are a bit higher than predicted by table 3b, largely due to the misbehaviour in dectile 7. However, there is considerable scatter amongst the dectiles in the third and fourth moments, and the results are actually reasonably good, statistically. This will be confirmed later when the statistics for ten sequences are compiled.

The program repeats the output shown in listing 1b ten times, each time using a different seed for the random number generator. Lack of space precludes presenting these listings here. However, they are partially summarized in listings 1c through 1e.

Listing 1c shows some of the cumulative statistics for the frequency of occurrence. The standard estimate of the error, assuming that the results for each sample seed are normally distributed about the population value, is equal to DEVIATION/$(10)^{1/2}$. The calculated (observed) frequency distribution data vary from the expected values by a little more than indicated by the standard error. However, the disagreement is not severe. The

grand average mean is low by .0035. The standard error of the estimate is 0.001 (as calculated either by using the observed deviation or using the theoretical prediction for an ideal uniform distribution). It appears that the random number generator being tested has a population mean lower than the ideal by roughly 0.7%. In using this generator in a simulation which requires 1% accuracy, this lack of perfection should be kept in mind. However, in most personal computer applications the effect is probably not significant.

The observed grand average second moment agrees with the predicted value within the estimate of the expected error. The grand average third and fourth moments also look reasonably good.

After compiling the cumulative sample statistics on the frequency distribution, the program goes on to printing out the cumulative sample statistics on the gap distribution for each dectile. Listing 1d shows the printout for the first dectile. Again the expected error may be estimated by dividing the standard deviation by $(10)^{1/2}$. The mean, second and third scaled moments are in very good agreement with the predictions given in table 3b. The fourth scaled moment is high, but within the expected error.

The cumulative statistics for each of the gap distribution dectiles are comparable and are not shown to conserve space. The conclusion is that the discrete sequence numbers appear to be spaced apart in a sufficiently random manner that any nonrandomness cannot be detected by the tests employed.

The final printout (see listing 1e) is a comparison between the expected population distribution of Chi-Square values and the observed sample distribution. The distributions are similar but consistently and obviously different; the North Star generator is not ideal by this test. There were hints of this partial failure earlier when the sample mean was observed to be lower than anticipated. However, the Chi-Square comparison plot makes the variance much easier to see.

From what the test program has shown, the tacit conclusion is that the North Star random number generator is reasonably good, particularly with respect to gap distributions. The frequency distribution appears to be inferior to the gap distribution, but the effect is not large. Later in this article we will examine other generators using the same test metric and we will find that the Chi-Square comparison plot appears to be quite sensitive.

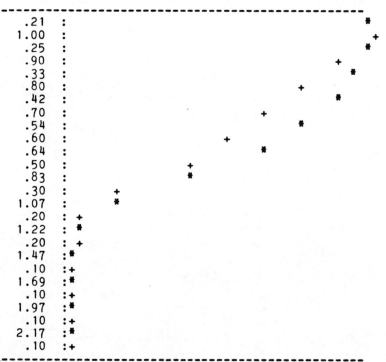

```
---------------------------------------------------
 .21  :                                         *
1.00  :                                          +
 .25  :                                        *
 .90  :                                     +
 .33  :                                    *
 .80  :                                +
 .42  :                               *
 .70  :                            +
 .54  :                           *
 .60  :                        +
 .64  :                        *
 .50  :                     +
 .83  :                     *
 .30  :              +
1.07  :              *
 .20  :        +
1.22  :        *
 .20  :        +
1.47  :  *
 .10  :  +
1.69  :  *
 .10  :  +
1.97  :  *
 .10  :  +
2.17  :  *
 .10  :  +
---------------------------------------------------
READY
```

Listing 1e: Comparison of Chi-Square sample statistics observed with the population distribution expected for an ideal generator. The asterisks (*) represent the expected (or hoped for) distribution, and the plus signs (+) the observations. The numbers in line with the asterisks are the χ^2 values corresponding to the cumulative distribution values listed in table 4. For example, 99% of the χ^2 observations are expected to be above $\chi^2 = 0.21$. The number in line with the plus sign is the actual fraction observed for the χ^2 value shown just prior to that. For example, 100% of the χ^2 values observed were greater than 0.21.

Hybrid North Star Random Number Generator

My interest in testing random numbe

generators initially stemmed from a desire to perform a statistical sampling analysis at work using the North Star generator. To be sure that the created sequences were "even more random", I had decided to use the previous number output of the North Star generator as the seed for the next number in the sequence. Buried in the thought process related to this approach was the intuitive idea that adding more confusion could only do good things. After making some simple Monte Carlo runs it dawned on me that there might be something very wrong with this technique; its success appeared to depend on the first number in each sequence itself being a random function of the seed, which hopefully was the case. Also, if adding an extra step to the randomization was such

a good idea, it probably was already in use in the software. Perhaps I was making the generator *less* random! Thus the testing exercise.

Listing 2a shows the modified generator which uses prior numbers as seeds. (This technique is used in many large computer random number generators. See "Random Number Generation and Testing".) Listing 2b shows the cumulative frequency distribution results for the test. The standard deviation values observed for the number frequency distribution are roughly twice those shown in listing 1c; the variation is a little large. The mean is excellent, but it also has a large deviation. The moments are as good as or better than those found using the generator the "proper" way, but the deviations are

Listing 2a: Statement changes for hybrid random number generator which, after the initial seed, uses the previous number as a seed for the next number.

```
240 X(1)=(J-1)/10
250 REM CREATE RANDOM NUMBERS AND MEAN
260 FOR I=2 TO 1001
270 X(I)=RND(X(I-1))
280 M(J)=M(J)+X(I)
290 NEXT I
```

Listing 2b: Cumulative frequency of occurrence results for the hybrid generator.

```
-------------------------------------------
CUMULATIVE DISTRIBUTION RESULTS

NUMBER FREQUENCY DISTRIBUTION

PERCENT BELOW  .1 IS  10.08 WITH DEV.  1.07
PERCENT BELOW  .2 IS  19.28 WITH DEV.  1.61
PERCENT BELOW  .3 IS  29.66 WITH DEV.  1.87
PERCENT BELOW  .4 IS  40.17 WITH DEV.  1.89
PERCENT BELOW  .5 IS  50.11 WITH DEV.  1.80
PERCENT BELOW  .6 IS  60.54 WITH DEV.  1.64
PERCENT BELOW  .7 IS  70.31 WITH DEV.  1.98
PERCENT BELOW  .8 IS  80.02 WITH DEV.  1.01
PERCENT BELOW  .9 IS  89.98 WITH DEV.   .85
PERCENT BELOW  1 IS 100.00 WITH DEV.   .00


NUMBER RECURSION FREQ. RESULTS

GRAND AVERAGE MEAN:    .5001   DEVIATION:    .0122
GRAND AVERAGE SECOND MOMENT:   .0827  DEVIATION:  .0021
GRAND AVERAGE THIRD MOMENT:  -.0002  DEVIATION:  .0013
GRAND AVERAGE FOURTH MOMENT:   .0125  DEVIATION:  .0004
SYNTAX ERROR IN LINE 2520
READY
```

Listing 2c: Cumulative results for the hybrid generator gap distribution (for dectile 10).

```
STATISTICS FOR DECTILE  10


NUMBER GAP RECURSION RESULTS

GRAND AVERAGE MEAN:    1.0001   DEVIATION:    .0928
GRAND AVERAGE SECOND MOMENT:   .8944  DEVIATION:   .2594
GRAND AVERAGE THIRD MOMENT:  1.7913  DEVIATION:  1.0889
GRAND AVERAGE FOURTH MOMENT: 7.6485  DEVIATION:  5.9769
```

Listing 2d: Comparison of observed and expected Chi-Square distribution for the hybrid generator.

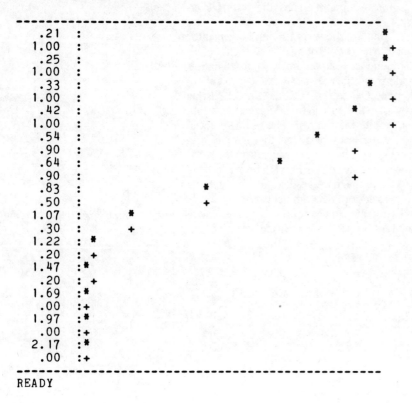

```
       .21 :                                                    *
      1.00 :                                                    +
       .25 :                                                  *
      1.00 :                                                  +
       .33 :                                               *
      1.00 :                                               +
       .42 :                                           *
      1.00 :                                           +
       .54 :                                     *
       .90 :                                   +
       .64 :                             *
       .90 :                           +
       .83 :                   *
       .50 :                 +
      1.07 :         *
       .30 :        +
      1.22 :    *
       .20 :    +
      1.47 :   *
       .20 :   +
      1.69 :  *
       .00 :  +
      1.97 :  *
       .00 :  +
      2.17 :  *
       .00 :  +
READY
```

Listing 3b: Complete printout for the test of the generator shown in listing 3a. Program failed when the fourth moment became too large to be printed.

NUMBER RECURSION FREQUENCY

```
SEED:  0
MEAN:      .5005
SECOND MOMENT:    .0833
THIRD MOMENT:   -.0000
FOURTH MOMENT:    .0125

PER CENT BELOW  .1 IS   10
PER CENT BELOW  .2 IS   20
PER CENT BELOW  .3 IS   30
PER CENT BELOW  .4 IS   40
PER CENT BELOW  .5 IS   50
PER CENT BELOW  .6 IS   60
PER CENT BELOW  .7 IS   70
PER CENT BELOW  .8 IS   80
PER CENT BELOW  .9 IS   90
PER CENT BELOW  1 IS   100
```

NUMBER SPACING DECTILE DISTRIBUTIONS

```
DECTILE/MOMENT (1,2,3,4)
   1     .11      .00       .00       .00   ( 99)
   2     .21     1.09     11.23    116.76   (100)
   3     .31     4.16     83.58   1696.51   (100)
   4     .41     9.21    275.27   8312.67   (100)
   5     .51    16.24    644.51 25844.07    (100)
   6     .61    25.25   1249.50 62475.10    (100)
   7     .71    36.24   2148.46
FORMAT ERROR IN LINE 690
READY
```

greater. However, the gap distribution results (listing 2c) on the whole look superior to those in listing 1d. The Chi-Square comparison shown in listing 2d bears this out. The difference is not large, however.

As pointed out in the literature, (see "Uniform Random Number Generators"), the next level of tests should involve the statistics associated with n-tuples. That is probably where the key differences between the "normal" and "confused" generators would become apparent.

Uniform, Ordered Sequence

As a probe for how sensitive the program is in weeding out poor generators, an obviously bad generator was tested (see listing 3a). This generator puts out the sequence .001, .002, .003, ..., 1. When converted to segments (dectiles) the sequence becomes 0,0,0,0,0,0,0,0,0,0, ..., 1,1,1,1,1, ..., 2,2,2,2,2,2, ..., 9,9,9,9,9. What does the test program have to say about this generator?

Listing 3b indicates that the number recursion frequency statistics are what one would predict (see table 2). However, they are *too* good for a random number generator as there is no statistical variation. Further, the program crashes during the number spacing dectile distribution test as the calculated moments go out of format range. The key item wrong with this generator is that the numbers aren't scrambled as they should be, and the program picks out the flaw immediately.

Square Root Generator

Now that we have a program which will perform some basic tests on purported random number generators, it is interesting and instructive to attempt to create a generator and examine how well it does in the test.

One of the simplest algorithmic forms which can be used is the *residue* generator (see "Random Number Generation and Testing"). In this type of generator we create multidigit numbers and use only some of the trailing digits. The particular case examined is the square root generator:

$$X(I) = A*I*SQRT(2), MOD(1)$$

Listing 3a: Program modification for testing a uniform, but non-random sequence.

```
250 REM CREATE RANDOM NUMBERS AND MEA
260 FOR I=2 TO 1001
270 X(I)=(I-1)/1000
280 M(J)=M(J)+X(I)
290 NEXT I
```

The modulus modifier (MOD) means that we take the resulting number and subtract off as many integer multiples of the modulus (in this case, 1) as possible. The residue is then used as the random number. For example, for A=1, X(1)=0.414214, X(2)=0.828427, X(3)=0.242641, etc. "A" can be used as the seed. The square root of 2 was chosen as a constant multiplier because it is irrational.

The software implementation of this generator is shown in listing 4a. The results for A=1 are shown in listing 4b. The number recursion frequency results observed are (almost) exactly what we would expect from the ideal population statistics; a big mark *against* the generator. The number gap distribution has the right mean (see table 3b), but the moments are quite different from the expected values. The Chi-Square statistic is also very condemning. Therefore we can conclude that this is a poor generator.

The above conclusion is not particular to A=1. The cumulative statistics shown in listing 4c indicates that this poor behaviour is characteristic; the frequency distribution

```
240 X(1)=(J-1)/10
250 REM CREATE RANDOM NUMBERS AND MEAN
260 FOR I=2 TO 1001
270 N9=I*(1+X(1))*SQRT(2)
271 N9=N9-INT(N9)
272 X(I)=N9
280 M(J)=M(J)+X(I)
290 NEXT I
```

Listing 4a: Program change for testing a simple generator based on multiples of an irrational number. In this case A=1+X(1), but X(1)=0 was chosen for the example (i.e., J=1).

results are too tight and the gap distribution moments wrong. The Chi-Square comparison in listing 4d makes the failure very obvious.

The square root generator was used to create the 1000 number sequence shown in table 1, sequence A. The North Star generator was used for sequence B. It is not immediately obvious to the eye that sequence A is representative of a poor generator. In fact, sequence A is more appealing to the eye since it has fewer repeats (doublets, triplets, etc).

Experimental Random Number Generator

As an experiment to determine how much the square root generator could be improved upon, the revised generator shown in listing 5a was attempted. The changes to the square root generator are:
- The seed is a multiple of an irrational number.
- The modulus is with respect to π, an irrational number, rather than unity.
- The frequency distribution is adjusted to make it more uniform. This was only approximately corrected for.

```
NUMBER RECURSION FREQUENCY
---------------------------

SEED:   0
MEAN:       .5001
SECOND MOMENT:      .0833
THIRD MOMENT:       .0000
FOURTH MOMENT:      .0125

PER CENT BELOW  .1 IS   10
PER CENT BELOW  .2 IS   19.9
PER CENT BELOW  .3 IS   30
PER CENT BELOW  .4 IS   40
PER CENT BELOW  .5 IS   50
PER CENT BELOW  .6 IS   59.9
PER CENT BELOW  .7 IS   70
PER CENT BELOW  .8 IS   80
PER CENT BELOW  .9 IS   90.1
PER CENT BELOW  1 IS    100
```

```
NUMBER SPACING DECTILE DISTRIBUTIONS
------------------------------------

DECTILE/MOMENT (1,2,3,4)
   1    1.00    .10   -.03    .02   (100)
   2    1.01    .11   -.03    .02   ( 99)
   3    1.00    .10   -.03    .02   (101)
   4    1.00    .11   -.03    .02   (100)
   5    1.00    .10   -.03    .02   (100)
   6    1.01    .11   -.03    .02   ( 99)
   7     .99    .10   -.03    .02   (100)
   8    1.00    .11   -.03    .02   (100)
   9     .99    .10   -.03    .02   (101)
  10    1.01    .11   -.03    .02   ( 99)
```

Listing 4b: Test results for the simple square root generator shown on listing 4a. A=1

```
CHI-SQUARE TEST
PROBABILITY:    99%  98%  95%  90%  80%  70%  50%  30%  20%  10%   5%   2%   1%
                ---  ---  ---  ---  ---  ---  ---  ---  ---  ---  ---  ---  ---
DISTRIBUTION:   .21  .25  .33  .42  .54  .64  .83 1.07 1.22 1.47 1.69 1.97 2.17

CHI-SQUARE RESULT:     .01
```

```
------------------------------------------------
CUMULATIVE DISTRIBUTION RESULTS

NUMBER FREQUENCY DISTRIBUTION

PERCENT BELOW  .1 IS   10.15 WITH DEV.    .40
PERCENT BELOW  .2 IS   20.29 WITH DEV.    .79
PERCENT BELOW  .3 IS   30.42 WITH DEV.   1.06
PERCENT BELOW  .4 IS   40.39 WITH DEV.    .96
PERCENT BELOW  .5 IS   50.35 WITH DEV.    .81
PERCENT BELOW  .6 IS   60.27 WITH DEV.    .69
PERCENT BELOW  .7 IS   70.20 WITH DEV.    .54
PERCENT BELOW  .8 IS   80.13 WITH DEV.    .38
PERCENT BELOW  .9 IS   90.09 WITH DEV.    .19
PERCENT BELOW  1 IS  100.00 WITH DEV.    .00


NUMBER RECURSION FREQ. RESULTS

GRAND AVERAGE MEAN:        .4978   DEVIATION:     .0058
GRAND AVERAGE SECOND MOMENT:     .0833  DEVIATION:    .0002
GRAND AVERAGE THIRD MOMENT:      .0000  DEVIATION:    .0001
GRAND AVERAGE FOURTH MOMENT:     .0125  DEVIATION:    .0001


------------------------------------------------
GAP CUMULATIVE DISTRIBUTION RESULTS

STATISTICS FOR DECTILE  1


NUMBER GAP RECURSION RESULTS

GRAND AVERAGE MEAN:       1.0008   DEVIATION:     .0086
GRAND AVERAGE SECOND MOMENT:     .1038  DEVIATION:    .0032
GRAND AVERAGE THIRD MOMENT:     -.0283  DEVIATION:    .0008
GRAND AVERAGE FOURTH MOMENT:     .0208  DEVIATION:    .0026
```

Listing 4c: Cumulative frequency of occurrence and gap (dectile 1) distribution results for the simple square root generator shown in listing 4a.

```
------------------------------------------------------
   .21  :                                          *
   .10  :+
   .25  :                                          *
   .10  :+
   .33  :                                       *
   .10  :+
   .42  :                                    *
   .10  :+
   .54  :                               *
   .00  :+
   .64  :                           *
   .00  :+
   .83  :                      *
   .00  :+
  1.07  :            *
   .00  :+
  1.22  :  *
   .00  :+
  1.47  :*
   .00  :+
  1.69  :*
   .00  :+
  1.97  :*
   .00  :+
  2.17  :*
   .00  :+
------------------------------------------------------
READY
```

Listing 4d: Chi-Square test comparison for the simple square root generator.

The tests of this generator for each seed value look very similar to the results obtained with the North Star generator and are not presented. The cumulative statistics are shown in listing 5b. They are comparable to those calculated for the North Star generator. The important test is the Chi-Square comparison shown in listing 5c. It looks good!

Conclusion

The random number generator testing program presented serves as a tool to weed out poor generators from more capable ones. However, the test is not complete. No test is. Additions to the program would probably include more Chi-Square tests, particularly with respect to the gap distribution statistics, and perhaps also include a pair and triplet frequency and gap distribution test along the same lines.

The addition of more tests leads to greater computer execution time. With the current program, ten 1000 number long sequences can be examined in six to seven hours.

```
240 X(1)=(J-1)/10
250 REM CREATE RANDOM NUMBERS AND MEAN
260 FOR I=2 TO 1001
270 N9=N9+(1+X(1)/2.7182818)*SQRT(2)
271 N9=N9*I
272 N9=N9-3.1415927*INT(N9/3.1415927)
273 N9=N9-INT(N9)
274 IF N9<.1 THEN N9=N9+.018
275 IF N9<.2 THEN IF N9>.1 THEN N9=N9+.027
276 IF N9<.3 THEN IF N9>.2 THEN N9=N9+.025
277 IF N9<.4 THEN IF N9>.3 THEN N9=N9+.02
278 IF N9<.5 THEN IF N9>.4 THEN N9=N9+.015
279 X(I)=N9
280 M(J)=M(J)+X(I)
290 NEXT I
```

Listing 5a: Experimental random number generator.

The brief discussion of the experimental generator holds out the hope that personal computer experimenters not having a random number generator can implement one in a rather simple manner similar to the example shown. For the more serious experimenters and users, the references given at the end of this article should prove helpful.■

```
--------------------------------------
CUMULATIVE DISTRIBUTION RESULTS

NUMBER FREQUENCY DISTRIBUTION

PERCENT BELOW  .1 IS   10.32 WITH DEV.    .86
PERCENT BELOW  .2 IS   20.91 WITH DEV.   1.44
PERCENT BELOW  .3 IS   30.83 WITH DEV.   1.66
PERCENT BELOW  .4 IS   40.68 WITH DEV.   1.98
PERCENT BELOW  .5 IS   50.59 WITH DEV.   1.89
PERCENT BELOW  .6 IS   61.77 WITH DEV.   1.64
PERCENT BELOW  .7 IS   71.03 WITH DEV.   1.25
PERCENT BELOW  .8 IS   80.87 WITH DEV.   1.32
PERCENT BELOW  .9 IS   90.65 WITH DEV.    .81
PERCENT BELOW  1 IS  100.00 WITH DEV.    .00


NUMBER RECURSION FREQ. RESULTS

GRAND AVERAGE MEAN:        .4943   DEVIATION:     .0106
GRAND AVERAGE SECOND MOMENT:     .0808   DEVIATION:   .0019
GRAND AVERAGE THIRD MOMENT:    -.0010   DEVIATION:    .0012
GRAND AVERAGE FOURTH MOMENT:     .0118   DEVIATION:    .0004


--------------------------------------
GAP CUMULATIVE DISTRIBUTION RESULTS

STATISTICS FOR DECTILE   1


NUMBER GAP RECURSION RESULTS

RAND AVERAGE MEAN:      1.0004   DEVIATION:     .0805
RAND AVERAGE SECOND MOMENT:    .9326   DEVIATION:    .3064
RAND AVERAGE THIRD MOMENT:   1.9479   DEVIATION:   2.1998
RAND AVERAGE FOURTH MOMENT:  10.2863   DEVIATION:  19.0110
```

Listing 5b: Cumulative results for the frequency of occurence and gap (dectile 1) distributions for the experimental random number generator.

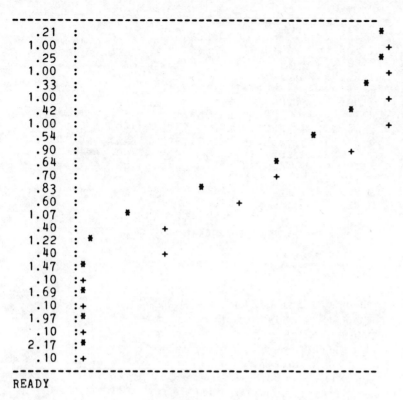

```
-------------------------------------------------------
 .21 :                                               *
1.00 :                                                +
 .25 :                                              *
1.00 :                                               +
 .33 :                                             *
1.00 :                                              +
 .42 :                                           *
1.00 :                                            +
 .54 :                                      *
 .90 :                                       +
 .64 :                                 *
 .70 :                                 +
 .83 :                            *
 .60 :                           +
1.07 :                   *
 .40 :                      +
1.22 :   *
 .40 :                      +
1.47 :*
 .10 :+
1.69 :*
 .10 :+
1.97 :*
 .10 :+
2.17 :*
 .10 :+
-------------------------------------------------------
READY
```

Listing 5c: Chi-Square test comparison for the experimental random number generator. Note, the observed statistic ("+" signs) is shifted one line in printing; the comparison is better than immediately apparent from looking at the plot.

REFERENCES

1. Abramowitz, M. and Stegum, I. A., *Handbook of Mathematical Functions*, Dover Publications, 1970.

2. Grappel, R., "Randomize Your Program", *Byte Magazine*, Sept. 1976.

3. Greiser, D., "Pseudorandom Number Generator", *Byte Magazine*, Sept. 1977.

4. Gruenberger, F., and Babcock, D., *Computing with Minicomputers*, Melville Publishing Co., Los Angeles, Ca., 1973.

5. Horowitz, *Elements of Statistics for Psychology and Education*, McGraw-Hill, 1974.

6. Knuth, D. E., *The Art of Computer Programming*, Addison-Wesley Publishing, Reading, Ma., 1971.

7. MacLaren, M. D. and Marsaglia, G., "Uniform Random Number Generators", *Journal of the Association for Computing Machinery*, Vol. 12, No. 1, 1965.

8. "Random Number Generation and Testing", *IBM Data Processing Techniques Pamphlet*, (C20-8011-0).

9. Rugg, T., "Games and Things", *SCCS Interface Magazine*, April 1976.

10. Sidall, J. N., *Analytical Decision Making in Engineering Design*, Prentice-Hall, Inc., Englewood Cliffs, NJ, 1972.

11. Soucek, B., *Minicomputers in Data Processing and Simulation*, Wiley Interscience, New York, 1972.

GRAPHICS

AND MATHEMATICS

About This Section

Computer graphics is one of those areas nearly everyone who deals with computers would like to know something about, and, since the advent of the microcomputer, computer graphics have been carried into the home, with the graphic video display becoming an intricate part of games and simulations. Also, a new form of expression has been opened to those whose ability lies in the area of programming rather than art. Computer art has become a field of its own.

Much computer art employs the calculating ability of the machine to make drawings expressing mathematical relationships. Kurt Schmucker defines two classes of such drawings and describes methods for producing them in "The Mathematics of Computer Art."

A background in vectors and matrices can give you a set of powerful tools for manipulating shapes on a graphics display. After reading Jeffrey L Posdamer's "The Mathematics of Computer Graphics," you may find that the mathematics is not as difficult as you think.

In "Graphic Manipulations Using Matrices" by Joel Hungerford, you'll discover that a displayed object can be defined within a matrix in a program. Once the object has been so defined, it is a simple matter to do intricate rotations or other operations on the object.

Finally, another type of computer graphics is the plotted image created either by using a regular printer or a special plotting device. A problem that plagues plots, however, is the infamous "hidden line", a line continued behind surfaces, and which in real life one would not be able to see in a computer generated plot of a solid object in two dimensions. A hidden line subroutine for your plotter can make the difference between an average plot and a professional looking one. The algorithms discussed in Mark Gottlieb's "Hidden Line Subroutines for Three-Dimensional Plotting" aren't as difficult as you might think.

The Mathematics of

Computer Art

Kurt Schmucker

Computer scientists and personal computer enthusiasts have a great appreciation of the beauty and form of art. They often use the tools of their trade, the computer and its associated peripheral devices, to create works of art. These works express particular, somewhat algorithmic and mathematical tastes in art forms. Since the late 1960s the use of computers and computer controlled devices for the generation of this artwork (often in three dimensions) has been firmly established. (See references 3, 4, 8, 9, and 14.) A great portion of this artwork has relied heavily on the computer's ability to precisely manipulate numerical quantities to produce drawings or sculptures that express complex mathematical relationships. Drawings in this category include figures which show the relationships between the phase, amplitude, and periods of different trigonometric functions; graphs of functions of two or more variables; and moiré patterns that can express complex relationships by interaction between families of similar simple curves (see reference 13).

This is not to say that all or even the majority of computer art is inherently mathematical. Two of the latest crazes in computer art, the recreation of natural scenes and the randomly drawn picture (called "controlled serendipity" by one artist in reference 11), are in essence nonmathematical. This article, however, will be concerned only with those figures which have mathematics as their basis.

Among figures which rely heavily on mathematics, two classes can easily be separated. One class is distinguished by the fact that it is precisely the equations themselves which give the figures beauty and appeal. While even the mathematically uninitiated can perceive the beauty of these forms, only those who understand the underlying mathematics can fully appreciate the plots. Some

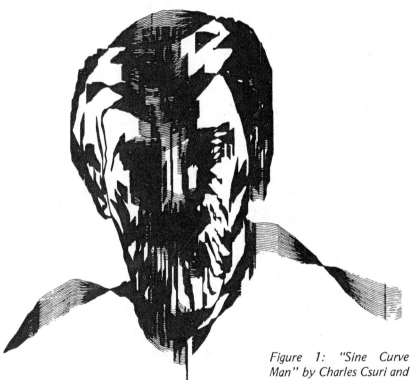

Figure 1: "Sine Curve Man" by Charles Csuri and James Shaffer, a trigonometrically based plot. Reprinted with permission from Computers and Automation, *August 1967, Copyright 1967 and published by Berkeley Enterprises Inc, 815 Washington St, Newtonville MA 02160.*

examples of this class are the endless varieties of lissajous figures (see references 2 and 6), and two other famous trigonometrically based plots, "Sine Curve Man" (shown in figure 1; see reference 15) and "Christmas Wreath" (see reference 1). The beauty of "Sine Curve Man" is in part due to the undulating sine curves, differences in the phase between the different curves, and the variation in the amplitudes. These form the mathematical base for the figure.

The other class of figures relies on mathematics not for the positioning of the actual

Illustrated by:
Alexander A Ames
Systems Analyst
Dept of Defense
Washington DC
20755

lines but for the meaning or the importance of the resulting total plot. For these figures, the actual equations which are plotted are not as important as the relationships which are revealed. Some examples of this class are moiré patterns and projection plots of multi-dimensional figures (see reference 12).

An example of a moiré figure is shown in figure 2. Notice that the lines in this figure are nothing more than regularly spaced radii of two circles — lines whose equations are easily determined. What *is* fascinating is the complex interference pattern, a pattern which can express complex relationships between those lines. In this article, these two classes of figures will be discussed by examining in detail one example of each.

Crest

An example of a computer generated figure which relies on complex mathematical relationships for its beauty is the crest, shown in figure 3 (see reference 5). While the beauty of this figure can be appreciated without examining its mathematics, a more complete understanding is necessary in order to reproduce it on a different computer or to fully comprehend the complexity of the figure. One can easily examine figure 3 and

Figure 2: Moiré figure, an interference pattern between regularly spaced radii of two circles.

determine by its symmetry the decomposition which is shown in figure 4.

The basic unit of figure 3 is shown in figure 5. If the equations which generate the basic unit can be found, then the entire figure can be generated by appropriately manipulating these equations. In an analysis of the unit in figure 5, one can see that the equation of the outer envelope of lines is the only portion of real importance. An examination of this curve brings to mind the spirals studied when one first encounters the use of polar coordinates. There are a number of different kinds of such spirals, most notably the spiral of Archimedes, the parabolic spiral, and the logarithmic spiral. By comparing the graphs of these spirals to figure 5 it can be seen that the logarithmic spiral closely approximates the desired curve. Recall that a logarithmic spiral (shown in figure 6) has an equation of the form $r = ae^{-\theta/b}$, where a and b are positive real numbers. By a suitable choice of the constants a and b, along with some transformations applied to the equations of two such spirals, we will be able to obtain the equation of the desired envelope.

To find the equation of this envelope, the graph of the logarithmic spiral must be rotated, translated, and reflected. The fact that the curve is usually expressed in polar form simplifies this task considerably. All three of these transformations can be expressed much more easily in that system than in Cartesian coordinates. Figure 7 shows the resulting graphs and their equations as the graph of the spiral is progressively reflected about the y axis, rotated clockwise by 60°, and translated.

Superimposing the graph of:

$$x = -ae^{-\theta/b} \cos(\theta - \pi/3) + a \cos \pi/3$$

$$y = ae^{-\theta/b} \sin(\theta - \pi/3) + a \sin \pi/3$$

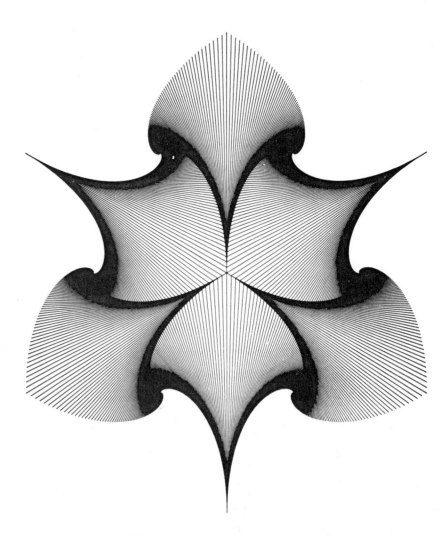

Figure 3: "Crest." This figure is composed of fundamental units shown in figure 5, and the author's algorithm is explained in the text.

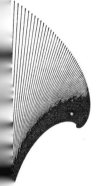

Figure 5: Fundamental building block of the crest figure. The form of the curves resembles a logarithmic spiral.

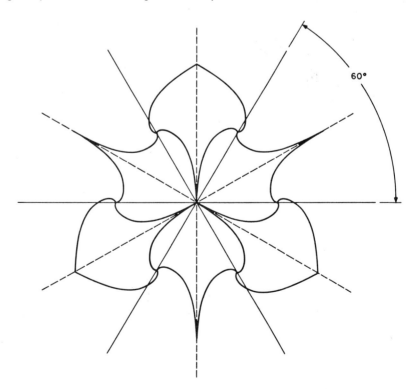

Figure 4: Decomposition of crest in figure 3.

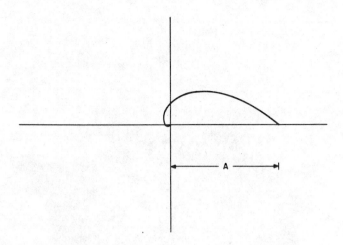

Figure 6: Logarithmic spiral with equation of form r = ae$^{-\theta/b}$ using polar coordinates.

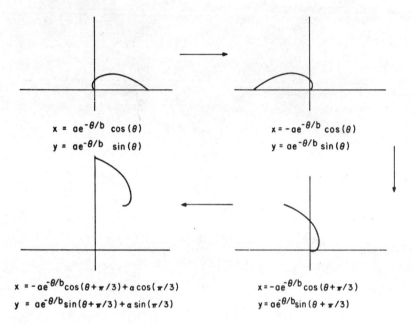

$x = ae^{-\theta/b} \cos(\theta)$
$y = ae^{-\theta/b} \sin(\theta)$

$x = -ae^{-\theta/b} \cos(\theta)$
$y = ae^{-\theta/b} \sin(\theta)$

$x = -ae^{-\theta/b}\cos(\theta+\pi/3)+a\cos(\pi/3)$
$y = ae^{-\theta/b}\sin(\theta+\pi/3)+a\sin(\pi/3)$

$x = -ae^{-\theta/b}\cos(\theta+\pi/3)$
$y = ae^{-\theta/b}\sin(\theta+\pi/3)$

Figure 7: Graphs and equations of a logarithmic spiral as it is reflected about the y axis, rotated clockwise by 60°, and translated.

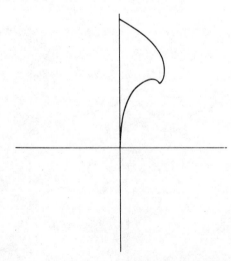

Figure 8: Superimposition of graph of: x= −ae$^{-\theta/b}$ cos(θ − π/3) + a cos π/3; and y= ae$^{-\theta/b}$ sin(θ − π/3) + a sin π/3; which yields the desired envelope shape.

upon the last portion of figure 7, the graph in figure 8 is obtained, which is precisely the desired envelope.

By redoing this work in rectangular coordinates, we can see how much easier it is to manipulate these equations in the polar coordinate system. The reflected, rotated, and translated coordinates of a point (X,Y) can be calculated with the matrix equation which is called *a* in table 1.

Substituting the specific values needed to repeat the previous work and multiplying the three 3 by 3 matrices together, we obtain equation *b* in table 1. This is the same result obtained earlier.

It is now a trivial matter to obtain the lines in figure 5 by drawing chords between points selected equiangularly along each of the two curves. One can extend this by similar modifications to the equation r = ae$^{-\theta/b}$ to obtain the crest in figure 3. The constants *a* and *b* determine the size of the resulting plot and the curvature of each of the six "leaves" respectively.

The Dissected Square

The plot in figure 9 is not too difficult to understand at first glance (see reference 7). In essence it is a set of concentric squares with the area between the squares divided into smaller squares. Postponing the detailed discussion until later, the figure can be constructed in the following manner: given a square with a side of length X, construct a concentric square with a smaller side of length Y. The value of Y is determined by X in a manner to be explained later, but note that Y < X. Extend the sides of the smaller square until they meet the edges of the square of side X. The intermediate result is shown in figure 10. Divide the shaded regions into squares. (It will be shown that this is always possible when X and Y are chosen carefully.) At this point, consider the square of side Y to be the outer square and begin again by choosing a suitable Y' where Y' < Y. This process is terminated when Y assumes a certain specified value. What significant about this plot, however, is the mathematics that it represents. This figure proves the following theorem:

$$\sum_{i=1}^{n} i^3 = \left(\sum_{i=1}^{n} i\right)^2$$

for all positive integers, *n* (an offshoot of the theorem of Nicomachus) for the case n = 2

To see this, it is easier to examine the associated figure for a smaller *n* than 26, say n = 6 (see figure 11). If the smallest square in the center of the figure are taken as unit squares, then the area of the large square c be calculated in two different ways. In the first way, the lengths of two sides can be multiplied. Since we are dealing with squares, any two sides can be used. The left side is of length $6(6 + 1)$ or in general $n(n + 1)$, as can be seen by considering the shaded squares which lie along the left side. The length of the opposite side can be calculated by considering the shaded squares which extend diagonally from the center to the right side to obtain:

$$b = 2(6 + 5 + 4 + 3 + 2 + 1)$$

or in general:

$$b = 2 \sum_{i=1}^{n} i$$

Therefore the area of the square is:

$$ab = 6(6 + 1) \times 2(6 + 5 + 4 + 3 + 2 + 1)$$

or in general:

$$ab = n(n + 1) \times 2 \sum_{i=1}^{n} i = 4 \left(\sum_{i=1}^{n} i \right)^2$$

However, the area of the square can also be calculated by summing the areas of all the component squares. There are four squares of area 1, eight squares of area 4, twelve of area 9, etc. Therefore the area of the large square is:

$$4 \times 1 \times 1^2 + 4 \times 2 \times 2^2 + 4 \times 3 \times 3^2 + 4 \times 4 \times 4^2$$
$$+ 4 \times 5 \times 5^2 + 4 \times 6 \times 6^2$$

or in general:

$$4 \sum_{i=1}^{n} i^3$$

By equating these computations of area, the desired theorem is obtained.

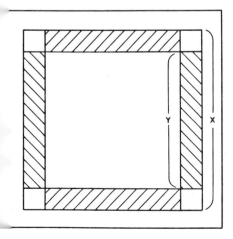

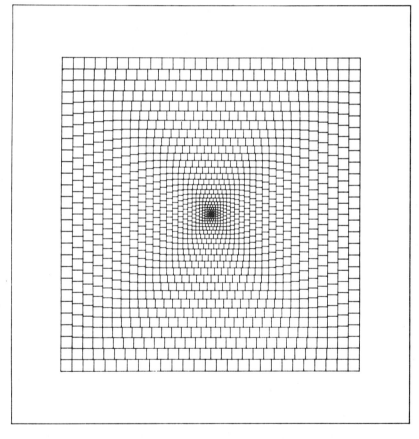

$$
a \quad [x'\,y'\,1] = [x\,y\,1]
\begin{bmatrix} -1 & 0 & 0 \\ 0 & 1 & 0 \\ 0 & 0 & 1 \end{bmatrix}
\begin{bmatrix} \cos\gamma & -\sin\gamma & 0 \\ \sin\gamma & \cos\gamma & 0 \\ 0 & 0 & 1 \end{bmatrix}
\begin{bmatrix} 1 & 0 & 0 \\ 0 & 1 & 0 \\ T_x & T_y & 1 \end{bmatrix}
$$

new point	old point	reflection	rotation by γ	translation

$$
b \quad [x'\,y'\,1] = [r\cos\theta \; r\sin\theta \; 1]
\begin{bmatrix} -\cos \pi/3 & \sin \pi/3 & 0 \\ \sin \pi/3 & \cos \pi/3 & 0 \\ a\cos \pi/3 & a\sin \pi/3 & 1 \end{bmatrix}
$$

$$= [-r\cos(\theta + \pi/3) + a\cos \pi/3 \quad r\sin(\theta + \pi/3) + a\sin \pi/3 \quad 1]$$

$$= [-ae^{-\theta/b}\cos(\theta + \pi/3) + a\cos \pi/3$$
$$ae^{-\theta/b}\sin(\theta + \pi/3) \quad + a\sin \pi/3 \quad 1]$$

Table 1: Matrix equation a reflects, rotates, and translates coordinates of a point (X, Y). Matrix equation b has substituted in it the specific values needed to repeat the earlier equations. We obtain the same result.

Figure 9: Dissected square, a set of concentric squares with the area between the squares divided into smaller squares.

Figure 10: A square with sides of length X has constructed within it a concentric square with sides of length Y. The sides of the smaller square are extended until they meet the edges of the square of side X. The shaded regions are next divided into squares.

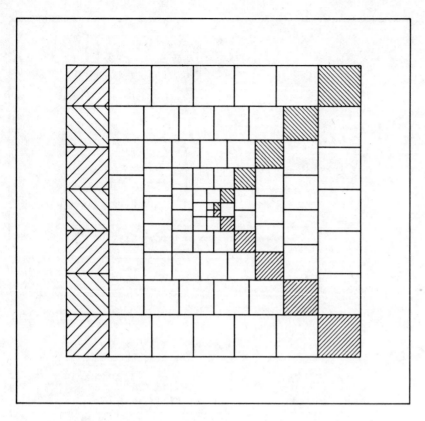

Figure 11: Dissected square for n = 6. *The left side is of length 6(6+1).*

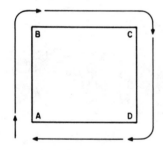 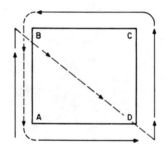

Figure 12: Two plotting procedures for a square with vertices ABCD. The smallest amount of pen motion occurs at left when plotting begins at point A with consecutive drawing movements to B, C, D, and then back to A. In this method the length of nondrawing moves is 0.

At right is seen a nonoptimal plotting scheme. Starting at A, the pen draws to B, a nondrawing move is made to point D, the pen draws from D to C and then to B, a move is made to A, and then pen draws from A to D.

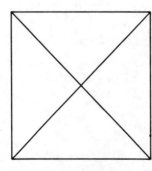

Figure 13: A simple plot for which the best possible scheme includes some nondrawing pen moves.

In drawing this figure, one need only choose an X of the form $n(n + 1)$ for the side of the largest square, where n is an integer greater than 3. The sides of the inner squares are also numbers of this form, obtained by decrementing n by 1 for each successive new square. When $Y' = 2$, the last two lines are drawn, completing the figure. This choice of X and Y always allows the shaded areas of figure 10 to be decomposed into squares, as they are all rectangles with one side of length n and the other of $n(n - 1)$. A rectangle with these proportions is dissectible into $(n - 1)$ squares of side n.

Plotting Considerations and Implementation

In developing the software to produce these drawings, the logic used to understand the generation of the figures was extended into the implementation of the code. Although this solution to the problem works, it turns out to be grossly inefficient in construction and plotting time.

These figures are best plotted on a high speed incremental plotter using ink rather than a ballpoint pen. The use of ink in plotting immediately causes a 50% reduction in plotting speed in order to avoid smears on the final plot. This and the high density of lines required to produce an aesthetically pleasing picture resulted in an average plot time of two hours per figure.

With these two considerations in mind, it became desirable to optimize the required plot time by minimizing pen movement. In the plotting of figures like those above, the total pen movement is comprised of the movement used to reposition the pen prior to the drawing of a new line (ie: when the pen tip is in the up position) and the actual drawing of the line (ie: when the pen tip is in the down position, that is, is in contact with the plotting surface and is drawing). While the total length of the "draws" (ie: when the pen tip is down and drawing) is fixed for any given figure, the length of the "moves" is variable. The total plot time can be diminished by minimizing these moves.

Consider the plotting of a square whose vertices are ABCD (see figure 12). Let us assume that vertex A is the origin of the plot. Clearly, the smallest amount of pen movement possible is $4s$, where s is the length of the side of the square. The value of $4s$ is obtained when the plotting begins at point A (ie: the origin) with consecutive draws to B, C, D, and then a final draw to A. In this case the length of the moves is 0. A nonoptimal plotting scheme for this figure would be to start at A, and then draw to B, move to D and draw to C and then to B, move to A and then draw to D. The total pen movement for this scheme is $5s$

$\sqrt{2}s$, where again s is the length of the square. It should be clear that there is no upper limit on the total pen movement, as the moves have no effect on the resulting plot and can be increased without bound.

Unfortunately, it is not always possible to find a plotting scheme in which the length of the pen moves is 0. A simple plot for which the best possible plotting scheme includes some moves is shown in figure 13. If s is the side of the square, the best possible plotting scheme has a total pen movement of $5s + 2\sqrt{2}s$ (see reference 10).

Of the two figures discussed in detail, the crest and the dissected square, only the crest can be drawn with zero moves. The plotting scheme which obtains this optimal solution is shown in figure 14. Using this strategy resulted in a substantial savings in total plotting time.

Unfortunately, no plotting scheme for the dissected square which has zero moves is possible. In fact, no scheme was found which significantly reduced the total plot time from that obtained by using the notions explained in detail above. It is felt that this is because all the plotting schemes we tried involved decomposing long line segments into a number of smaller such segments which were not drawn consecutively. With an on line incremental plotter this requires the processor controlling the pen to issue a much larger number of plot commands. In a multiprocessing environment, any advantage gained in the total length of the moves was completely eliminated by the increased processing time with its associated overhead.■

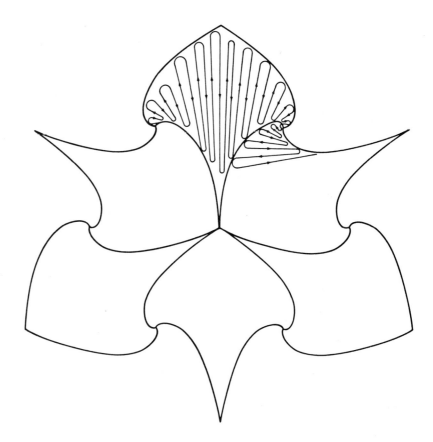

Figure 14: Optimal plotting scheme for drawing the crest with no wasted pen movement.

7. Gardner, Martin, *Scientific American,* volume 229, number 10, October 1973, pages 114 thru 118.

8. Hertlein, Grace C, "Computer Art for Computer People — A Syllabus," *SIGGRAPH '77 Proceedings, Computer Graphics,* volume 11, number 2, Summer 1977, pages 249 thru 254.

9. Ives, Roger, "Computer-Aided Sculpture," *Computers and Automation,* volume 18, number 9, August 1969, page 33.

10. Lewis, Harry R, and Papadimitriou, Christos H, "The Efficiency of Algorithms," *Scientific American,* volume 238, number 1, January 1978, pages 96 thru 109.

11. Mueller, Robert E, "Idols of Computer Art," *Art in America,* May-June 1972; reprinted in *Creative Computing,* May-June 1978, pages 100 thru 106.

12. Noll, A Michael, "Computer Animation and the Fourth Dimension," *AFIPS Fall Joint Computer Conference 1968,* pages 1279 thru 1283.

13. Oster, Gerald, and Nishijima, Yasunori, "Moire' Patterns," *Scientific American,* volume 208, number 5, May 1963, pages 54 thru 63.

14. Prueitt, Melvin L, *Computer Graphics,* Dover Publications Inc, New York, 1975.

15. "Sine Curve Man," First prize winner in the 5th Annual Computer Art Contest, *Computers and Automation,* volume 16, number 8, August 1967, pages 8 thru 21.

REFERENCES

"Christmas Wreath," Entry in the 6th Annual Computer Art Contest, *Computers and Automation,* volume 17, number 8, August 1968, pages 8 thru 27.

"Circus," First prize winner in the 8th Annual Computer Art Contest, *Computers and Automation,* volume 18, number 9, August 1969, pages 12 thru 32.

Csuri, Charles, "Computer Graphics and Art," *Proceedings of the IEEE,* volume 62, number 4, April 1974, pages 503 thru 515.

Franke, Herbert W, *Computer Graphics — Computer Art,* Phaidon, 1972.

Franke, Herbert W, *op cit,* page 18.

Franke, Herbert W, *op cit,* pages 20 thru 22.

The Mathematics of
Computer Graphics

Jeffrey L Posdamer

The personal computing literature is filled with material describing the hardware of microprocessors using video graphics. A great deal has also been written about specific graphic applications including video games, computer art, etc. Computer graphics is, however, a powerful tool that requires for its use an understanding of a set of underlying computing and mathematical principles. The purpose of this article is to present some of these principles in the context of personal computing.

The screen of a video display is essentially a space with two dimensions. While a number of schemes exist for dealing with two-dimensional spaces, the most common is Cartesian coordinates. Each point in the space is represented by a pair of numbers corresponding to its distance from two axes at right angles to each other. On a video display this pair of numbers corresponds to the scan line number and picture element within the scan line. The notation [x y] will be used here to denote the element number and scan line number. Due to the nature of displays, the values for x and y are integers of limited range. Each pair of values corresponds to a unique point in the *display space*.

For many problems in which computer graphics is useful, a second space is used. This is the *problem space* (see figure 1). This corresponds to the description of the problem geometry as opposed to the screen. The representation [u v] will be used here for problem spaces. For Space War its dimen-

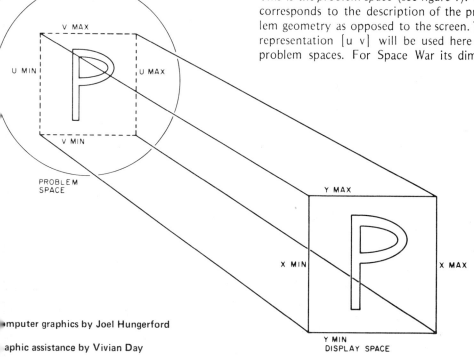

PROBLEM SPACE

DISPLAY SPACE

Figure 1: Problem space versus display space. The screen of a video display is essentially a space with two dimensions, commonly addressed by integer Cartesian coordinates. In creating graphics images, it is often useful to perform calculations in what is called a problem space and later map onto the display space. For instance, if you are creating a game of action football for your graphics display, it may be more useful to perform the calculations with u and v coordinates measured in yards (your problem space) and later convert to the display space with its integer coordinates.

Computer graphics by Joel Hungerford

Graphic assistance by Vivian Day

151

sions may be measured in parsecs, for a tennis simulation it may be measured in inches, etc. Problem spaces may be integer or real, bounded or unbounded and are defined by the nature of the problem, not the use of computer graphics as a tool.

Naturally, there must be a way to convert from one space to the other when both are used. If

$xsmin$ = left screen value
$xsmax$ = right screen value
$ysmin$ = bottom screen value
$ysmax$ = top screen value

and

$upmin$ = minimum problem space u coordinate value
$upmax$ = maximum problem space u coordinate value
$vpmin$ = minimum problem space v coordinate value
$vpmax$ = maximum problem space v coordinate value

then the point $[u\ v]$ in problem space maps into a point $[x\ y]$ in screen space as follows:

$$x = (\frac{u\text{-}upmin}{upmax\text{-}upmin}) \times (xsmax\text{-}xsmin) + (xsmin)$$

$$y = (\frac{v\text{-}vpmin}{vpmax\text{-}vpmin}) \times (ysmax\text{-}ysmin) + (ysmin)$$

In most cases, operating on individual points is only a beginning. Generally, techniques are needed to deal with line segments that connect points to define figures and regions.

If two points $P_0 = [x_0\ y_0]$ and $P_1 = [x_1\ y_1]$ are to be connected by a line segment, it is often necessary to compute every point on the connecting line (see figure 2). A traditional representation of the straight line is of the form:

$$y = mx + b$$

where

$$m = \frac{y_1 - y_0}{x_1 - x_0} \text{ and } b = y_0 - (x_0 \times m).$$

To compute the series of points that would represent the line segment connecting P_0 and P_1, a program would start with the point at (x_0, y_0) add $m \times \Delta x$ to y_0 and Δx to x_0 enough times to reach x_1 and y_1 (Δx means a small increment of x). It is important to realize that m, b and the intermediate values of x and y may take on non-integer values. For each intermediate point, the rounded values of x and y are used to designate a picture element to be displayed as part of the line's representation.

An alternative to this scheme is the "parametric" line representation. Here, the mathematical representation of the infinite line that passes through P_0 and P_1 is not used.

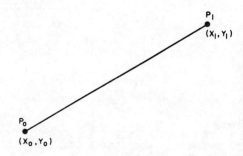

Figure 2: The straight line, a basic element in many displays. If two points are to be connected by a line segment, in a raster graphic display it is necessary to calculate every point on the connecting line. In the case of a vector display, only the endpoints of the vector need be computed.

Instead, we represent only the points between P_0 and P_1:

$$x = (1-t)x_0 + tx_1 = x_0 + t(x_1 - x_0)$$

$$y = (1-t)y_0 + t y_1 = y_0 + t(y_1 - y_0)$$

where t varies from 0 to 1

$$(x,y) = (x_0, y_0) \text{ at } t = 0$$

$$(x,y) = (x_1, y_1) \text{ at } t = 1$$

A line similar to the above line is generated but with simpler, more direct computations

For more advanced systems, a number of hardware schemes for line generation exist Since hardware is not the topic of discussion in this article, refer to reference 1 for a discussion of binary rate multipliers, digital differential analyzers and multiplying digital to analog converters.

Another basic graphics element is the polygon. The polygon is a plane figure consisting of all points inside and on the boundary of a simply connected series of straight lines. For our purposes it is more convenient to represent a polygon by a list of its vertices than by a list of the entire set of displayed points. Polygons raise the issue of the differences between video or raster displays and line drawing vector or calligraphic displays.

The line drawing display has been standard graphics device. It contains hardware to draw lines between points in the screen space. The image is drawn by tracing over each line in the image in the order the lines were specified. Thus, only points on displayed lines are scanned.

The raster display uses a fixed scanning pattern that covers the entire screen. At screen positions which are parts of the displayed image, the scanning beam intensified, causing images to appear on the screen. On a line drawing display, polygon can be represented by their boundaries; on a raster display they can be "colored in."

Displaying Polygons

A polygon is represented by an ordered set of points: $(x_0, y_0), (x_1, y_1), \ldots (x_n, y_n)$. An alternative notation for this collection is a matrix:

$$M = \begin{bmatrix} x_o\, y_o \\ x_1\, y_1 \\ \cdot \\ \cdot \\ \cdot \\ y_1\, y_n \end{bmatrix} = \begin{bmatrix} m_{11}\, m_{12} \\ m_{21}\, m_{22} \\ \cdot \\ \cdot \\ \cdot \\ m_{n1}\, m_{n2} \end{bmatrix}$$

Each element of the matrix is a number, specified by its row index and column index. In memory, arrays are typically stored in consecutive locations in either row or column order. It is necessary to calculate an element address from the row and column indices of a particular element in order to access it.

Given the vertices, how can the displayed interior points be calculated? Let us assume (as is usually the case) that the display scans from top to bottom and from left to right. For each line segment in the polygon, determine the vertex with the maximum y value and sort the edges in descending order by the maximum y value. Every vertex in the polygon is now represented in two places: as the beginning and end of two lines. Beginning with the topmost vertex, a line generation algorithm is used on any line that crosses the current y value. Because of the sort that was performed, line segments which begin lower on the screen may be ignored. Since both ends of the line segment are present, a line is dropped from the computation when its "lower" end is passed. For every line passing through the current y value, the x value has been calculated. The points generated are now sorted by x value.

Starting with the minimum x value, fill in picture elements on the scan line until the next value is encountered; leave empty picture elements until another picture element (if any) is encountered. As the program scans from left to right, the x values occupying odd numbered positions (1st, 3rd. . .) in the x-sorted list cause picture element insertion to begin; the even position elements cause picture element insertion to be superseded. Figure 3 shows how this process can be generalized and applied to an arbitrary plane figure in outline form, ie: a letter "P." This procedure is repeated as the y value is stepped down the screen space

for each scan line until the "lowest" vertex is encountered, ending the figure.

Transformations

Now that the basic graphic elements have been defined in terms of points and a set of algorithms which generate lines and arbitrary figures from the points, it is necessary to examine the operations needed to manipulate points to perform useful tasks. There are three basic *transformations* in two dimensions: translation, rotation, and scaling or magnification.

Translation is the movement of a point or points by an amount in x and an amount in y. The motion is such that neither the shape, size nor orientation is changed. It may be expressed as:

$$x' = x + changex$$
$$y' = y + changey$$

where the *changex* need not equal *changey*.

If all of the points associated with a line or figure are translated by an equal amount, the graphic element is translated without change in size, shape or orientation. Figure 4 shows the effect of a translation applied to our arbitrary figure, the letter "P." Rotation is a somewhat different problem. It involves a computation which maintains shape

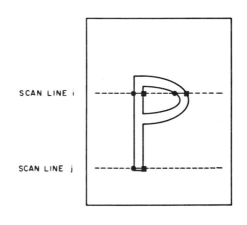

● ODD INTERSECTIONS
■ EVEN INTERSECTIONS

Figure 3: Creating a letter P with a raster scanning video display. During each scan line the program creates blanks until it comes to the first line. After this point it creates solid picture elements until it encounters the next line, whereupon it switches back to blanks. The algorithm states that solid picture elements should follow odd numbered line intersections and that blanks should follow even numbered line intersections.

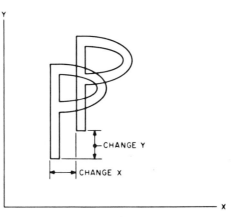

Figure 4: translation in the xy plane.

but changes orientation. A rotation will generally leave only one point in the two-dimensional space with its position unchanged: the center of rotation. For the sake of simplicity, the rotation computation is developed with the point (0,0) as the center of rotation. The polar coordinate representation is used (see figure 5). Later it will be shown how to rotate about any arbitrary point. The point to be rotated, P_0, is at position (x_0, y_0) (see figure 6). This is at a distance r from (0,0) and the line from the origin to P makes an angle of a with the x axis. From trigonometry we know that:

$$x_0 = r \cos(a)$$
$$y_0 = r \sin(a)$$

If P_0 is rotated about (0,0) by an angle of b to become P_1 then

$$x_1 = r \cos(a+b)$$
$$y_1 = r \sin(a+b)$$

but from trigonometry we may substitute for the sum-of-angles form:

$$x_1 = r \cos(a) \cos(b) - r \sin(a) \sin(b)$$
$$y_1 = r \cos(a) \sin(b) + r \sin(a) \cos(b)$$

but from above we get

$$x_1 = x_0 \cos(b) - y_0 \sin(b)$$
$$y_1 = x_0 \sin(b) + y_0 \cos(b)$$

The last of the basic transformations is scaling or magnification. This involves a change in size without change in orientation. Depending on the definition of shape, it is either unchanged or changed "without distortion." As in rotation, only a single point in the plane is unchanged by a particular scaling transformation and once again, for convenience, the origin [0 0] is left unchanged. The equations:

$$x_1 = s x_0$$
$$y_1 = s y_0$$

will scale x and y by a factor s. The factor may be greater than or less than 1. If a

negative value is used for s, then *reflection* about the origin is performed. If the scale factors for x and y are different, then "stretching" is accomplished. Figure 7 illustrates several scaling transformations applied to the "P" figure seen in several earlier illustrations.

Vectors and Matrices

The use of matrix notation allows simplified extensions and combinations of the basic transformations. A matrix is a rectangular array of numbers identified by row and column numbers. Every row in a particular matrix has the same number of entries, as does every column. The notation $A(I,J)$ refers to the element of matrix **A** in the Ith row and Jth column. A matrix has a size associated with it, $[r \, c]$, which defines the number of rows and number of columns. For matrices **A**, **B** and **C** each having the same number of rows and columns, the following rules are true:

A = **B** if $A(I,J) = B(I,J)$ for all elements
A = **B**+**C** when $A(I,J) = B(I,J) + C(I,J)$ for al elements
A = **B**−**C** when $A(I,J) = B(I,J) - C(I,J)$ for all elements

While addition and subtraction of matrices follow in fairly simple fashion from scalar (nonmatrix) arithmetic rules, multiplication and operations similar to division are not at all similar. (A scalar is a quantity that i completely specified by a single number compared with multiple number data constructs, which are vectors and matrices.)

A matrix with only one row is called a *row vector*. Similarly, a matrix with only one column is called a *column vector*. The subject of matrix multiplication is first examined with these simplified forms. While there are two forms of vector multiplication, only the *dot product* (also called the *vector inner-product*) is presented here. Again

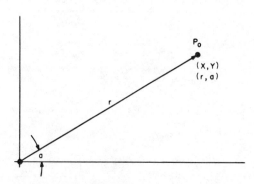

Figure 5: Polar coordinate representation of a point in the xy plane.

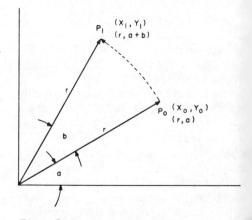

Figure 6: Rotation of vector about the orig

154

using a matrix **A** (the row vector), **B** (the column vector) and **C** (their product) the vector product computation will be described. A vector product can exist only if the number of elements in **A** and the number of elements in **B** are equal. If each of these has N elements then

$$C = A(1,1) \times B(1,1) + A(2,1) \times B(1,2) \ldots + A(N,1) \times B(N,1).$$

This is called the *dot product* of the two vectors. It is the sum of the pairwise products of their elements. C, the dot product of the two vectors, is a single number (a scalar) not a vector or matrix. For example:

let

$$\mathbf{A} = [1\ 2\ 3\ 4] \qquad \text{row vector}$$

$$\mathbf{B} = \begin{bmatrix} 3 \\ 5 \\ 7 \\ 11 \end{bmatrix} \qquad \text{column vector}$$

then

$$\mathbf{A \cdot B} = C = 1 \times 3 + 2 \times 5 + 3 \times 7 + 4 \times 11 = 78$$

Now suppose that **A** and **B** are not restricted to one column and one row, respectively. Instead, we let **A** have size $[r_A\ c_A]$ and **B** have size $[r_B\ c_B]$. The matrix product can only be computed if $c_A = r_B$: that is, the number of columns in **A** is equal to the number of rows of **B**. Two matrices for which this is true are called *conformable*. C will now have size $[r_A\ c_B]$, inheriting its size from both **A** and **B**. Each element in C (which is no longer a scalar) results from the dot product of a row in **A** with a column in **B**:

$$C(I,J) = A(I,1) \times B(1,J) + A(I,2) \times B(2,J) \ldots + A(I,N) \times B(N,J)$$

where

$$N = c_A = r_B$$

and where I takes on all integer values from 1 to r_A and J takes on all integer values from 1 to c_B. For example:

let

$$\mathbf{A} = \begin{bmatrix} 1 & 2 \\ 5 & 7 \\ 3 & -1 \end{bmatrix}$$

$$r_A = 3$$
$$c_A = 2$$

$$\mathbf{B} = \begin{bmatrix} 3 & 1 & 4 & 1 \\ 5 & 9 & 2 & 6 \end{bmatrix}$$

$$r_B = 2$$
$$c_B = 4$$

The number of columns in matrix **A** is equal to the number of rows in matrix **B**. In equation form, this means that:

$$c_A = r_B = 2$$
$$[r_c\ c_c] = [3\ 4]$$

Therefore, we can calculate the matrix result C:

$$\mathbf{C} = \begin{bmatrix} 1\times3+ & 1\times1+ & 1\times4+ & 1\times1+ \\ 2\times5 & 2\times9 & 2\times2 & 2\times6 \\ 5\times3+ & 5\times1+ & 5\times4+ & 5\times1+ \\ 7\times5 & 7\times9 & 7\times2 & 7\times6 \\ 3\times3- & 3\times1- & 3\times4- & 3\times1- \\ 1\times5 & 1\times9 & 1\times2 & 1\times6 \end{bmatrix}$$

$$\mathbf{C} = \begin{bmatrix} 13 & 19 & 8 & 13 \\ 50 & 68 & 34 & 47 \\ 4 & -6 & 10 & -3 \end{bmatrix}$$

For any matrix M there is a special matrix which, when multiplied by M, yields **M**. This is called the *identity* matrix (**I**). It is similar in role to the value 1 in scalar multiplication. Naturally, the identity matrix must be conformable with a particular M. **I** is a square matrix, with zeros everywhere but on the diagonal, where the value 1 is placed. The

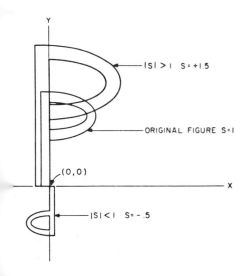

Figure 7: Scaling an arbitrary figure in the xy plane.

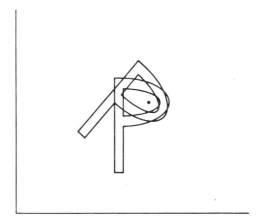

Figure 8: Rotation of an arbitrary figure about an arbitrary point.

diagonal is the set of elements where the row index equals the column index. For example, if I and M are both 3 by 3 matrices, then $IM = M$:

$$\begin{bmatrix} 1 & 0 & 0 \\ 0 & 1 & 0 \\ 0 & 0 & 1 \end{bmatrix} M = M$$

Now let's turn back to rotations, and see how these may be applied to a collection of points describing a figure on the display screen.

Two comments are worth noting at this stage. It is often useful and necessary to apply the same transformation to several points. This occurs when applying a transformation to items such as polygons or more complex collections of points. Additionally, it is useful to combine basic transformations to create more complex transformations.

A collection of points may be represented as a matrix:

$$\begin{bmatrix} x_0 & y_0 \\ x_1 & y_1 \\ \cdot \\ \cdot \\ \cdot \\ x_n & y_n \end{bmatrix}$$

Recall the basic operations of scaling, rotation and translation:

Scaling (about the origin)
$$x_1 = s_x x_0$$
$$y_1 = s_y y_0$$

Rotation (about the origin)
$$x_1 = x_0 \cos(b) - y_0 \sin(b)$$
$$y_1 = x_0 \sin(b) + y_0 \cos(b)$$

Translation
$$x_1 = x_0 + changex$$
$$y_1 = y_0 + changey.$$

If these transformations could be represented as appropriate matrices, they could be applied simultaneously to all points in the collection. Scaling may be represented in matrix form as:

$$[x' \ y'] = [x \ y] \begin{bmatrix} s_x & 0 \\ 0 & s_y \end{bmatrix}$$

or, for a collection of points:

$$\begin{bmatrix} x_0' & y_0' \\ \cdot \\ \cdot \\ \cdot \\ x_n' & y_n' \end{bmatrix} = \begin{bmatrix} x_0 & y_0 \\ \cdot \\ \cdot \\ \cdot \\ x_n & y_n \end{bmatrix} \begin{bmatrix} s_x & 0 \\ 0 & s_y \end{bmatrix}$$

Rotation through angle b about the origin may be represented as:

$$\begin{bmatrix} x_0' & y_0' \\ \cdot \\ \cdot \\ \cdot \\ x_n' & y_n' \end{bmatrix} = \begin{bmatrix} x_0 & y_0 \\ \cdot \\ \cdot \\ \cdot \\ x_n & y_n \end{bmatrix} \begin{bmatrix} \cos(b) & \sin(b) \\ -\sin(b) & \cos(b) \end{bmatrix}$$

Translation presents a somewhat more difficult problem. No 2 by 2 transformation matrix can be devised that will transform a group of points by a uniform displacement. An alternative representation of the translation is:

$$x' = (x)1 + (y)0 + 1 \cdot changex$$
$$y' = (x)0 + (y)1 + 1 \cdot changey$$

If we now represent all points in two-dimensional space with a 3 element vector of the form $[x \ y \ 1]$ for the point at $[x \ y]$, then the translation operation may be represented in matrix form as

$$\begin{bmatrix} x_0' & y_0' & 1 \\ \cdot \\ \cdot \\ x_n' & y_n' & 1 \end{bmatrix} = \begin{bmatrix} x_0 & y_0 & 1 \\ \cdot \\ \cdot \\ x_n & y_n & 1 \end{bmatrix}$$

$$\begin{bmatrix} 1 & 0 & 0 \\ 0 & 1 & 0 \\ changex & changey & 1 \end{bmatrix}$$

Note that a third (unnecessary) column is added to the translation matrix to make the results have the same dimensions as the input points.

The scaling matrix is now rewritten as:

$$\begin{bmatrix} s_x & 0 & 0 \\ 0 & s_y & 0 \\ 0 & 0 & 1 \end{bmatrix}$$

The rotation matrix is now:

$$\begin{bmatrix} \cos(b) & \sin(b) & 0 \\ -\sin(b) & \cos(b) & 0 \\ 0 & 0 & 1 \end{bmatrix}$$

The use of an n+1 element vector to represent a point in n-dimensional space is known as the use of *homogeneous coordinates*.

Now that a uniform representation, the 3 by 3 matrix, is available for transformations, two questions arise: (1) How can more complex transformations be implemented? (2) What effects are obtained from matrices which do not fit into the special structure generated for the basic transformations?

Most complex geometric operations may be implemented as a sequence of basic operations. A few examples are examined next.

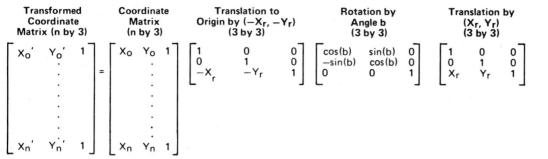

| Transformed Coordinate Matrix (n by 3) | Coordinate Matrix (n by 3) | Translation to Origin by $(-X_r, -Y_r)$ (3 by 3) | Rotation by Angle b (3 by 3) | Translation by (X_r, Y_r) (3 by 3) |

$$\begin{bmatrix} X_0' & Y_0' & 1 \\ & \cdot & \\ & \cdot & \\ & \cdot & \\ & \cdot & \\ & \cdot & \\ X_n' & Y_n' & 1 \end{bmatrix} = \begin{bmatrix} X_0 & Y_0 & 1 \\ & \cdot & \\ & \cdot & \\ & \cdot & \\ & \cdot & \\ & \cdot & \\ X_n & Y_n & 1 \end{bmatrix} \begin{bmatrix} 1 & 0 & 0 \\ 0 & 1 & 0 \\ -X_r & -Y_r & 1 \end{bmatrix} \begin{bmatrix} \cos(b) & \sin(b) & 0 \\ -\sin(b) & \cos(b) & 0 \\ 0 & 0 & 1 \end{bmatrix} \begin{bmatrix} 1 & 0 & 0 \\ 0 & 1 & 0 \\ X_r & Y_r & 1 \end{bmatrix}$$

Example 1.

Rotation About an Arbitrary Point $[x_r \, y_r \, 1]$

Since we know how to rotate about the origin, the point R and the object are first moved to the origin. The object is then rotated and the system moved back so that R is at its original location. A matrix representation of this procedure is shown in example 1. The point R will be unchanged by this sequence of transformations. Transformations are *not* generally commutative; ie: the order of application of the transformations *is fixed* to achieve a particular combined result.

A similar statement is true for matrix multiplication:

$$AB \neq BA \quad \text{in general.}$$

But, matrix multiplication is *associative*. That is, if the order of the matrices is fixed, the order in which the individual multiplications is performed does not matter as far as the value of the result is concerned. Thus, in the example shown, we could combine the last three (transformation) matrices by multiplication to yield a single 3 by 3 matrix which represents the combined transformation. If more than three points are represented in the coordinate matrix, this technique will reduce the amount of computation necessary to calculate the result.

As a general comment, it is useful to decompose complex transformations into a series of basic transformations. Any transformation which preserves shape in the sense discussed above can be decomposed into a series of basic transformations represented as matrices. The product of these matrices will be the matrix representation of the complex transformation.

A general 3 by 3 matrix might be represented by:

$$T_3 = \begin{bmatrix} a & b & c \\ d & e & f \\ g & i & j \end{bmatrix}$$

(h intentionally omitted)

Three special cases of this matrix have been presented that represent the basic transformations. While the products of such basic transformations can yield many of the cases of the general T_3 matrix, it is useful to examine some other simple cases. The 3 by 3 identity matrix:

$$I_3 = \begin{bmatrix} 1 & 0 & 0 \\ 0 & 1 & 0 \\ 0 & 0 & 1 \end{bmatrix}$$

yields a result identical to the original set of points. This is a *null* transformation. The effect of setting elements *a* and *e* (referring to the general T_3 matrix elements) equal to other values results in scaling. Setting elements *g* and *i* to nonzero values creates a translation. The process of setting element *b* to a nonzero value is shown in the following equations:

$$x' = x$$
$$y' = bx + y$$

The effect of this change on our figure "P" test pattern is shown in figure 9. This type of transformation is known as a y shear. Note how the "P" has been distorted in the y direction only by this operation.

Similarly, setting element *d* equal to a nonzero value causes an x shear as shown in figure 10:

$$x' = x + dy$$
$$y' = y$$

If element *c* or element *f* is nonzero, or if element *i* is not one, the result of the transformation is of the form:

$$h \neq 1$$
$$[hx \, hy \, h]$$

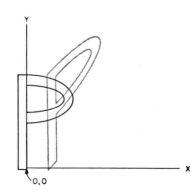

Figure 9: An example of y shear.

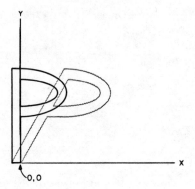

Figure 10: An example of x shear.

Here, *hx* and *hy* are considered to be *biliteral* (2 letter) symbols or variable names, *not* products of *h* and *x* or *y*. In this case, we divide each element of the vector by the last (or homogeneous) element. Thus, the coordinates of the point (x,y) in two-space may be represented by an infinite number of homogeneous representations $[hx\ hy\ h]$. The process of dividing through by the homogeneous coordinate is known as homogeneous normalization (see table 1).

A particular problem arises when $h = 0$. In this case, division is undefined. An understanding of this situation is attained by letting *h* go to zero.

The value of the normalized point in table 1 goes out along a line from the origin through the point $[a\ b]$; as *h* approaches zero, the point goes to infinity. Thus the representation $[a\ b\ 0]$ defines a point at infinity along the line from the origin through $[a\ b]$. This representation of points at infinity is completely consistent with all previous discussion and definitions of transformations. The only truly undefined homogeneous value in two-dimensional space is $[0\ 0\ 0]$.

In transforming graphic elements, a problem may arise regarding the screen space boundaries. Portions of objects may fall outside the screen space after transformation. A similar situation may arise when objects are converted from problem space to screen space. It is therefore necessary to have a procedure for "clipping" the portions of objects outside the screen space so that the on-screen portion is accurately portrayed. The procedure described operates on the typical 4 sided rectangular screen.

The screen may be defined by four inequalities:

$$x \geqslant x_\ell \qquad x_\ell = \text{leftmost x value}$$
$$x \leqslant x_r \qquad x_r = \text{rightmost x value}$$
$$y \geqslant y_b \qquad y_b = \text{bottom y value}$$
$$y \leqslant y_t \qquad y_t = \text{top y value}$$

The procedure operates on each line segment in the image and determines what portion, if any, lies in the screen space.

The two endpoints of each line segment are classified as satisfying or not satisfying each of the four inequalities. Three specific cases may result from this endpoint coding:

(a) Both endpoints satisfy all inequalities.
(b) Both endpoints do not satisfy the same inequality.
(c) Neither of the above.

In case (a) the entire line lies within the screen space and is therefore displayed. In case (b) the entire line lies outside the screen space and is therefore not displayed. Case (c) requires further treatment.

The visible portion (if any) of each case (c) line is determined by cutting it with every inequality line (screen boundary) which is violated by either endpoint. Each inequality or clipping boundary not satisfied will cut the line into two portions, visible and invisible. The portion remaining, if any, will be the line segment visible in the screen space.

One approach to determining the point at which a line is cut by a boundary is derived from geometry (see figure 12a). The formulas for the left x boundary can be derived and the x_r, y_b and y_t results follow in similar fashion. By similar triangles:

$$\frac{y_s - y_0}{x_c - x_0} = \frac{y_1 - y_0}{x_1 - x_0}$$

but

$$x_c = x_\ell$$

so

$$y_c = y_0 + \left(\frac{y_1 - y_0}{x_1 - x_0}\right)(x_\ell - x_0)$$

The visible portion of the line is from (x_ℓ, y) to (x_1, y_1).

An alternative approach, the clipping divider, is more suitable for microprocessor implementation since it uses neither multiplication nor division. It is actually a type of

Homogeneous Representation			Normalized Representation	
hx	hy	h	x	y
a	b	1	a	b
a	b	.1	10a	10b
a	b	.01	100a	100b
.	.	.	.	.
.	.	.	.	.
.	.	.	.	.
a	b	0	undefined	undefined

Table 1: Homogeneous versus normalized representation of coordinates in two-dimensional space. The homogeneous representation of the coordinate pairs is a way of encoding the numbers in a general manner using the extra element h in the matrix row. The values of the coordinates are found by dividing h into each coordinate (expressed here as variable names, ie: "hx"; this does not mean "h times x"). The results are shown in the right side of the table. The extra column in the homogeneous form of the matrix is needed to make the matrix conformable with other matrices used for translation operations.

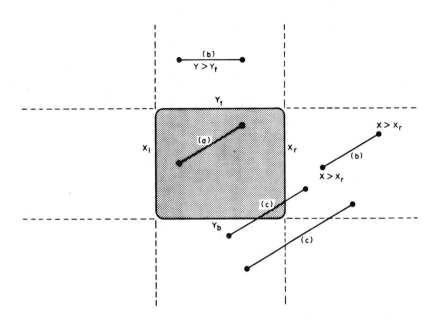

Figure 11: Three different ways a line can appear. Line (a) is completely within the borders of the video screen. The lines labeled (b) are completely outside of the screen area, and the lines labeled (c) are partially within the screen area.

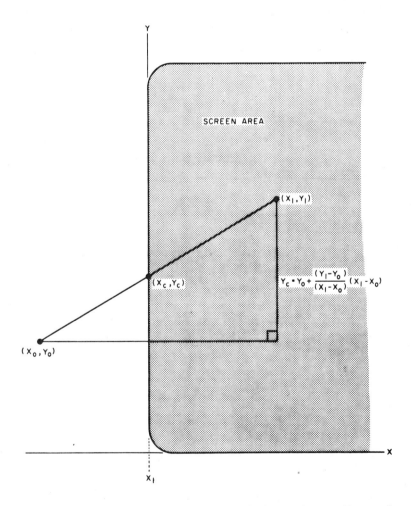

Figure 12a: Clipping. One way of calculating the cutoff point for a line is to use the traditional method of similar triangles. A disadvantage of this method is that it requires multiplicaton, a relatively time consuming operation on a computer.

Figure 12b: Clipping. Another method of calculating the cutoff point of a line on the screen is to use a form of binary search. The method involves halving the line segment successively until the y value converges to the correct answer. This method only requires adding and shifting and is thus quicker to compute than the method of similar triangles.

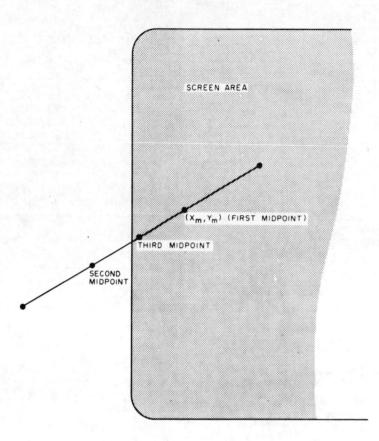

SCREEN AREA

(x_m, y_m) (FIRST MIDPOINT)

THIRD MIDPOINT

SECOND MIDPOINT

binary search. Using the example in figure 12b, we define (x_m, y_m) as the midpoint of the line to be clipped. (x_m, y_m) is calculated as follows:

$$x_m = (x_0 + x_1)/2 \quad \text{(add and 1 bit shift)}$$
$$y_m = (y_0 + y_1)/2 \quad \text{(add and 1 bit shift)}$$

If $x_m = x_\ell$, then y_m is the y coordinate of the clipped endpoint and the process is completed. If x_m violates the inequality, then replace (x_0, y_0) with (x_m, y_m). Recalculate (x_m, y_m). If the new x_m satisfies the inequality, then replace (x_1, y_1) with (x_m, y_m). In either of the last two cases, repeat the procedure with the new line, either (x_m, y_m) to (x_1, y_1) or (x_0, y_0) to (x_m, y_m). Because of the shifting used to calculate (x_m, y_m), the process continues no more times than the number of bits in a word and the y coordinate will converge to the correct value.

This clipping process completes the set of basic operations necessary to operate on two-dimensional information to produce graphic output.

I hope readers will be encouraged to use these practical techniques in their experiments with computer graphics.■

REFERENCES

1. Newman, W, and Sproull, R, *Principles of Interactive Computer Graphics,* McGraw-Hill Book Company, New York, 1973.

2. Rogers, D F, and Adams, J A, *Mathematical Elements for Computer Graphics,* McGraw-Hill Book Company, New York, 1976 (paperback uses BASIC).

Graphic Manipulations Using Matrices

Joel C Hungerford

One definition of graphics might be "a means to convert data into information." Our computers create printed data at a great rate, but all this data is not information until it conveys to a person some trend or fact about the world we live in. A small part of graphics is the conversion of data representing the position in space of the surface of an object into a three-dimensional picture of that object. The picture may be useful for itself as computer art, or it may help understand something about the object.

Imagine looking down the length of a pencil, using only one eye. With the eraser held away from the viewer, the pencil appears as a polygon with a dark place in the center where the lead is. The length of the pencil and the eraser are invisible. Now imagine the pencil rotated about its point until it is pointed toward the viewer's shoulder. The length of the pencil and the eraser are now visible, and appear in the form of translations to the side and up of the surface of the pencil. The relation between the position of a point on the pencil, specified in three dimensions X, Y and Z, and the apparent translation of that point as the pencil is rotated is expressed by standard equations. These can be written in an organized fashion using matrices. These matrices are called *coordinate transform matrices*. They are powerful tools because they separate the mathematics associated with the angle of observation from the data describing the surface of an object. The small computers available today make it easy to convert surface data to pictorial information using matrices. This article will show how.

Definitions

The Cartesian coordinate system will be used in this discussion. On a computer graphic screen, X is the horizontal dimension, Y is defined as the vertical dimension, and Z is depth into the screen. Positive values are to the right, up, and away from the viewer. The origin will usually be in the center of the screen. A plane is described by any two axes. Thus, the X,Y plane is the surface of the computer screen, the Y,Z plane is seen edge on as the Y axis, and the X,Z plane is seen edge on as the X axis.

An equation which does not specifically include a particular coordinate direction will be interpreted to mean that the described line or point may exist anywhere along the unmentioned axis. Thus, X=1 represents the entire Y,Z plane located at 1 along the X axis. The line defined by Y=X may exist anywhere along the Z axis; therefore this equation defines a plane tilted 45 degrees from the horizontal, seen edge on at Z equal to zero on the computer screen. A surface may be made parallel to an axis by omitting that axis, as above, or may be specified at all values of X, Y and Z. Thus, Y=X+Z is a surface defined for all space.

Two kinds of matrices will be used here. The first kind is a matrix which represents the coordinates of a point in space, described by X, Y and Z. This matrix, P, is a column matrix, with one column and three rows as shown in figure 1. It will be used to hold the values for a point on the surface, both before and after transformation. All drawing commands will

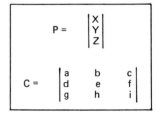

Figure 1: *Two types of matrices used in graphics applications. P represents a point in space. The matrix C contains equations to relate the transformed values of X, Y, and Z to the original values.*

161

use the X and Y from this matrix.

The second kind of matrix contains the standard equations which relate the transformed values for X, Y and Z to the original values. This matrix, C, has three rows and three columns. The numbers at each position in this matrix are derived from the standard equations for some specific coordinate transformation type, such as a rotation. If the angle of observation of the object is arrived at by two successive operations, such as a rotation in each of two planes, then the matrix, C, which controls this view may have numbers in it that are derived from two matrix equations. The procedure which produces a single matrix combining several operations is called matrix multiplication. Matrix multiplication is used both to produce the particular numbers in the 3 by 3 matrix, C, which describe a point of observation, and then to apply those numbers to derive a transformed 3 by 1 matrix, P, which gives the apparent position of some part of the object's surface.

Computing Procedure

Given the ability to do matrix multiplication (the details will be presented below), the sequence of operations to produce a three-dimensional picture of an object is short and easily stated:

1. Generate an array of data consisting of the X, Y and Z coordinates of the object to be drawn. This may be either computed as the drawing progresses, or done all at once and stored. The latter way is faster if the viewpoint is to be adjusted to find the most pleasing picture.

2. Define the viewpoint. For this part a matrix is generated for each motion required to arrive at the desired point of view. The matrices are then multiplied together to produce a single 3 by 3 matrix to be used in the main routine. The order of multiplication may be important.

3. Write a program to draw the object in its untransformed state. This will be a sequence of commands which move the graphic cursor to a spot on the object at the beginning of an edge of other feature, then draw (move leaving a line behind) to another spot on the object. Specify the move and draw coordinates in terms of column matrix element rather than X, Y and Z. Define the elements at each spot by using each of the points in the array.

4. When the untransformed picture is accurate and understood, then the picture is reoriented by simply inserting a matrix multiplication between the specification of each column matrix and the associated graphic command. The original X, Y, Z coordinates of the spot on the object are thereby transformed into a new set of X, Y, Z numbers representing the spot seen from the new viewpoint. Each set of coordinates from step 3 is multiplied by the matrix generated in step 2.

4a. An alternate method is to do all the transformations at once, changing

---

Matrix Multiplication

What information is necessary to write a subroutine to perform the matrix transformations described in this article? The general theory of matrix algebra and its interpretation is beyond the scope of this discussion. For more information and a very clear description of many other uses for matrices, the reader is referred to The Mathematics of Matrices *by Philip J Davis. Here are some brief notes on the subject:*

Two aspects of matrices are important in matrix multiplication. These are the order of the matrices being multiplied (which one comes first), and the shape of each matrix. The elements in the output matrix resulting from a multiplication of two matrices are each formed by combining numbers in the columns of the first matrix and rows of the second matrix, done in a standard order. All the necessary rows and columns have to exist for the output to exist. Thus, some matrices may be multiplied in one order, but not in the opposite order. The rule is: the number of columns of the first matrix must equal the number of rows of the second matrix.

In table 1, the two matrices may be multiplied in the order (C) (P) but not in the order (P) (C). The result of multiplying (C) (P) is a new column matrix P'. A mathematician would say that two matrices are "conformable for multiplication" when the order and shape requirements are met. He would also say "(C) is multiplied by (P)" here. The requirement for conformability leaves one dimension of the shape of each matrix unrestricted. The unrestricted dimensions establish the shape of the output matrix. Tables 1 and 2 summarize the necessary arithmetic. The elements in (C) are numbers, which are each computed in various ways depending upon the desired transformation.

$$
\begin{vmatrix} A & B & C \\ D & E & F \\ G & H & I \end{vmatrix}
\begin{vmatrix} X \\ Y \\ Z \end{vmatrix}
=
\begin{vmatrix} X' \\ Y' \\ Z' \end{vmatrix}
$$

$X' = (X*A+Y*B+Z*C)$
$Y' = (X*D+Y*E+Z*F)$
$Z' = (X*G+Y*H+Z*I)$

Table 1: Matrix multiplication format.

$$
\begin{vmatrix} A & B & C \\ D & E & F \\ G & H & I \end{vmatrix}
\begin{vmatrix} J & K & L \\ M & N & O \\ P & Q & R \end{vmatrix}
=
\begin{vmatrix} A' & B' & C' \\ D' & E' & F' \\ G' & H' & I' \end{vmatrix}
$$

$A' = (A*J+B*M+C*P)$ $B' = (A*K+B*N+C*Q)$ $C' = (A*L+B*O+C*R)$
$D' = (D*J+E*M+F*P)$ $E' = (D*K+E*N+F*Q)$ $F' = (D*L+E*O+F*R)$
$G' = (G*J+H*M+I*P)$ $H' = (G*K+H*N+I*Q)$ $I' = (G*L+H*O+I*R)$

Table 2: 3 by 3 matrix multiplication format.

the X, Y and Z points in the array formed in step 1 into transformed X, Y and Z numbers in the same array.

Since the computer screen is really only two-dimensional, only the X and Y elements are used in step 3. After transformation, these numbers are shifted about and contain depth information. The drawing made in this fashion is a projected view rather than a three-dimensional drawing. The difference is that in the projected view sides which are parallel on the object remain parallel in the projected view, but in the three-dimensional view all lines converge at infinity along the Z axis. The difference is minor. The observer perceives a three-dimensional picture in most cases; the projected view in some figures is perceived either as having relief or depth without the visual clue of lines meeting at infinity. This leads to some interesting optical illusions using projected views.

The rest of this article discusses some of the transformations available and shows the pictorial results of each.

Unit Matrix

Table 3 shows the unit matrix. This transformation reproduces the picture of the object in its original view as defined above. Figure 2 shows a side view of a coffee cup.

Scaling

The object may be defined with some shape which is not quite the final version, but which uses easily verified dimensions. Thus, in our example, the height is equal to the diameter, and the square outline in figure 2 quickly shows that the array of data defining the cup is correct in the X and Y dimensions.

Selective magnification along any axis may be used to alter the proportions of

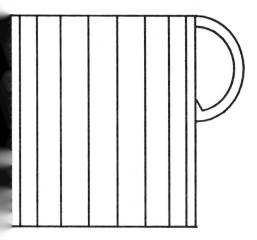

Figure 2: The standard view (untransformed).

$$
\begin{Vmatrix} 1 & 0 & 0 \\ 0 & 1 & 0 \\ 0 & 0 & 1 \end{Vmatrix} \begin{Vmatrix} X \\ Y \\ Z \end{Vmatrix} = \begin{Vmatrix} X' \\ Y' \\ Z' \end{Vmatrix}
$$

$X' = (X*1+Y*0+Z*0)$
$Y' = (X*0+Y*1+Z*0)$
$Z' = (X*0+Y*0+Z*1)$

Table 3: The unit matrix.

$$
\begin{Vmatrix} 1 & 0 & 0 \\ 0 & K & 0 \\ 0 & 0 & 1 \end{Vmatrix} \begin{Vmatrix} X \\ Y \\ Z \end{Vmatrix} = \begin{Vmatrix} X' \\ Y' \\ Z' \end{Vmatrix}
$$

$X' = (X*1+Y*0+Z*0)$
$Y' = (X*0+Y*K+Z*0)$
$Z' = (X*0+Y*0+Z*1)$

Table 4: Expansion along the Y axis by a factor K.

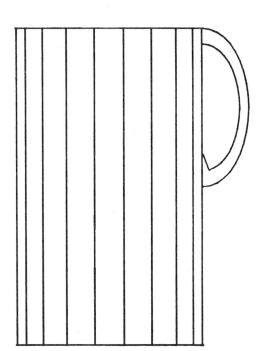

Figure 3: Expanded along the Y axis by a factor of 1.5.

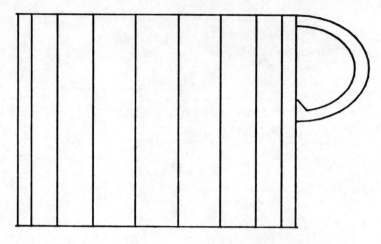

Figure 4: Expanded along the X axis by a factor of 1.5.

Figure 5: Magnified by a factor of 0.5.

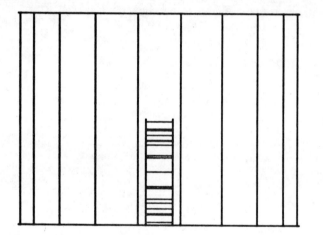

Figure 6: Rotated 90 degrees and expanded along Z axis by a factor of 1.5.

the object to a shape that may be nearer that required by the user. Thus, table 4 and figure 3 are appropriate for users with large capacities; table 5 and figure 4 produce a cup for those with wide mouths, while table 6 and figure 6 produce a cup which could be used for filling a pie plate with whipped cream.

If the proportions are correct but the user wants to create several different sizes, table 7 will allow the same magnification to take place along all the axes. One such magnified cup is shown in figure 5.

Shear

The object in its original shape may be boring and conventional in shape and lack individuality. This failing may be rectified as in table 8 and figure 7. To shear the object the position of a point on the object is displaced from its original position by a function of the point's position along an orthogonal axis. These figures displace the point upward by a value equal to half the horizontal distance to each point.

Table 9 and figures 8 and 9 show shear along the horizontal axis. Figure 9 shows the same object as figure 8 rotated 90° to illustrate that the third axis is unchanged by this operation. As in the other operations, shear along all axes may be combined.

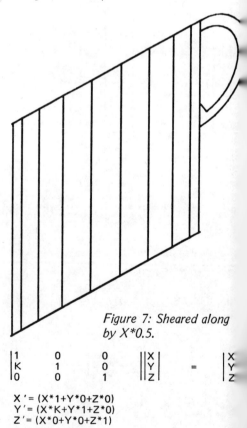

Figure 7: Sheared along by X*0.5.

$$
\begin{vmatrix} K & 0 & 0 \\ 0 & 1 & 0 \\ 0 & 0 & 1 \end{vmatrix}
\begin{Vmatrix} X \\ Y \\ Z \end{Vmatrix} =
\begin{vmatrix} X' \\ Y' \\ Z' \end{vmatrix}
$$

X'= (X*K+Y*0+Z*0)
Y'= (X*0+Y*1+Z*0)
Z'= (X*0+Y*0+Z*1)

Table 5: Expansion along the X axis by a factor K.

$$
\begin{vmatrix} 1 & 0 & 0 \\ 0 & 1 & 0 \\ 0 & 0 & K \end{vmatrix}
\begin{Vmatrix} X \\ Y \\ Z \end{Vmatrix} =
\begin{vmatrix} X' \\ Y' \\ Z' \end{vmatrix}
$$

X'= (X*1+Y*0+Z*0)
Y'= (X*0+Y*1+Z*0)
Z'= (X*0+Y*0+Z*K)

Table 6: Expansion along the Z axis by a factor K.

$$
\begin{vmatrix} K & 0 & 0 \\ 0 & K & 0 \\ 0 & 0 & K \end{vmatrix}
\begin{Vmatrix} X \\ Y \\ Z \end{Vmatrix} =
\begin{vmatrix} X' \\ Y' \\ Z' \end{vmatrix}
$$

X'= (X*K+Y*0+Z*0)
Y'= (X*0+Y*K+Z*0)
Z'= (X*0+Y*0+Z*K)

Table 7: Magnification by a factor K.

$$
\begin{vmatrix} 1 & 0 & 0 \\ K & 1 & 0 \\ 0 & 0 & 1 \end{vmatrix}
\begin{Vmatrix} X \\ Y \\ Z \end{Vmatrix} =
\begin{vmatrix} X \\ Y \\ Z \end{vmatrix}
$$

X'= (X*1+Y*0+Z*0)
Y'= (X*K+Y*1+Z*0)
Z'= (X*0+Y*0+Z*1)

Table 8: Shear along the Y axis in the Y plane by a factor K.

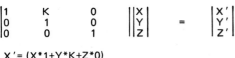

$$\begin{vmatrix} 1 & K & 0 \\ 0 & 1 & 0 \\ 0 & 0 & 1 \end{vmatrix} \begin{vmatrix} X \\ Y \\ Z \end{vmatrix} = \begin{vmatrix} X' \\ Y' \\ Z' \end{vmatrix}$$

X'= (X*1+Y*K+Z*0)
Y'= (X*0+Y*1+Z*0)
Z'= (X*0+Y*0+Z*1)

Table 9: Shear along the X axis in the X,Y plane by a factor K.

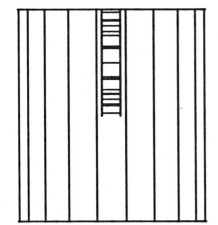

Figure 9: Rotated 90 degrees, sheared along X.

Rotations

The object may be reoriented in space by rotating it about any axis. A particular angle of view may be arrived at by some sequence of rotations about each axis. This is easily accomplished using the matrices in the following tables.

A point of confusion occurs when using rotations. The order of multiplication of the matrices (or the order of applying the operations to the object) is important. The axes remain associated with the object, not the screen. This means, for instance, that if the rotation in the X, Y plane shown in table 10 is applied first to the object, then subsequent rotations in the other planes happen in the slanted planes (X,Z and Y,Z) shown in figure 10.

It required some care to accurately predict the final picture after several rotations, especially since projected views lack the usual clue due to lines converging at infinity. Tables 11 and 12 along with figures 11 and 12 show the effects of rotation in the other two planes.

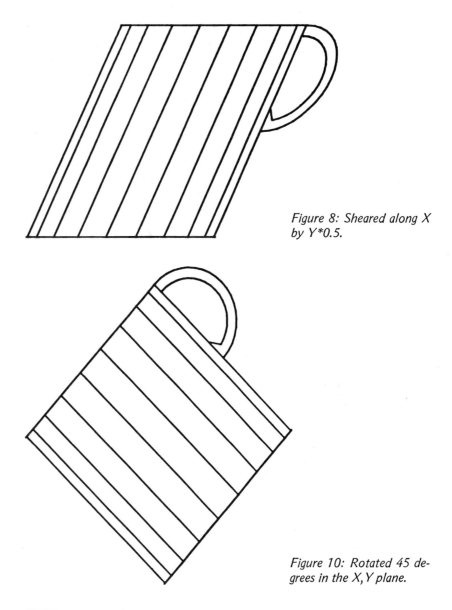

*Figure 8: Sheared along X by Y*0.5.*

Figure 10: Rotated 45 degrees in the X,Y plane.

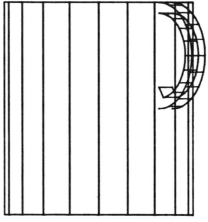

Figure 11: Rotated 45 degrees in the X,Z plane.

$$\begin{vmatrix} COS(T) & -SIN(T) & 0 \\ SIN(T) & COS(T) & 0 \\ 0 & 0 & 1 \end{vmatrix} \begin{vmatrix} X \\ Y \\ Z \end{vmatrix} = \begin{vmatrix} X' \\ Y' \\ Z' \end{vmatrix}$$

X'= (X*COS(T)+Y*-SIN(T)+Z*0)
Y'= (X*SIN(T)+Y*COS(T)+Z*0)
Z'= (X*0+Y*0+Z*1)

Table 10: Rotation in the X,Y plane.

$$\begin{vmatrix} COS(T) & 0 & -SIN(T) \\ 0 & 1 & 0 \\ SIN(T) & 0 & COS(T) \end{vmatrix} \begin{vmatrix} X \\ Y \\ Z \end{vmatrix} = \begin{vmatrix} X' \\ Y' \\ Z' \end{vmatrix}$$

X'= (X*COS(T)+Y*0+Z*-SIN(T))
Y'= (X*0+Y*1+Z*0)
Z'= (X*SIN(T)+Y*0+Z*COS(T))

Table 11: Rotation in the X,Z plane.

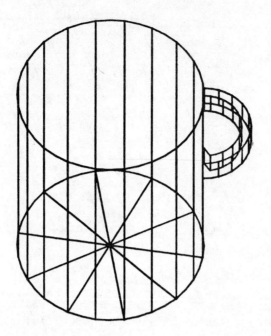

Figure 12: Rotated 45 degrees in the Y,Z plane.

$$\begin{vmatrix} 1 & 0 & 0 \\ 0 & COS(T) & -SIN(T) \\ 0 & SIN(T) & COS(T) \end{vmatrix} \begin{vmatrix} X \\ Y \\ Z \end{vmatrix} = \begin{vmatrix} X' \\ Y' \\ Z' \end{vmatrix}$$

$X' = (X*1 + Y*0 + Z*0)$
$Y' = (X*0 + Y*COS(T) + Z*-SIN(T))$
$Z' = (X*0 + Y*SIN(T) + Z*COS(T))$

Table 12: Rotation in the Y,Z plane.

Combinations

Table 13 shows an example of the sequential application of two rotations using the procedure shown in table 2 to define the elements. Figure 13 combines the three rotations, a magnification and two scale changes along individual axes. Figure 14 applies shear and rotation. Figure 15 shows just the rotation for comparison purposes.

Figure 13: Magnified, expanded, and rotated.

Table 13: Rotation in the X,Y and Y,Z planes sequentially.

$$\begin{vmatrix} 1 & 0 & 0 \\ 0 & COS(T) & -SIN(T) \\ 0 & SIN(T) & COS(T) \end{vmatrix} \begin{vmatrix} COS(S) & -SIN(S) & 0 \\ SIN(S) & COS(S) & 0 \\ 0 & 0 & 1 \end{vmatrix} = \begin{vmatrix} A' & B' & C' \\ D' & E' & F' \\ G' & H' & I' \end{vmatrix}$$

$A' = (1*COS(S) + 0*SIN(S) + 0*0)$
$B' = (1*-SIN(S) + 0*COS(S) + 0*0)$
$C' = (1*0 + 0*0 + 0*1)$
$D = (0*COS(S) + COS(T)*SIN(S) - SIN(T)*0)$
$E' = (0*-SIN(S) + COS(T)*COS(S) - SIN(T)*0)$
$F' = (0*0 + COS(T)*0 - SIN(T)*1)$
$G' = (0*COS(S) + SIN(T)*SIN(S) + COS(T)*0)$
$H' = (0*-SIN(S) + SIN(T)*COS(S) + COS(T)*0)$
$I' = (0*0 + SIN(T)*0 + COS(T)*1)$

Figure 14: Rotated and sheared.

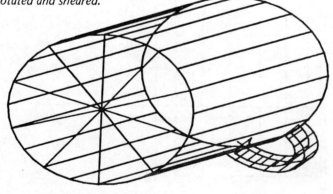

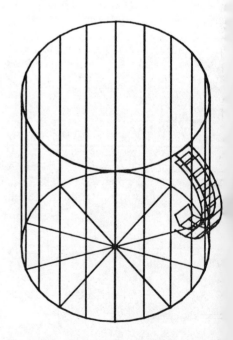

$$\begin{vmatrix} X+k \\ Y+m \\ Z+n \end{vmatrix} = \begin{vmatrix} X' \\ Y' \\ Z' \end{vmatrix}$$

$X' = X+k$
$Y' = Y+m$
$Z' = Z+n$

Table 14: Translation matrix.

Translation

Moving the object sideways is not shown but is accomplished by adding the translation value to the original value for each axis as shown in table 14.

Figure 15: Rotated but not sheared.

Mapping

All of the examples shown so far have applied the same operation to every point on the surface of the object. The coordinate transform matrix contains the same numbers for all parts of the object. A more complicated operation results when the value (X,Y, Z) associated with a point on the surface of the object is replaced by a function of X, Y, and Z at each point. The result maps the object onto some surface. Thus, if X is replaced by sin(X), for instance, the object will experience a change in scale which changes with X, and the output position of a point on the object which has a value of X equal to zero, and an arbitrary Y and Z is the same as a point with a value of X equal to 180 or 360 if the computer interprets the value of X as degrees.

The result of replacing X by sin(X) pictorially is identical to the projected view of a cylinder, parallel to the Y axis, which has the original view (such as figure 2) painted onto its surface. If the dimensions of the object for this example are such that the width is equal to 360 units, then the cylinder is completely circumscribed by the original view of the object.

In order to make a three-dimensional picture of the mapped figure, the other two dimensions must also be specified. For the example here, the depth must also be mapped by setting Z equal to cos(X). Since the new surface is a cylinder, Y is unchanged.

Mapping Example

Figure 16 shows a label to be pasted on the coffee cup. This label, like the cup itself, is defined by an array of data giving the X, Y and Z coordinates of each point. The standard view is in the Z equal to zero plane. A subroutine then replaces the X and Z values with the mapped values in all the points of the array. Since the standard view of the cup is a side view, and the label is to be pasted opposite the handle, 180° is added to X before computing the mapped functions. The lower left corner of figure 16 is coordinate (0,0).

The mapped array of data is now subjected to whatever coordinate transforms are applied to the cup. Figure 17 shows the result as applied to the label alone. Figure 18 shows the completed picture.

Illusions

Figure 19 shows the same object as figure 18, rotated 180°. While most viewers see the cup with the handle toward them, "looking down into it" in figure 18, many find that figure 19 alternates between looking *down* into it with the handle away from the viewer, and looking *up* at it from the bottom, with the handle at the top. This example shows that a relatively minor change in viewpoint may produce a great change in terms of the clarity of the information presented.

Figure 19.

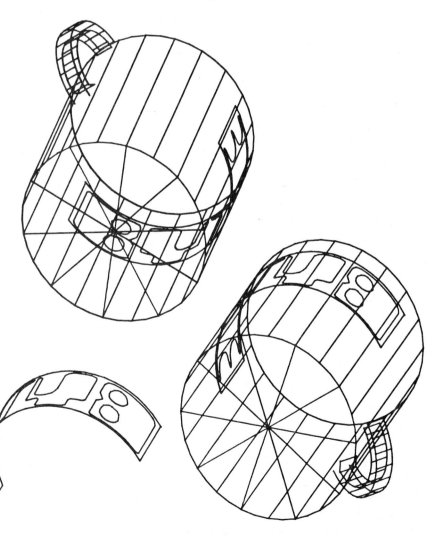

Figure 16.   *Figure 17.*   *Figure 18.*

Mapping Uses

Mapping may be used to compress the picture of an object to fit it into a particular space, to selectively emphasize some part while compressing the rest, such as the region near X equal to zero or 180° in this example. Or it may be used to picture some complicated configuration which is more easily defined in a rectangular coordinate system. Thus, a simple rectangular electrode configuration expressed in Cartesian coordinates may be used to compute the electric field lines at each point in the configuration. Mapping processes plus the coordinate transforms may then be used to change the known field picture into one for a complicated electron gun in a cathode ray tube.

Excerpts from the BASIC program which produced the pictures in this article are shown in listing 1. The machine used is a Tektronix 4051 graphic computer with a 4662 plotter, with matrix read only memory. The matrix command A MPY B is specific to this equipment. The rest of the program is in a fairly standard BASIC.

Lines 2000 to 2490 comprise the main program which draws the coffee cup. The purpose of each subroutine is noted. The program defining the various matrices in terms of viewpoint parameters is shown in lines 2535 to 3010. The program to combine the matrices into a single 3 by 3 matrix, C4, which is applied to the drawing is listed in lines 3120 to 3200. The A MPY B format does the matrix multiplication. In a machine without this extension, a subroutine using the equation listed in the various figures would do the same job, but take much more space.

Lines 4000 to 4300 show part of the much longer listing which defines the cup: A1 (N,1) = X, A1 (N,2) = Y, A1 (N,3) = Z. The variable A1 (N,4) is a secondary address used with a form of the print command to make it move (21) or draw (20). This is a faster way to draw on the Tektronix machine. Lines 4050 to 4140 draw the top and bottom circle.

Lines 5240 to 5270 convert the cup dimensions to graphics display units (GDUs) which are required to use this style of drawing commands. This program, with all arrays, filled, uses about 28,500 bytes of memory. Incidentally, lacking a printer, I printed the program using the plotter.

Listing 1.

```
2000 DELETE A1,A2,B1,B2,B3,B4,B5,B6,B7,B8,B9,C1,C2,C3,V1,C4,V2
2002 DIM A1(262,4),A2(262,4),B1(3,3),B2(3,3),B3(3,3),B4(3,3),B5(3,3)
2003 DIM B6(3,3),B7(3,3),B8(3,3),B9(3,3),C1(3,3),C2(3,3),C3(3,3),C4(3,3)
2004 DIM V1(3,1),V2(3,1)
2005 REM THIS SUBROUTINE DEFINES THE CUP
2010 GOSUB 2500
2090 REM THIS SUBROUTINE DEFINES THE TRANSFORM MATRICES
2100 GOSUB 2540
2140 REM THIS SUBROUTINE MULTIPLIES ALL THE MATRICES TOGETHER
2150 GOSUB 3120
2160 REM THIS SUBROUTINE CHANGES A1 TO A NEW VIEW,A2
2170 GOSUB 5500
2180 REM THIS SUBROUTINE CHANGES THE CUP FROM USER DATA UNITS TO GDU'S
2190 GOSUB 5240
2195 REM THIS SUBROUTINE DRAWS THE FIGURE
2200 GOSUB 5200
2490 END

2535 REM B1 ROTATES IN THE X,Y PLANE BY T1 DEGREES
2540 B1=0
2550 B1(1,1)=COS(T1)
2560 B1(1,2)=-SIN(T1)
2570 B1(2,1)=SIN(T1)
2580 B1(2,2)=COS(T1)
2590 B1(3,3)=1
2600 REM B2 ROTATES IN THE X,Z PLANE BY T2 DEGREES
2610 B2=0
2620 B2(1,1)=COS(T2)
2630 B2(1,3)=-SIN(T2)
2640 B2(2,2)=1
2650 B2(3,1)=SIN(T2)
2660 B2(3,3)=COS(T2)
2670 REM B3 ROTATES IN THE Y,Z PLANE BY T3 DEGREES
2680 B3=0
2690 B3(1,1)=1
2700 B3(2,2)=COS(T3)
2710 B3(2,3)=-SIN(T3)
2720 B3(3,2)=SIN(T3)
2730 B3(3,3)=COS(T3)
2740 REM B4 IS THE UNIT MATRIX
2750 B4=0
2760 B4(1,1)=1
2770 B4(2,2)=1
2780 B4(3,3)=1
2790 REM B5 EXPANDS ALONG THE X AXIS BY K1
2800 B5=B4
2810 B5(1,1)=K1
2820 REM B6 EXPANDS ALONG THE Y AXIS BY K2
2830 B6=B4
2840 B6(2,2)=K2
2850 REM B7 EXPANDS ALONG THE Z AXIS BY K3
2860 B7=B4
2870 B7(3,3)=K3
2880 REM B8 MAGNIFIES BY K4
2890 B8=K4*B4
2900 REM B9 REFLECTS IN THE Y=X PLANE
2910 B9=0
2920 B9(1,2)=1
2930 B9(2,1)=1
2940 B9(3,3)=1
2950 REM C1 SHEARS ALONG THE X AXIS BY K5 X/Y RATIO
2960 C1=B4
2970 C1(1,2)=K5
```

```
2980 REM C2 SHEARS ALONG THE Y AXIS BY K6 X/Y RATIO
2990 C2=B4
3000 C2(2,1)=K6
3010 RETURN

3120 C3=B6 MPY B5
3130 C4=B7 MPY C3
3140 C3=B8 MPY C4
3150 C4=C1 MPY C3
3160 C3=C2 MPY C4
3170 C4=B2 MPY C3
3180 C3=B3 MPY C4
3190 C4=B1 MPY C3
3200 RETURN

4000 REM THIS PART FORMS THE TOP AND BOTTOM EDGE OF THE CUP
4010 A1(1,1)=10
4020 A1(1,2)=10
4030 A1(1,3)=0
4040 A1(1,4)=21
4050 FOR N=0 TO 360 STEP 9
4060 A1(N/9+2,1)=10*COS(N)
4070 A1(N/9+2,3)=10*SIN(N)
4080 A1(N/9+2,2)=10
4090 A1(N/9+2,4)=20
4100 A1(N/9+44,1)=A1(N/9+2,1)
4110 A1(N/9+44,3)=A1(N/9+2,3)
4120 A1(N/9+44,2)=-10
4130 A1(N/9+44,4)=20
4140 NEXT N
4142 A1(43,1)=A1(44,1)
4144 A1(43,2)=A1(44,2)
4146 A1(43,3)=A1(44,3)
4148 A1(43,4)=21
4150 REM A1 IS FILLED TO #84 AT THIS POINT
```

```
4160 A1(85,1)=10
4170 A1(85,2)=0
4180 A1(85,3)=1
4190 A1(85,4)=21
4200 REM THIS PART DRAWS THE OUTSIDE OF THE HANDLE
4210 FOR N=0 TO 180 STEP 9
4220 A1(N/9+86,1)=5*SIN(N)+10
4230 A1(N/9+86,2)=5-5*COS(N)
4240 A1(N/9+86,3)=1
4250 A1(N/9+86,4)=20
4260 A1(N/9+107,1)=A1(N/9+86,1)
4270 A1(N/9+107,2)=A1(N/9+86,2)
4280 A1(N/9+107,3)=-1
4290 A1(N/9+107,4)=20
4300 NEXT N

5200 FOR N=1 TO 262
5210 PRINT @I,A2(N,4):A2(N,1),A2(N,2)
5220 NEXT N
5230 RETURN
5240 FOR N=1 TO 262
5250 A2(N,1)=A2(N,1)/15*40+50
5260 A2(N,2)=A2(N,2)/15*40+50
5270 A2(N,3)=A2(N,3)/15*40
5280 NEXT N
5290 RETURN
5500 FOR N=1 TO 262
5510 V1(1,1)=A1(N,1)
5520 V1(2,1)=A1(N,2)
5530 V1(3,1)=A1(N,3)
5540 V2=C4 MPY V1
5550 A2(N,1)=V2(1,1)
5560 A2(N,2)=V2(2,1)
5570 A2(N,3)=V2(3,1)
5580 A2(N,4)=A1(N,4)
5600 NEXT N
5610 RETURN ■
```

169

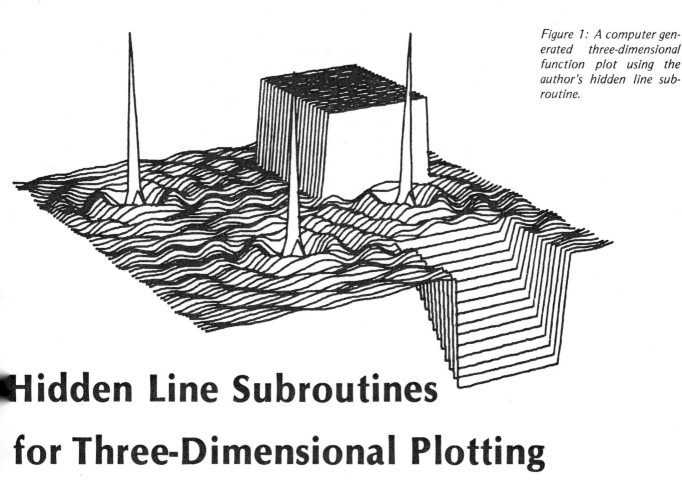

Figure 1: A computer generated three-dimensional function plot using the author's hidden line subroutine.

Hidden Line Subroutines for Three-Dimensional Plotting

Mark Gottlieb

A hidden line subroutine is used to eliminate lines which are behind surfaces and which in real life one would not be able to see in a computer generated plot of a solid object in two dimensions. A hidden line subroutine makes the final picture more realistic.

A three-dimensional Cartesian function is a function such as

$$F(x,y) = 4x\cos(3y) + 1/e^x$$

where the value for the z coordinate is a function of both X and Y.

This article considers the various steps necessary for a hidden line routine that handles functions of this kind. The algorithm will *not* work for functions plotted in spherical coordinates or for complex three-dimensional figures such as a house.

The hidden line subroutine should be written in a general form so that the user can attach the subroutine to any appropriate program without having to rewrite it.

First, one must have a program that generates the X and Y values that the hidden line subroutine will operate on. Briefly, this involves a program to generate an X and a Y FOR NEXT loop; generate a Z value; rotate

to get a new (x',y',z'); scale; put through a perspective function and come out with an (x,y) point. This is the point on the screen (or paper) to which one would normally draw a line. However, we now take this (x,y) point and GOSUB to our hidden line subroutine.

Let us first draw a function of this kind without hiding any lines (see figure 2). Note that one point seems to ruin the appearance of the graph because the viewer sees immediately that a surface is being formed. When a point goes "behind" the small mound, the subjective feeling is that it should be hidden. We need a rule that will handle all points that should be hidden and leave other points alone.

One difference between this point and all the previous points is that it is lower (along the Y axis) than the corresponding point in the previous line. "Corresponding" here means the *same X value*. Thus, our rule states that if for any point (x,y), the Y value is lower than any previous Y value for the same X value, it should be hidden. To do this, we must save the necessary values; for the above rule, we need to know the highest valued Y for every X.

Let us assume the screen has a resolution of 1024 along the X axis and 800 along the Y axis (such as in the case of the Textronix 4013 graphics terminal). Thus, we have 1024 possible X locations. But we need to know only the highest valued Y for each X. This means that if we have a 1 by 1024 matrix we can store the highest valued Y in the corresponding X location. We can keep our matrix updated with the following BASIC statement:

$$100 \ B(X,1) = B(X,1) \ MAX \ Y$$

This statement always keeps the matrix full of the highest valued Y for each X location.

In order to implement our rule in the hidden line program, we need a check such as:

If $Y < B(x,1)$
    Then *don't draw this line.*

Implementing what is already known, the graph might look like the one in figure 3.

The program hides all of the lines shown as broken lines because all the Y values for those X values are less than the highest Y value for that X value. However, we see that we would like to have seen the part of the dip which comes out beneath the graph. In other words, we want our graph to look like the one in figure 4.

Instead of hiding all the lines whose Y value is less than the highest Y value for that particular X, we should say "Hide all lines whose Y value is less than the highest Y and greater than the lowest Y value for that particular X." This involves storing the lowest Y value, also. We do this by using the matrix with dimensions (1024,2). In column 1 we store the highest Y value and in column 2 the lowest Y value for that X. The matrix can be kept up-to-date this way:

$$B(X,1) = B(X,1) \ MAX \ Y$$
$$B(X,2) = B(X,2) \ MIN \ Y$$

This statement keeps the matrix full of the highest and the lowest valued Y for each X location. Thus, the new check for the hidden line routine looks like this:

If $Y < B(X,1)$ AND $Y > B(X,2)$
    Then *don't draw.*

One small technical problem arises which is easily solved. We need to solve for our two points in order to get a line between them, but our (1024,2) matrix has not been told what is between these two points. Thus for each new point solved, we must go through the matrix, starting from the value where we last left off, and fill in the Y values for each of these new Xs until we get to the X value of our new point (x,y).

This process involves solving the equation for a straight line given the two points and then filling in the Y values for each X along that line for our matrix. This routine is called upon almost every time a new point

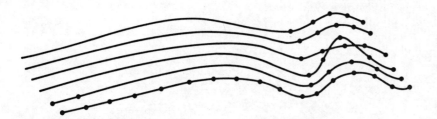

Figure 2: The first crude plot function shows problems encountered when no hidden line algorithm is used. The subroutine would hide that portion of the fourth line from the front that "goes behind" the high point in front of it.

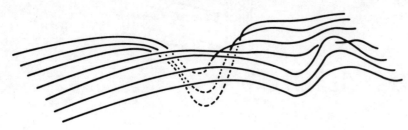

Figure 3: In this case the algorithm has correctly hidden some points but has failed to show others which emerge at the bottom of the plot.

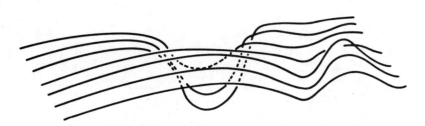

Figure 4: Improved algorithm reveals the bottom of the curve as a series of solid lines (compare with figure 3).

A Note About the BASIC Employed in These Examples:

The BASIC employed in these examples is the interpreter available with the author's computer. Most features are similar to a typical extended BASIC which includes matrix operations (MAT keyword). As noted in text, the file oriented operations which are used to initialize the matrix B can be replaced by a FOR ... NEXT loop at lines 310 and 320 in listing 6. (Lines 130 and 140 would then be deleted.)

```
5505    U6=SGN(X—X9)
5510    IF U6=0 THEN 5535
5515    FOR U7=X9 TO X STEP U6
5520        S8=Y9+S9*(U7—X9),B[U7,2]=B[U7,2] MIN S8,B[U7,1]=B[U7,1] MAX S8
5530    NEXT U7
5535    RETURN
```

Listing 1: A BASIC program used to calculate points between the endpoints of a line segment for plotting purposes.

is generated, and, therefore, is executed many times. This is the one step that makes this method of hidden line processing slow, and thus should be made as condensed as possible. A suggested routine is shown in listing 1. In this routine, U6 causes the FOR NEXT loop to go forward or backward depending on where X is in relation to X9. X9 and Y9 are set equal to the previous points throughout the program. U7 becomes the X value for each point along the line and S8 the corresponding Y value. S9 is the slope of the line and is determined earlier in the subroutine. Matrix B is the 1024 by 2 matrix for storing the high and low Ys.

One small item which must not be overlooked is that the initial values of the 1024 by 2 matrix elements must be set. Suppose we initially set each element to 0. While drawing the first line, suppose the first point is (300,200). When the program executes the line which reads

$$100 \; B(X,1) = B(X,1) \; \text{MAX} \; Y$$
$$B(X,2) = B(X,2) \; \text{MIN} \; Y$$

element B(300,1) will take the MAX of 0 and 200 which is 200; this is correct. However, element B(300,2) will take the MIN of 0 and 200 which is 0. This is incorrect; the desired answer is 200. We can solve the problem by filling all of the elements in the second column with the highest value we might need, 800 in this case.

One way (used in my program) to fill the first column with 0s and the second with 800s is to use a file. The initial conditions are read from the file onto the matrix at the beginning of each program. Another way, of course, would be to employ a FOR ... NEXT loop.

The few techniques learned so far form a good basis for a hidden line subroutine. Plotting a function with a hidden line subroutine and incorporating what has been determined so far gives a graph like the one shown in figure 4. An outline for the hidden line subroutine would be similar to this:

- If Y < B(X, 1) and Y > B(X, 2)
  Then *don't draw.*
  Otherwise draw.
- *Fill in points in matrix.*
- *Return to main program.*

Figure 4 looks respectable; at least the right lines are hidden. However, something is not quite right. When we need to hide a point, we cannot simply draw a line to that point. This leads to the problem seen in the graph; the lines do not meet the surface of the graph when they go behind; when coming out, they start emerging before they are completely clear of the surface. Obviously, some improvement on our

hidden line subroutine is needed.

We need an algorithm to find the intersection. When a point lies behind the surface, we must find a new point on the surface of the graph. If we draw a line to a point that should be hidden, we will intersect the surface at this new point which we are trying to locate: the point of intersection. This becomes tricky. The basic procedures necessary to determine the point of intersection are as follows:

- Find the equation for the line which passes through the previous point and the new point behind the surface.
- Step along this line from the old X value to the new X value until we find an X where the Y for that X is the same (within one point of resolution) as the highest (or lowest) Y for that same X. This is the intersection point to which we draw to intersect the surface, or from which we start drawing when coming from behind the surface.

Suppose the point outside of the surface is (505,200) and the new point which goes

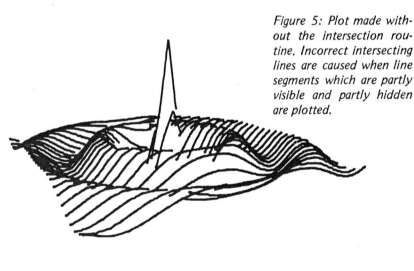

Figure 5: Plot made without the intersection routine. Incorrect intersecting lines are caused when line segments which are partly visible and partly hidden are plotted.

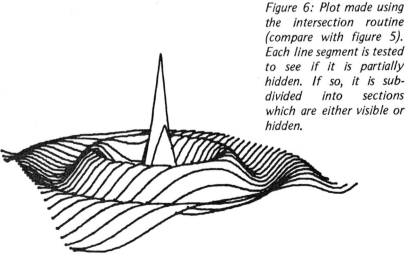

Figure 6: Plot made using the intersection routine (compare with figure 5). Each line segment is tested to see if it is partially hidden. If so, it is subdivided into sections which are either visible or hidden.

behind the surface is (575,188). If we step along the line joining them in the X direction, from X = 505 to X = 575, it could take up to 70 steps until the intersection point is found.

A much more elegant and time saving approach is to perform a "binary search" along the line to find the intersection point. For the previous example in which there were 70 steps, we could get to within one point of resolution from the point of intersection in seven steps. I go through the binary search method eight times to accommodate longer line segments.

Listing 2 shows the segment of my hidden line subroutine that searches for the intersection point. U1 is a binary loop; U2 tells whether to go forward or backward along the line segment whose length is S7; X1 is the new X location along the line segment as the search continues; Y7 is the solution to the line equation between the two points at the new X value X1; and U3 calls a further

nested subroutine if one is trying to find the intersection point while coming out from behind the surface. Finally, after the program executes the loop eight times, X1 and Y7 are the coordinates of the intersection point (X1,Y7). Figures 5 and 6 show the before and after effects of the intersection routine.

Figures 7 and 8 show what happens to a graph with and without a process called "left and right side fill-in." The edges of the graph in figure 8 appear messy. This is because on the left edge, for example, when a line comes into the preceding left edge, it does not appear to intersect it; instead it goes a bit too far. This can be seen with the aid of the dotted line. The problem is solved by adding an imaginary dotted line into the matrix of 1024 by 2. Although we do not draw the edge lines on the screen, which we *could* do, we "draw" them into

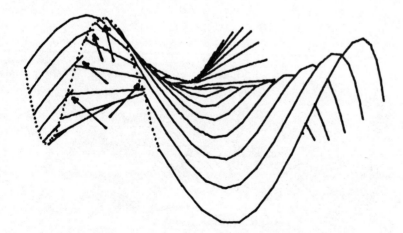

Figure 7: Graph made with "left and right side fill-in." The term refers to an imaginary "edge" at the borders of the surface (shown in dotted lines). This edge enables the algorithm to accurately handle lines drawn near the edges.

Figure 8: Graph made without the "left and right side fill-in" feature in the algorithm. In this case the routine cannot accurately handle intersections.

```
5205    S7=X−X9,U2=0,X1=X9,U1=1
5210    UNTIL U1>128 DO
5215       U1=U1*2
5220       IF U2 THEN 5235
5225       X1=X1+S7/U1
5230       GOTO 5240
5235       X1=X1−S7/U1
5240       Y7=S9*(X1−X9)+Y9
5245       IF U3 THEN 5456
5250       IF Y9>B[X9,2] THEN 5270
5255       IF Y7>B[X1,2] THEN U2=1
5260       IF Y7<B[X1,2] THEN U2=0
5265       GOTO 5280
5270       IF Y7<B[X1,1] THEN U2=1
5275       IF Y7>B[X1,1] THEN U2=0
5280    DOEND
5285    X5=X,Y5=Y
5290    X=X1,Y=Y7
5455    REM ** FOR U3=1:COMING OUT ***
5456    IF Y>B[X,1] THEN 5460
5457    IF Y7<B[X1,2] THEN U2=1
5458    IF Y7>B[X1,2] THEN U2=0
5459    GOTO 5280
5460    IF Y7>B[X1,1] THEN U2=1
5465    IF Y7<B[X1,1] THEN U2=0
5470    GOTO 5280
```

Listing 2: A BASIC routine that searches for intersections between line segments.

```
5600    REM ** FILL IN LEFT SIDE **
5610    IF X4#−1 THEN GOTO 5640
5620    X4=X,Y4=Y
5630    RETURN
5640    X8=X9,Y8=Y9
5650    X9=X4,Y9=Y4
5660    S9=(Y−Y9)/(X−X9)
5670    GOSUB 5500
5680    X9=X8,Y9=Y8
5690    GOTO 5620
5700    REM ** FILL IN RIGHT SIDE **
5710    IF X3#−1 THEN 5740
5720    X3=X,Y3=Y
5730    RETURN
5740    X8=X9,Y8=Y9
5750    X9=X3,Y9=Y3
5760    S9=(Y−Y9)/(X−X9)
5770    GOSUB 5500
5780    X9=X8,Y9=Y8
5790    GOTO 5720
```

Listing 3: Two routines used to "fill in" the left and right sides of the graph so that line intersections occur (see figures 7 and 8).

the matrix. Thus, when a line is about to intersect with an edge, it will have an imaginary boundary in the matrix with which to intersect.

The matrix fill-in is accomplished by taking the point at the beginning of a new line and the point for the beginning of the previous line and calling them (X,Y) and (X9,Y9), respectively. Then GOSUB 5500 (the fill-in points for the matrix subroutine) will fill in all the Y values for each X value along this line segment. Do the same thing for the right side, or the last point in each line.

The subroutine in listing 3 is accessed at the beginning and end of each line for the left side and the right side, respectively. X3 and X4 are initially set equal to −1 at the beginning of the program. This tells the routine that it is the first point in the graph and thus a line cannot be drawn between it and the previous point, which does not exist. After the first line is drawn, the previous points become (X4,Y4) and (X3,Y3) for the left and right sides respectively. S9 is the slope of the line needed in the fill-in routine.

Crosshatching is a method of drawing graphs with sets of orthogonal lines. For many graphs, this enhances the overall appearance and definition. The crosshatch program draws two separate graphs, one for the horizontal direction, and the other for the vertical. When the graph in the horizontal direction is completed, all initial conditions used in the hidden line subroutine must be reset. This includes reinitializing by placing the 0s and 800s into the 1024 by matrix as described earlier.

One must also change the FOR NEXT loops for the X and Y axis: instead of keeping the Y value constant while stepping along in the X direction for a complete line, we hold the X value constant while stepping along in the Y direction.

A more efficient method consists of assuming the X to be the Y and the Y to be the X the second time around. An example shown in listing 4. Matrix A contains the X,Y and Z values for use in rotation. Matrix is the final three-dimensional rotation matrix calculated elsewhere in the program. In the B loop, B = 0 is for the horizontal direction, B = 1 for the vertical direction. Notice the values assigned to matrix A when changes from 0 to 1. Function FNP is the perspective function defined in the beginning of the program. GOSUB 5000 is for the hidden line subroutine. The function is for the graph shown in figure 7. Figures 9 and 10 show the effects of crosshatching.

In certain graphs, such as figure 11, lines must go behind very narrow regions. Here in the upper portion of the spikes we encounter

```
300     FOR B=0 TO 1
302       X3=Y3=X4=Y4=−1
303       READ #2,1
305       MAT READ #2;B
310       FOR T=−E TO E STEP E/K
320         FOR G=−E TO E STEP E/K
330           U9=G
340           IF B=0 THEN 370
350           A[1,1]=T
355           A[1,2]=G
360           A[1,3]=T*G*(T*T−G*G)/(T*T+G*G)
365           GOTO 400
370           A[1,1]=G
380           A[1,2]=T
390           A[1,3]=T*G*(G*G−T*T)/(G*G+T*T)
400           MAT C=A*Q
410           X=FNP(C[1,1]*300/E)+512
420           Y=FNP(C[1,2]*300/E)+400
430           GOSUB 5000
440         NEXT G
450       NEXT T
455     NEXT B
```

Listing 4: A routine to create crosshatched plots.

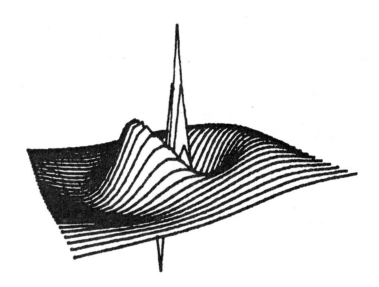

Figure 9: A plot made without crosshatching.

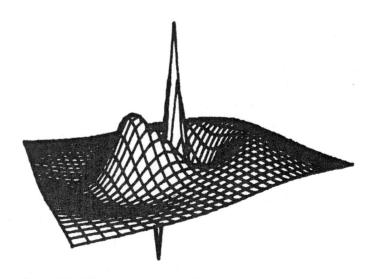

Figure 10: The same function as figure 9, but with crosshatching.

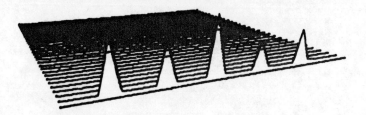

Figure 11: Problems can occur when lines go behind very narrow regions, but the line's endpoints are both visible.

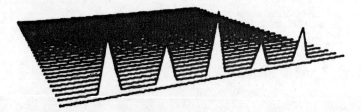

Figure 12: Solution to the problem illustrated in figure 11. The routine checks additional points along the line segment and makes changes accordingly.

```
100     00=1
110     U4=0,F=U5=1
120     L9=75
130     FILES *,*
140     ASSIGN "BLANK",2,T2
150     DIM A[1,3],C[1,3]
160     DIM Q[3,3],B[1024,2]
165     REM PERSPECTIVE FUNCTION
170     DEF FNP(F)=D7*F/(D7-C[1,3])
180     REM E=STEP VALUE AND K= # STEPS
190     E=10,K=20
200     I=-E,I2=E
210     REM D7=DISTANCE FROM (0,0,0) FOR PERSPECTIVE
220     D7=30
230     REM X2,Y2,Z2 ARE DEG. TURN AROUND X,Y,&Z AXIS
240     X2=-75,Y2=0,Z2=30
250     W=3.1416/180
260     X2=W*X2
270     Y2=W*Y2
280     Z2=W*Z2
290     GOSUB 6000
300     X3=Y3=X4=Y4=-1
310     READ #2,1
320     MAT READ #2;B
325     REM Y AXIS LOOP
330     FOR T=-E TO E STEP E/K
340       IF T>-.05 AND T<.05 THEN T=0
345       REM X AXIS LOOP
350       FOR G=-E TO E STEP E/K
360         IF G>-.05 AND G<.05 THEN G=0
370         U9=G
380         R=SQR(G*G+T*T)
390         A[1,1]=G
400         A[1,2]=T
405         REM ACTUAL FUNCTION
410         A[1,3]=8/(R+1)*COS(R*1.2)
420         MAT C=A*Q
425         REM SCALING, PERSPECTIVE & OFFSET
426         REM GOSUB TO HIDDEN LINE ROUTINE
430         X=FNP(C[1,1]*300/E)+512
440         Y=FNP(C[1,2]*300/E)+400
450         GOSUB 5000
460       NEXT G
470     NEXT T
480     END
```

Listing 6: A BASIC program used to create the plot shown in figure 13. Two subroutines, at line numbers 8100 and 8200, are not included in this listing, but must be supplied by the user. These are a routine to draw an invisible vector to point (x,y) at line number 8100, and a routine to draw a visible vector to point (x,y). These correspond respectively to the movement of a plotter's pen without contact and with contact. The details of the routines depend on the display hardware used.

```
5035    L8=SQR((X-X9)^2+(Y-Y9)^2)
5040    IF L8>L9 THEN DO
5045      L2=X9,L5=X,L6=Y,S6=(Y-Y9)/(X-X9)
5050      L7=(X-X9)/(L8/L9),L4=Y9-S6*X9
5060      FOR X=L2 TO L5-L7 STEP L7
5065        Y=S6*X+L4
5070        GOSUB 5090
5075      NEXT X
5080      X=L5,Y=L6
5085    DOEND
```

Listing 5: A routine used to refine the hidden line algorithm so it can correctly handle line segments which are visible at each end but obscured in the middle (see figures 11 and 12).

difficulties. Using the method described so far for hidden lines, we solve for a new point and test to see whether that point is behind something. We can now determine if it should be hidden. Let us see what happens when we approach and go behind the upper portion of one of the spikes in figure 11.

Suppose the new point is just to the left of one of the spikes. The hidden line routine sees that the point is visible and should therefore have a line drawn to it from the previous point. Suppose the next point is behind the spike: the hidden line routine will see this and draw a line to the intersection point on the left edge of the spike. All is well and the graph continues.

But suppose on the next pass (near the tip of the spike) that the next point is again just to the left of the spike. It should be visible, so we draw a line to that point from the previous point. If the next point is to the right of the spike, the hidden line routine sees that this point on the graph should be seen, and thus a line is drawn from the previous point (which is to the left of the spike) to the point on the right of the spike. A line is drawn across the spike. This problem is apparent in the figure.

The problem of lines going through narrow regions which are in front is caused by the fact that the hidden line routine checks only to see if a line should be hidden at the end points of each line. If both endpoints are outside of the spike, it does not know that it is crossing the spike and draws a line across the spike.

The only way to overcome this problem is to check at points between the two endpoints to see if they go behind any region. If so, draw the line accordingly to hide any portion of the line that goes behind the region.

Here is a method for solving this problem. At the beginning of the program, decide on a maximum length of segment you wish to draw. If you are using a length of 5, for example, and the length of a normal line from endpoint to endpoint is 60, the program would divide this line into 12 segments.

Listing 6, continued:

```
4985   REM U1 Thru U9;S7-S8-S9;X1,Y1 Thru X9,Y9 ** }
4987   REM U8=0 (Last In); U8=1 (Last out) *********** }   Variables used in the Hidden Line Routine
4990   REM ***SET I=1ST X & I2=LAST X *********** }
4992   REM ***U4=0,F=U5=1 * X4=Y4=X3=Y3=-1 **** }        Variables to set at beginning of Program
4995   REM ***** Let U9 = Value of X step ***********
4997   REM SET L9= MAXIMUM LENGTH OF LINE ****
5000   IF X>1023 OR X<1 THEN U4=1
5005   IF X>1023 OR X<1 THEN RETURN
5010   IF U9=I AND Y<B[X,1] and Y >B[X,2] THEN 5140
5015   IF U9=I OR U4 THEN GOSUB 5600
5020   IF U9=I2 THEN GOSUB 5700
5025   U3=0
5030   IF U9=I OR U4 THEN 5155
5033   IF X-X9=0 THEN 5125
5034   REM STEPS 5035-5085 DIVIDE LINES INTO LINES OF LENGTH L9
5035   L8=SQR((X-X9)^2+(Y-Y9)^2)
5040   IF L8>L9 THEN DO
5045      L2=X9,L5=X,L6=Y,S6=(Y-Y9)/(X-X9)
5050      L7=(X-X9)/(L8/L9),L4=Y9-S6*X9
5060      FOR X=L2 TO L5-L7 STEP L7
5065         Y=S6*X+L4
5070         GOSUB 5090
5075      NEXT X
5080      X=L5,Y=L6
5085   DOEND
5090   IF X-X9=0 THEN 5145
5099   U3=0
5100   S9=(Y-Y9)/(X-X9)
5105   IF U8=0 THEN 5400
5110   IF Y<B[X,1] AND Y>B[X,2] THEN 5205
5115   U8=1
5120   IF U9=I THEN 5155
5125   GOSUB 8200
5130   GOSUB 5500
5135   GOTO 5145
5140   U8=0
5145   X9=X,Y9=Y
5150   RETURN
5151   REM RETURN TO MAIN PROGRAM
5155   X9=X,Y9=Y
5160   GOSUB 8100
5165   GOSUB 8200
5170   U4=0
5175   U8=1
5180   RETURN
5181   REM RETURN TO MAIN PROGRAM
5200   REM *** FIND INTERSECT ***
5205   S7=X-X9,U2=0,X1=X9,U1=1
5210   UNTIL U1>128 DO
5215      U1=U1*2
5220      IF U2 THEN 5235
5225      X1=X1+S7/U1
5230      GOTO 5240
5235      X1=X1-S7/U1
5240      Y7=S9*(X1-X9)+Y9
5245      IF U3 THEN 5456
5250      IF Y9>B[X9,2] THEN 5270
5255      IF Y7>B[X1,2] THEN U2=1
5260      IF Y7<B[X1,2] THEN U2=0
5265      GOTO 5280
5270      IF Y7<B[X1,1] THEN U2=1
5275      IF Y7>B[X1,1] THEN U2=0
5280   DOEND
5285   X5=X,Y5=Y
5290   X=X1,Y=Y7
5295   IF U3 THEN GOTO 5425
5300   U8=0
5305   GOSUB 8200
5310   GOSUB 5500
5315   X9=X5,Y9=Y5
5320   RETURN
5321   REM RETURN TO MAIN PROGRAM
5400   REM ***TEST U8=0***
5401   REM U8=0 IF LAST POINT WAS HIDDEN
5405   IF Y>B[X,2] AND Y<B[X,1] THEN 5145
5410   U8=1,U3=1
5415   X8=X,Y8=Y
5420   GOTO 5205
5425   GOSUB 8100
5430   GOSUB 8200
5435   X=X8,Y=Y8,U8=1
5450   GOTO 5125
5454   REM PART OF THE INTERSECTION ROUTINE
5455   REM ** FOR U3=1:COMING OUT ***
5456   IF Y>B[X1,1] THEN 5460
5457   IF Y7<B[X1,2] THEN U2=1
5458   IF Y7>B[X1,2] THEN U2=0
```

Figure 13: A representative plot with the hidden line subroutine. The program to generate it is shown in listing 6.

```
5459   GOTO 5280
5460   IF Y7>B[X1,1] THEN U2=1
5465   IF Y7<B[X1,1] THEN U2=0
5470   GOTO 5280
5500   REM ***** FILL IN POINTS *****
5505   U6=SGN(X-X9)
5510   IF U6=0 THEN 5535
5515   FOR U7=X9 TO X STEP U6
5520      S8=Y9+S9*(U7-X9),B[U7,2]=B[U7,2] MIN S8,B[U7,1]=B[U7,1] MAX S8
5530   NEXT U7
5535   RETURN
5600   REM ** FILL IN LEFT SIDE **
5610   IF X4#-1 THEN GOTO 5640
5620   X4=X,Y4=Y
5630   RETURN
5640   X8=X9,Y8=Y9
5650   X9=X4,Y9=Y4
5660   S9=(Y-Y9)/(X-X9)
5670   GOSUB 5500
5680   X9=X8,Y9=Y8
5690   GOTO 5620
5700   REM ** FILL IN RIGHT SIDE **
5710   IF X3#-1 THEN 5740
5720   X3=X,Y3=Y
5730   RETURN
5740   X8=X9,Y8=Y9
5750   X9=X3,Y9=Y3
5760   S9=(Y-Y9)/(X-X9)
5770   GOSUB 5500
5780   X9=X8,Y9=Y8
5790   GOTO 5720
6000   REM MAT ROTATE
6001   REM 6010-6110 MAKES MATRIX Q THE
6002   REM FINAL ROTATIONAL MATRIX
6010   MAT Q=ZER
6020   Q[1,1]=COS(Z2)*COS(Y2)
6030   Q[2,1]=-1*SIN(Z2)*COS(Y2)
6040   Q[3,1]=-1*SIN(Y2)
6050   Q[1,2]=COS(Z2)*(-1)*SIN(X2)*SIN(Y2)+SIN(Z2)*COS(X2)
6060   Q[2,2]=SIN(Z2)*SIN(X2)*SIN(Y2)+COS(Z2)*COS(X2)
6070   Q[3,2]=-1*SIN(X2)*COS(Y2)
6080   Q[1,3]=COS(Z2)*COS(X2)*SIN(Y2)+SIN(Z2)*SIN(X2)
6090   Q[2,3]=-1*SIN(Z2)*COS(X2)*SIN(Y2)+COS(Z2)*SIN(X2)
6100   Q[3,3]=COS(X2)*COS(Y2)
6110   RETURN

8100   REM A ROUTINE TO DRAW AN INVISIBLE VECTOR TO (X,Y)
8101   REM OR TO PICK THE PEN UP TO LOCATION (X,Y) (NOT INCLUDED)
8200   A ROUTINE TO DRAW A VISIBLE VECTOR TO (X,Y) (NOT INCLUDED)
9999   END
```

and use the hidden line routine as though these were 12 consecutive lines. One should choose the maximum length of line on the basis of the screen resolution and the accuracy desired. For greatest accuracy, use 1 as the greatest length of a line. This would, however, take a very long time to compute and draw. A happy medium should be chosen depending on the graph being drawn. Figure 12 shows the results of using this method.

Listing 5 is the routine used in the hidden line routine to divide each line into lengths no longer than L9. X9 and Y9 are the coordinates for the previous point. L8 is the length of the line being tested. GOSUB 5090 sends the new coordinates into the remaining portion of the hidden line routine. This routine may not be elegant, but it does work.

Listing 6 is the complete listing for the graph plotted in figure 13. I have given a complete program to help the programmer when any specific obstacles come up which are not explained in this article.

The program still contains a few "bugs" which crop up occasionally due to the simplicity of the algorithms used, so it is by no means the ultimate hidden line program. If any readers can write that ultimate hidden line routine, please let me know.■

About the Authors

Webb Simmons (1559 Alcala Place, San Diego CA 92111) discovered computers after 19 years in electronics. At first his work involved scientific programming in FORTRAN on large computers, but over the years he has used many languages on all sizes of computers, from programmable pocket calculators on up. Webb enjoys mathematical algorithms and computer language translation.

Wayne Ledder (8 Overlook Drive, Medway MA 02053) received his BSEE from the University of Buffalo in 1960. He is presently a senior electrical engineer in the Components Group at Digital Equipment Corporation using various microprocessors in intelligent terminal applications. Formerly he was an engineer with Sylvania involved with digital circuits using discrete components, and spent 10 years designing high frequency communications receivers for National Radio. His hobbies include amateur radio, photography, and sports car rallying.

Raymond B Bagley (714-637-5965) is a self-employed software consultant in the microcomputer field and is presently developing language processors for microcomputers. Ray received his BS in EE from Pacific State in 1962 and MS in Mathematics from Pepperdine in 1966. His personal systems include an Alpha AM 100 with 64 K memory, Wangco dual floppy disk drives, and Control Data hard disk drive. His interests include computer chess and abstract mathematics.

Geoffrey Gass (5240 S.W. Disch Road, Portland OR 97201) is currently employed by Custom Modifications Engineering as a specification writer and design engineer. His chief interests are interactive systems and applications software written for the convenience of the programmer or the programming language, rather than the interest and needs of the user. His personal system consists of a SwTPC 6800 personal computer with 24 K bytes of memory, a floppy disk drive, homebrew cassette interface, printer with paper tape punch and reader, and SwTPC CT-64 terminal. He totes this system to work each week to run department reports and assist in development work, and back home on weekends for fun, games, word processing, and program development.

Michael Finerty (%Dr Walter Miller, Department of General Biology, University of Arizona, Tucson AZ) is pursuing a PhD in Chemistry from the University of Arizona. His current project involves making methane from methanol. In addition he will soon be teaching chemistry at the university. He holds a bachelor's degree in mathematics, a master's degree in creative writing, and a master's in drama. His interests include astronomy, chemistry, and physics.

Daniel R Buskirk (POB 211, Rockefeller University, New York NY 10021) is currently a graduate fellow at Rockefeller University where he is studying neuronal biology. He has a bachelor's degree in mathematics and zoology. His current professional interest is the application of mathematical and computer methods to the study of neuronal structure. When not working, he enjoys photography, playing the piano, and, of course, fiddling with microcomputers.

Joel Boney (Motorola Inc, 6707 LaSalle, Austin TX 78723) is currently employed by Motorola in its Integrated Circuits Division plant. He is responsible for the software input in the system and architectural design for future Motorola processors and peripheral integrated circuits, and is currently involved in the MC6809 MC6805 projects.

Sheldon Linker (6399 Wilshire Blvd, #1010, Los Angeles CA 90048) is a member of the technical staff at TRW, where he is responsible for various aspects of program design and implementation. His personal system consists of an 8080 based machine with 32 K memory, Micropolis disk drives, and HyType terminal. His hobbies include Science Fiction, wargaming, and programming.

Burt Hashizume (POB 447, Maynard MA 01754) received his Bachelors degree in both Electrical Engineering and Physics from MIT and his Masters degree in Electrical Engineering from USC. He is currently employed by Digital Equipment Corporation. His microcomputer interests are chiefly in the area of software and how microprocessor and systems architecture can help software.

Henry A Davis (1208 Lynbrook Way, San Jose CA 95129) is currently Section Manager for Microprocessor Applications for American Microsystems Inc. He received his BS in Computer Science from Furman University, and his MS in Computer Science from the New Mexico Insititute of Mining and Technology. He is a member of IEEE and the ACM. Henry's vocation and avocation is microelectronics.

Jef Raskin (10696 Flora Vista, Cupertino CA 95014) is Manager of Publications and New Products Review for Apple Computers Inc, directing the user level testing of hardware and software products and the writing of all manuals. Jef received a BS in Philosophy from SUNY at Stony Brook, an MS in Computer Science from Penn State, and a PhD in Music from the University of California at San Diego. His personal system includes a homebrew 8080, three Apple II computers, a Polymorphic 88, and a PDP 11/03.

Robert Grappel (148 Wood Street, Lexington MA 02173) obtained his Bachelors degree in Physics from the University of Michigan, where he also received his first exposure to computing. He went on to receive a Masters in Physics from Ohio University, but discovered that programming offered more opportunities. He is presently employed at Lincoln Laboratory of MIT writing programs for air-traffic control systems. He is also the designer of the STRUBAL programming language for the 6800 microprocessor, and is the joint author of two books, TRACER 6800 *and* LINK68: An M6800 Linking Loader. *His hobbies include ham radio, woodworking, and music.*

John Rheinstein (10 Gould Road, Lexington MA 02173) has a PhD in Physics, and presently works for Lincoln Laboratory in the general area of Radar Systems Analysis. His microcomputer is a Digital Group Z-80 with 32 K bytes of memory, two Phi-Deck cassette units, and a modified DURA Mach 10 (with Selectric 1) printer. His hobbies include ham radio, sailing, and scuba diving.

Alan B Forsythe (University of California, Health Sciences Computing Facilities, Los Angeles CA 90024), as a Supervising Statistician and Computer Systems Designer at UCLA, has been heavily involved with the development of the BMDP-77 package of statistical programs which are aimed at large and medium-sized computers. His interest in small systems increased when he built a Heath H-8 system for his personal use for statistical analysis and algorithm evaluation. His personal computer is shared with his wife, Dina, and their three children, Donna, Lane and Michael. Dr. Forsythe's undergraduate education was in mathematics at City University of New York and he was awarded a Ph.D. at Yale University in 1967. He is one of the founders of the Statistical Computing Section of the American Statistical Association and served the section as secretary and chairman. He is an Associate Editor for two professional journals and has authored over forty articles.

Fred R Ruckdeschel (773 John Glen Blvd, Webster NY 14580) is a Principal Scientist at the Xerox Corporation in Webster, New York, where he has been employed for the past eleven years. During this time he has been involved in physics and management. His first experience in computing was with the IBM 650. He later performed extensive thermal simulations using the IBM 360. More recently he has turned his interests to microcomputers for both data acquisition and personal use. Dr. Ruckdeschel's hobbies include sailing, woodworking, digital electronics, programming, and haunting computer stores.

Mark Zimmermann (CalTech 130-33, Pasadena CA 91125) is a graduate student at Caltech, where his studies have been mostly devoted to astrophysical sources of gravitational radiation (estimates of their intensity, waveforms, etc.). He has also done work on stellar models and nucleosynthesis. A large portion of this work has been on computers, both for model-building and algebraic calculations. His personal system is a Commodore PET.

George W Atkinson (University of Nevada Computing Center, 4505 Maryland Parkway, Las Vegas NV 89154) is by education a mathematician, with a BS from the University of New Mexico in 1965, an MS in 1970 and PhD in 1975 from Universität Heidelberg. He is by inclination a computer scientist and educator, having had positions with the International Computer Education Center in Budapest and New Mexico State University before his present position as Manager of an Academic User Services for UNS. His current research interests are in the areas of programming languages and artificial intelligence. His article of random number generation is a spinoff from work in local industry: the design of microprocessor controlled slot machines.

Richard Mickelsen (5744 Holden Street, Pittsburgh PA 15232) is a graduate student in political science at Carnegie-Mellon University. He previously earned a PhD in civil engineering from Cargnegie-Mellon and worked in industry for several years before returning to school. In addition to his studies, he is a consultant to the student user services.

Phillip J Ferrell (Seattle WA) received his BS in physics from CalTech in 1955 and his PhD in EE from the University of Washington in 1970. Before his present position as Principal Engineer for Boeing Aerospace, he was an Air Force officer in the research and development of communications. He is now involved in computer flight control systems for spacecraft. His personal system is a Digital Group Z-80 Computer.

About the Authors, continued

C Brian Honess (College of Business Adm, University of South Carolina, Columbia SC 29208) is currently assistant professor of management science in the College of Business Administration at the University of South Carolina. He reports that he has been an active "building" radio amateur (ham) for 20 years; his interest in computers goes back to programming scientific business applications on an IBM 1620. He learned about what was inside computers by buying a surplus IBM 704 from the government, and slowly taking it apart (donating, selling and scrapping the parts as he went). Another 704 was eventually purchased, and this time it was built back up, from the inside out. This is not exactly a typical personal computer.

William L Colsher (2110 Hassell Rd., Apt 308, Hoffman Estates IL 60195) spends his time building and writing about microcomputers as well as writing science fiction. He is a member of General Technics, a group of technically oriented science fiction fans who like to build what they read about. Mr Colsher has a BS degree in Computer and Information Science from Ohio State University.

Kurt J Schmucker (3571 Ft. Meade Road, Apt 519, Laurel MD 20810) has been employed as a mathematician at the Department of Defense in Washington, DC since 1974. He has an MS in mathematics from Michigan State University and an MS in computer science from Johns Hopkins University. He is now an advanced special student in the computer science department at the University of Maryland. Mr Schmucker's current interests are in natural language processing and computer graphics.

Jeffrey L Posdamer (Department of Computer Science, State University of New York at Buffalo, Ridge LEA Road, Amherst NY 14226) is an Associate Professor of Computer Science for SUNY at Buffalo. He received his BS in electrical engineering at Rensselaer Polytechnic and his PhD in computer science from Syracuse University. He is also a consultant in computer graphics, computational geometry, and computer aided design.

Joel C Hungerford (Stearns Road, Amherst NH 03031) received his BS from MIT in 1958 and his MS from Purdue in 1962. He is currently president and chief engineer of Joval Scientific, dealing with computer simulation of microwave and optical reflecting systems. Formerly he was a systems engineer in radar and related subjects. His hobbies include building steam engines and hiking.

Mark Gottlieb (4342 Sunset Beach Drive NW, Olympia WA 95902) is a graduate student at Stanford, working on his Masters in Engineering Management and in Product Design. He was formerly a partner of Northwest Computer Cinema which specialized in computer controlled special effects on film. His current hobbies include underwater violin playing, scuba diving, and inventing.

Edmond C. Kelly, Jr., publisher
Blaise W. Liffick, technical editor
William H. Hurlin, production manager
Patricia Curran, production editor
Tina M. Mion, production artist
Techart Associates, drafting
George Banta Company, printing
Dawson Advertising Agency, cover art